REINVENTING WORLD WAR II

RSA·STR

THE RSA SERIES IN TRANSDISCIPLINARY RHETORIC

The RSA Series in Transdisciplinary Rhetoric is a collaboration with the Rhetoric Society of America to publish innovative and rigorously argued scholarship on the tremendous disciplinary breadth of rhetoric. Books in the series take a variety of approaches, including theoretical, historical, interpretive, critical, or ethnographic, and examine rhetorical action in a way that appeals, first, to scholars in communication studies and English or writing, and, second, to at least one other discipline or subject area.

A complete list of books in this series is located at the back of this volume.

Barbara A. Biesecker

REINVENTING WORLD WAR II

Popular Memory in the Rise of the Ethnonationalist State

THE PENNSYLVANIA STATE UNIVERSITY PRESS
UNIVERSITY PARK, PENNSYLVANIA

Library of Congress Cataloging-in-Publication Data

Names: Biesecker, Barbara A., author.
Title: Reinventing World War II : popular memory in the rise of the ethnonationalist state / Barbara A. Biesecker.
Other titles: RSA series in transdisciplinary rhetoric.
Description: University Park, Pennsylvania : The Pennsylvania State University Press, [2024] | Series: The RSA series in transdisciplinary rhetoric | Includes bibliographical references and index.
Summary: "Explores how World War II was retooled in popular culture starting in the mid-1980s to redress a crisis in American identity and restore social equilibrium"— Provided by publisher.
Identifiers: LCCN 2024024552 | ISBN 9780271097824 (hardback)
Subjects: LCSH: World War, 1939–1945—Social aspects—United States. | World War, 1939–1945—United States—Influence. | Collective memory—United States—History—20th century. | National characteristics, American—History—20th century. | United States—Civilization—1970–
Classification: LCC D744.7.U6 B54 2024 | DDC 940.53/73—dc23/eng/20240604
LC record available at https://lccn.loc.gov/2024024552

Printed in the United States of America
Published by The Pennsylvania State University Press, University Park, PA 16802–1003

The Pennsylvania State University Press is a member of the Association of University Presses.

It is the policy of The Pennsylvania State University Press to use acid-free paper. Publications on uncoated stock satisfy the minimum requirements of American National Standard for Information Sciences—Permanence of Paper for Printed Library Material, ANSI Z39.48–1992.

For Timothy M. Randall

Contents

Illustrations

Acknowledgments

It has taken me a long time to finish this book. I will not even try to thank by name all the colleagues and graduate students with whom I have had the pleasure to read, write, and think these many years. I am especially grateful for the frequency of opportunities to share the work while it was in progress at my two home institutions—the University of Iowa and the University of Georgia—as well as at the Annenberg School of Communication at the University of Pennsylvania, Arizona State University, Bluffton College, Carleton University, the Center for Transcultural Studies at Northwestern University, Concordia University, Indiana University, the Peace Studies Institute at Florida Atlantic University, Syracuse University, the University of North Carolina at Chapel Hill, the University of South Carolina, the University of Texas at Austin, and Vanderbilt University. I also want to acknowledge the generous support for this project from the Obermann Center for Advanced Studies at the University of Iowa (where I enjoyed a semester of leave to read, write, and work with John Lucaites to put on the first Visual Rhetoric Workshop), the Discretionary Funding Advisory Group at the University of Iowa (whose funding made it possible for me to explore and research the Women in Military Services for America Memorial), the Franklin International Faculty Exchange at the University of Georgia (which supported travel to Carleton University in Ottawa, Canada, during which chapter 4 was greatly improved thanks to a series of lively exchanges during my visit), and the Department of Communication Studies at the University of Georgia (whose support made it possible to include color images in the book).

Working with people associated with the Transdisciplinary Rhetoric Series at the Pennsylvania State University Press has been a pleasure. Thank you, Leah and Michael, for your enthusiasm for the book from the very first read. Thanks also to the two expert external reviewers, one of whom remains anonymous and the other who has long been one of my most trusted readers and cherished friends, Carole Blair. Archna Patel, Josie DiNovo, and Alex Ramos, I am grateful for your professionalism, timeliness, and patience. And I remain in awe of

Nicholas Taylor, my copyeditor, whose meticulous work on the final manuscript saved me a host of embarrassments.

Work-life balance is a crippling ruse. It's better when it's all mixed up together, when you can't separate labor and love: Tim Randall, you had me at the first note and, again and again, each day you bring music into my life; Sue Trollinger, your extraordinary spirit gives me faith when I need it most; and Jan Odom, having you not only as a lifelong conversant and confidant but now also as a neighbor has been a gift from the gods. Chu Chu, you were next to me to the last word of the full draft. I so miss your constant company.

Chapter 3 was originally published as "Renovating the National Imaginary: A Prolegomenon on Contemporary Paregoric Rhetoric," in *Framing Public Memory*, edited by Kendall R. Phillips (University of Alabama Press, 2004), 212–47.

The concluding section of chapter 4 is derived in part from my article "Whither Ideology? Toward a Different Take on Enjoyment as a Political Factor," published in *Western Journal of Communication* © 2011 Western States Communication Association, available online at https://www.tandfonline.com/10.1080/10570314.2011.588904, reprinted by permission of Taylor & Francis Ltd., https://www.tandfonline.com/, on behalf of Western States Communication Association.

Introduction

You don't have to buy into Freud's account of hidden guilt to recognize the force in the real world of the unconscious dreams of nations.
—Jacqueline Rose

Following the release in 1970 of Franklin J. Schaffner's *Patton* and Richard Fleischer, Toshio Masuda, and Kinfi Fukasaku's *Tora! Tora! Tora!* WWII all but disappeared from US public culture.[1] For reasons at once common and complex, by the early 1970s Americans had lost their appetite for WWII.[2] It seems to have mattered little whether the enemy was the Germans or the Japanese, whether the battle was staged on land, on sea, or in the air, whether it was fact or fiction, tragedy or romance, or whether it was pitched in a complimentary or critical key: WWII's moment had passed. By the end of the American century, however, all of that changed, the "Good War" gaining a new lease on our collective life. Indeed, during the mid-eighties WWII returned with a vengeance and by the 1990s it was ubiquitous for a second time across US public and political culture. WWII appeared on the big screen and our flat screens; it stuffed our bookshelves and stocked our coffee tables; Carnival, Princess, and Viking cruise lines booked excursions centered around it, exhibition halls across the country curated it, the D-Day Museum in New Orleans was built on it, and Congress took the extraordinary step of reversing the law in order to break the once-sacred ground between the Washington Monument and the Lincoln Memorial in order to memorialize it.

Already I have begun to suggest that on the eve of the new millennium WWII redux was much more than a collective curiosity or national pastime. In fact, one of the primary tasks of this book is to explain why its return was one of the most significant events to have taken place in the United States between 1985 and 2005. I argue that this is true not merely because WWII was what happened and what kept happening day after day for twenty years but also because the return of WWII played a major role in restructuring the people's common sense and its sense of the common. This book might best be summed up, then, as an effort to take measure of the reintroduction and dramatic uptake of WWII in the United States. How exactly, I ask, was WWII being given back to us, and with what consequences for collective life? The short answer to that question and, hence, the central argument of the book is this: WWII popular remembrance was a primary means by which a distinctly ethnonational neoliberalism achieved not only intelligibility but also currency and legitimacy within and across the spheres that constitute civil society today.

In aiming to specify WWII redux's part in the transformation of ethnonational neoliberalism into the lingua franca, I spend the first section of this introduction describing in some detail the political, social, and economic conditions subtending WWII's reemergence in US public and political culture. Along the way—and taking several of my cues from American Studies scholar Donald Pease and psychoanalytic theorist and cultural critic Jacqueline Rose—I suggest that the late twentieth-century crisis of American identity is largely attributable to the radical decline in the symbolic efficiency of the national Cold War state fantasy. WWII remembrance, I then argue, filled that ideological gap, fashioning a "new" equilibrium in the United States whose authority and power will be shown to be owed to the rhetorical restoration of a certain *kind* of ethical state that I call ethnonationalist. I spend the second section of this introduction on preliminary remarks about the uses to which the archives of history may be put; I am intent on bringing into sharp focus the implications of deciphering WWII redux as an extended exercise in the reconstruction of *popular* memory. In the third section I address the always vexing question of method. In addition to offering an account of why and how I toggle methodologically between Derridean-, Foucaultian-, and Lacanian-inflected rhetorical readings of a rather wide range of (con)texts, I also provide a synopsis of the different ways I use the term "rhetoric" over the course of the book. I bring this introduction to a close by previewing very briefly the chapters that follow.

Crisis and National State Fantasies

From the beginning of President Ronald Reagan's second term in office until George W. Bush declared the War on Terror in 2001,[3] the US nation-state faced one challenge that outflanked all others: the potentially catastrophic crisis of national identity. According to almost everyone at the time, the "We" of "We the People" was splintering from within and our nation-ness was in free fall. Wracked by the question of what, if anything, makes this multiracial, multiethnic, and multicultural many a one, ours was an imagined community at loose ends.[4]

Given education's role in preparing young people for civic life, it is hardly surprising that America's collective identity crisis first surfaced as a protracted and impassioned curriculum debate, focused largely on history, social studies, and literary instruction. Beginning in the mid-eighties and throughout the nineties public school boards across the country wrestled fiercely over the virtues and vices of a common core and the textbooks that would be used to teach it. About which historical events, for example, would all students be required to learn? By what criteria would the decision be made? And should there be agreement on the inclusion of any given event, what exactly would students learn about it? Whose history would serve as ground for our collective sense of self? In 1991 the New York State system's review of its guidelines for teaching American history and social studies, with an eye to rewriting them in less orthodox terms, caught the public's collective attention and triggered rancorous debate. Even *Time* magazine weighed in with its 1991 Independence Day issue, the visual and verbal rhetoric of its cover depicting the relation between the received wisdom and those challenging it in unmistakably ruinous terms. The cover presented a multicultural fife-and-drum corps (led, not incidentally and quite literally, by an old white guy) over the heads of which was printed in large type the question "Who are we?" tagged with the byline "American kids are getting a new—and divisive—view of Thomas Jefferson, Thanksgiving and the Fourth of July." In response to this as well as other ongoing curricular contests, the George H. W. Bush administration launched its hotly contested and ultimately failed attempt to institutionalize a "culturally unifying set of U.S. history standards" under the leadership of Lynne Cheney, then chair of the National Endowment for the Humanities. As the end of the decade approached, the struggle intensified. The holding of public hearings in 1997 to air differences of opinion over the California State Board of Education's effort to adopt a new textbook series was like throwing gasoline on an already raging fire.

College and university curriculum committees and faculty went to battle as well. Most famously, perhaps, in 1988 the Stanford University faculty voted to diversify the course offerings from which undergraduate students would choose in order to satisfy the institution's long-standing "Western Culture" general education requirement. But Stanford was hardly alone. Across the country, at both public and private, elite and not, scores of faculty and administrators asked, about what should we, must we, feel a sense of national pride? Others asked, have we no shame? Conservatives decried the meltdown of the great melting pot, insisting on the irreducible necessity of "a unifying American identity" that trumps all other affiliations and refuses to cower, as Arthur M. Schlesinger Jr. put it at the time, at "the hullabaloo over 'multiculturalism' and 'political correctness,' over the notion that history and literature should be taught not as intellectual disciplines but as therapies whose function is to raise minority self-esteem."[5] Out of the cauldron of blistering debate emerged hundreds of essays and books, many of them pitched to the general public but all of them addressing the promise and perils of orthodox national allegiance. In 1987 literature professor E. D. Hirsch published his bestseller *Cultural Literacy: What Every American Needs to Know*. With the support of the Exxon Education Foundation, Hirsh turned a scholarly article into a manifesto for "functional literacy and effective national communication" whose appendix, as boldly noted on the front cover, comprised a list of five thousand essential names, phrases, dates, and concepts all Americans should know. As he explained in the preface, such shared knowledge "enables grandparents to communicate with grandchildren, southerners with Midwesterners, whites with blacks, Asians with Hispanics, and Republicans with Democrats—no matter where they were educated."[6] Other bestsellers fanned the flames, their authors keenly interested in inflating the stakes of our collective crisis of identity by insisting on the outcome's metaphysical rather than politico-cultural consequences. Most famously, Alan Bloom's 1986 book *The Closing of the American Mind* indicted an ostensibly overliberalized system of higher education in America for turning its back on the Western tradition and reason, mourning not only our "failed democracy" but the very "impoverish[ment of] the souls of today's students."[7] Such spirited prose, however, did not drip from the pens of conservatives alone. Following nearly ten more years of deep discontent and divisiveness, left-leaning activist and public intellectual Todd Gitlin published his book-length polemic on the fragmentation of the American polity, attributing "the twilight of [our] common dreams" to the demise of the New Left's "messianic faith" in "the universal destiny of human kind."[8] Metaphysical indeed!

The crisis of national identity was not, however, only a curricular, academic, or cultural affair. Although the mid to late eighties and nineties most often evoke the curriculum and canon wars, the history and monument wars, the NEA Four, Robert Mapplethorpe, and Andre Serrano, the destabilization of

American identity was keenly felt across all domains of civic life. Indeed, at the same time that battles over free speech and hate speech erupted on college and university campuses, clashes over immigration, affirmative action, gay rights, adoption rights, abortion rights, and fetal rights flared up on the streets and in the courts—all challenges to the "We" of "the People." Presidents, politicians, and political pundits from both parties spoke breathlessly about the dire need for reunification, the contested terms of which fueled season after season of fiery funding debates and policy disputes within and beyond their chambers' walls. The question of who is and who is not American functioned, too, as the pivot point of a host of hotly contested initiatives, from state laws declaring English their official language (House Speaker Newt Gingrich insisting that "without English as a common language, there is no [American] civilization")[9] to the Clinton administration's Department of Defense Directive "Don't Ask, Don't Tell." The imminent collapse of American identity and society was the topic du jour of local and national talk radio shows as well as regular fare on network and cable news shows. As we slouched toward the new century, we were dogged by one question above all others: what will keep America from breaking apart?[10] I use the words "WWII redux" as shorthand for that sizeable assemblage of *popular* memory practices, texts, places, and events that, over those twenty years, helped cultivate the "new" hegemonic response.

There exists an impressive literature explaining why the burning question of American identity emerged in the mid-eighties. Scholars tend to agree that the warming of relations between the United States and the Soviet Union and, ultimately, the termination of the Cold War are the key. Of course, conventional wisdom has long recommended that there is no force greater than war to inspire and sustain robust national allegiance. As Kenneth Burke put it, under the shadow of WWII, fierce conflict between groups strengthens the sense of belonging within each. Because the Cold War was a war unlike all that had preceded it—for the simple reason that a nuclear exchange between the United States and the Soviet Union truly would be the war-to-end-all-wars by ending all worlds—it unified Americans like none before. One way, then, to begin to explain the emergence of America's identity crisis is to notice that this national emergency gets its start at precisely the same time that the Cold War is winding down. It is during the early eighties that hostilities between the United States and the Soviet Union begin to ease and by 1989 the Cold War is declared over. As has often been remarked, absent that forty-six-year rivalry whose mythic proportions and potentially apocalyptic outcome had taken firm hold of the citizenry's attention, Americans across the political spectrum began to examine the state of their own union.

Although the dissolution of the Soviet Empire and the termination of the Cold War was formative, it is important to recall a number of other geopolitical events of the time. Since had it been only a matter of the demise of a single scapegoat, another nuclear-armed enemy Other could have been chosen or fabricated to serve in its place. (This was, of course, the second Bush administration's approach, about which I say more below). But as Francis Fukuyama was (too) quick to point out in the *National Interest* to great fanfare, 1989 did not only see the end of the Cold War between the United States and Russia, it also bore witness to what he famously dubbed "the end of history": in that single calendar year Poland embraced Solidarity, thousands of pro-democracy protesters marched in Tiananmen Square, Communist rule in Hungary, East Germany, Czechoslovakia, and Bulgaria collapsed, and the Berlin Wall was felled. Although it later would become clear that 1989 did not mark, as Fukuyama had wagered, "the end point of mankind's ideological evolution and the universalization of Western liberal democracy as the final form of human government" around the world, that impressive chain of political events nevertheless punctually drained from the Cold War rhetoric much of its persuasive force.[11]

At this point a perplexing question imposes itself: why did these "wins" for democracy and for capitalism (however provisional they later would prove to be) fuel a crisis of American identity rather than fortify the citizenry's positive self-image? American Studies scholar Donald E. Pease delivers a compelling answer: the crisis of American identity was caused not by the end of the Cold War, but by the collapse of the Cold War state fantasy that had structured and lent consistency to the citizenry's collective belonging for nearly half a century. In view of my interest in taking rhetorical stock and political measure of the return of WWII in this historical conjuncture, I briefly call attention to the theoretical scaffolding that bears most of the weight of Pease's claim and the persuasive case made on its behalf.

State fantasy is, of course, a technical term for Pease, but what may be less evident is that embedded in it is a triptych of analytics—state, fantasy, and state fantasy. In the Lacanian lexicon the most basic understanding of fantasy is a manufactured scenario that stages desire.[12] Contrary to its everyday use, then, fantasy does not signify a scene in which desire is fulfilled; rather, it is the stage on which desire is set to work by putting the subject in its place within a symbolic structure and giving that subject its desired objects. As Slavoj Žižek deftly put it, "Through fantasy, we learn 'how to desire,' which is to say, fantasy is the frame co-ordinating our desire."[13] Moreover, fantasy's function is to protect the subject from the fundamental disjointedness of its situated existence. Fantasy thus "constitutes the frame through which [the subject] experience[s] the world as consistent and meaningful."[14]

Fantasy in its psychoanalytic sense operates at the level not only of individuals but also of collectivities. That may seem obvious now, but it was Žižek who, with the publication of *The Sublime Object of Ideology* in 1989, renovated a long tradition of ideological analysis whose fortunes had declined precipitously with the ascendancy of the various post-structuralisms. And he did it by turning ideology critique inside out. "The fundamental level of ideology," he skillfully wrote, "is not of an illusion masking the real state of things but that of an (unconscious) fantasy structuring our social reality itself."[15] Because Pease's argument draws heavily on four additional Lacanian insights popularized by Žižek and his comrades, I identify them here. One, it is only by way of reference to a pure or empty signifier, what Lacanians dub a nodal or quilting point, that reality is retroactively configured as coherent and meaningful. Two, every (ideological) fantasy is structured around a fundamental antagonism, impossibility, or lack that is disavowed by the (collective) subject but which resurfaces as symptom. Three, the fundamental antagonism, impossibility, or lack is displaced inevitably onto an Other whose function within the (ideological) fantasy is to keep desiring subjects from achieving their aim. And four, fantasy therefore obliges an accounting of enjoyment as a political factor.

Now in the matter of ideological analysis, historicization has been a persistent problem. Psychoanalytic supplementation, critics have argued, only confounds it: to Class or History, add Unconscious or Symbolic. In every case a transcendental leads the way. As Jacqueline Rose has demonstrated, however, that need not be the case. In fact, it can be the radical contingency of history that bids us to leverage psychoanalysis for nuanced ideological critique. That is what I take to be the implicit argument of the very brief but powerful introduction to her *States of Fantasy* wherein Rose audaciously confronts what is perhaps the key question vexing the modern state: on what might its authority depend given that it can no longer trade on the transcendental or metaphysical guarantees that, heretofore, were embodied in the king or prince? The modern state, Rose reminds us by cunningly calling on the work of sociologists rather than psychoanalysts, marks a "decisive shift" in governance: "It is the point where the ruler, instead of 'maintaining his state,' serves a separate constitutional and legal state which it is his duty 'to maintain.' Once real authority is no longer invested in the prince and his trappings, it loses its face and disembodies itself: 'With this analysis of the state as an omnipotent yet impersonal power,' Quentin Skinner concludes his study of the foundations of modern political thought, 'we may be said to enter the modern world.'"[16]

It is precisely this splitting of the constitutional principles of governance and law from the executive charged with their upkeep that throws modern state authority radically into question. With the institution of this irreducibly discursive caesura, the modern state's authority, as Rose put it, "passes straight off the edge of the graspable, immediately knowable world."[17] This leaves the leadership to rely, to use Pease's words, on a ghostly, phantasmatic power or state fantasy for which standard modes of reason cannot account. State fantasies, however, do not directly infuse the state with authority (whatever that might mean). Authority is less an objective quality than a kind of subjective relation. Hence, state fantasies suture individuals to the state in a particular way, rendering them at once subjects of and subject to the state or actively governable. Simply put, state fantasy positions a bounded democratic polity as a certain kind of citizen-subject in relation to a certain kind of state. The mechanism of their governance is, as pointed out above, their own staged desire such that what the citizenry always gets from the state is what it already wants. Put in the terms with which this introduction began, state fantasies imaginatively lend the modern state its nation-ness and transform citizens into a consenting and patriotic people.

To return to Pease's account of American's identity crisis, by the time the United States entered the Cold War, American Exceptionalism already had enjoyed a long and storied history (the details of which Pease recounts but are not necessary to chronicle here). Suffice it for my purposes to say that not despite but thanks to American Exceptionalism's elasticity, the Cold War state fantasy of it was an iteration in the Derridean sense of the term: a repetition with a difference.[18] What remained the same was America as exemplar or model, the "Nation of Nations" (what Pease singles out as the keystone of Cold War foreign policy). What changed, however, was the primal event, understood as that which organizes lived reality (and, more specifically, the relations of the state and the polity) but must itself remain objectively impossible within it.[19] In this iteration of American Exceptionalism, global nuclear annihilation was the primal event, the "cause" to which every available state resource was expended to efface—and with more than just the blessing of the people. Indeed, because a decisively national Cold War state fantasy of American Exceptionalism positioned the citizenry, along with the entire planet, in mortal danger, it became possible for them to imagine themselves not just as beneficiaries of but also "enactors of the state's will" during an indefinite state of exception.[20]

Apart from the citizenry itself, the National Security State, a para-national military and security network declared exempt from the rules and norms of the legally constituted national and international orders, was the Cold War nation-state's most formidable apparatus. The warrant for that exemption was folded into its charge: to protect *our* exemplary democratic order from *their* evil empire whose aspirations for revolutionary socialism everywhere justified US intervention, covert or otherwise, constitutional or not, at home or abroad. Although a good bit already has been and remains to be said about the National Security State, I am most interested in making sense of the citizenry's (imaginary) relation to it. US public support for its expansive and extralegal charge defied reason then but may best be understood now by way of state fantasy. The Cold War iteration of American Exceptionalism positioned the citizenry not merely to look favorably on the National Security State but to collaborate with it, to also be its enactors. Pease explains how this relation was formed:

> Under Truman, the National Security State took existing social relations, reconstituted them in terms of its geopolitical imperatives, and then gave them back to the U.S. citizens as if these imperatives were the enactments of their own will. U.S. citizens embraced the state's exceptions by taking up liberal anticommunism as a homogenizing political ethos. Indeed, the energy for domestic politics was parasitic upon the state's projection of its irreconcilable internal political conflicts onto the arena of international conflict. Proponents of liberal (and conservative) anticommunism fostered a consensus about matters of political belief by actively soliciting the state to project fundamental antagonisms that emerged within the domestic political sphere onto the alien imperial state with whom the United States was engaged in an international war.[21]

This, then, was the frame coordinating the citizenry's internally contradictory desire: on the one hand, to continue to view the nation *as exceptional*, on the other hand, by willfully regarding even blatant violations of the nation's creed and laws as warranted exceptions.

It is now possible to explain not only the emergence but also the affective intensity of America's identity crisis. This, again, is Pease: "When the Soviet

Empire came apart and the United States lost its enemy Other, the entire overdetermined structure of the state fantasy was dismantled. When the cold war stopped justifying the state's production of exceptions [at home and around the globe], Carl Schmitt's diagnosis of the instability of the liberal political sphere proved all too accurate. Unable to project the antagonisms that plagued the exponents of the incompatible political positions within the U.S. political sphere onto an external enemy, the state was confronted with the irreconcilable differences internal to the liberal political realm."[22]

In other words, without the fabulous Cold War imperative,[23] the hyphen between the nation and the state lost its hold, the suture securing the phantasmatic identification frayed, and what had heretofore been seen by so many citizens as benevolent exceptions (to the rule of custom or ethics as well as to the rule of US constitutional and international law) suddenly became visible to them as violent inconsistencies. Indeed, a citizenry well rehearsed in seeing *as* and *for* the state found itself confronted by a legacy of contradictions enacted *by* the state that, at best, would be understood as a dumb bureaucratic apparatus and, at worst, as a cunning imperial capitalist machine. Where there was to have been equality, there was prejudice based on ethnicity, gender, race, and class. Where there was to have been rule of law, there was illegal search and seizure, false imprisonment, and forced confessions. Where there was to have been popular sovereignty, there was territorial expansion beyond the US borders and voter suppression and gerrymandering within them. And where there was to have been freedom, there was slavery, internment, and occupation. Summarily put, the demise of the symbolic efficiency of the Cold War national state fantasy made it increasingly difficult, and ultimately impossible, for many Americans to ignore the gap between America's democratic principles of equality, liberty, and freedom and what had been happening on the ground. The crisis of national identity that rattled the country from the mid-eighties until 2001 (and the culture wars that were its most conspicuous effect) is to be attributed, then, not to the precipitous positive presence of ethnic, sexual, racial, class, and cultural differences but to the absence of a state fantasy that had trained the citizenry to sublimate those differences to the national.

By the end of his book Pease will have made the case that it took the attacks on the World Trade Center and the Pentagon on September 11, 2001, and the George W. Bush administration's Global Homeland state fantasy to suture the ideological gap. In the aftermath of 9/11 and under the auspices of a new state of emergency, the Bush administration quickly established a new security state, declared its global War on Terror, and retooled American Exceptionalism yet again. Like the earlier Cold War state fantasy, the Global Homeland state fantasy was an imaginary scenario in which the American way of life was at stake. This time, however, the American people had already been exiled from that way of life, and the possibility of its return hinged on acts of "defensive aggression" by the state at home and abroad. Accordingly, the American people were positioned in/by the Global Homeland state fantasy both as denizens of the domestic emergency state and as mere spectators of the state's retributive violence in Iraq and Afghanistan (their enjoyment of the latter derived from their imaginatively bearing witness to the unfolding of America's Manifest Destiny in the Middle East). Importantly, for Pease, this national state fantasy owed its authority not to the subjective relation between the state and the people but to its special relation to God: Christian scripture read through a fundamentalist lens "instituted a version of American exceptionalism that was voided of the need for American exceptionalists."[24] Effectively denationalized (for they no longer had their "homeland"), the Global Homeland state fantasy repositioned the people as "naked biological life under the state's protection." As a newly biopoliticized population, the people "could play no active political role in the Homeland Security State's reordering of things."[25]

It is a mistake, on the one hand, to credit the Bush administration's discourse with so much hegemonic force and, on the other, to let the American people so easily off the hook. I want to suggest instead that the country had been primed for the kind of response to 9/11 the Bush administration issued, and that the people had long been positioned not simply to receive it but to act in concert on its behalf. Over the chapters that follow I argue that between 1985 and 2005 recuperations of WWII fueled a rebirth of American Exceptionalism, shaping both the public and the "ideal citizen" to fit the needs of the late neoliberal state and its endless War on Terror. I therefore want to insist on the necessity of attending to other material and social realities that, albeit less punctual than the passing of the Cold War national state fantasy, played a measurable role in the crisis of national identity and, similarly, affected its restructuring.[26]

The national Cold War state fantasy was not all that had gone missing in the United States by the mid to late eighties. The once-robust Fordist regime of production—characterized by mass production and standardization, monopoly capitalism and "Taylorism"—also had gone the way of the dodo, and by 1985 Post-Fordism was hitting its stride.[27] As Lisa Duggan usefully recalls, the ground for this economic mutation, whose pattern of upward redistribution continues into the present day, had long been in the making. During the 1950s and 1960s, for example, the New Deal coalition and progressive unionism came under increasingly hostile fire; during the 1960s and 1970s, downwardly redistributive social movements—such as civil rights, Black Power, feminism, as well as lesbian and gay liberation—were assailed by an increasingly vocal and organized right-wing opposition; it was also during the 1970s that the United States saw a surge in pro-business activism as big and small companies joined forces to face global competition and tilt the economic playing field in their favor.[28]

To most Americans, however, the new Post-Fordism felt less like an anticipated mutation in productive relations and more like a sudden shift—for better or worse, depending on one's station. Gone was the US manufacturing base and with it the prosperity in the Rust Belt states; this would be a day for computer-based, high-tech industries and regions like Silicon Valley and Seattle. Gone was the "in-house" corporate accountant, human resources staff, and help-line team; these services and others would be outsourced, often to offshore sites. Gone, too, were once-common skilled jobs for white middle-class men, and full-time white-collar jobs with benefits became increasingly scarce. The once-standard employee pension programs secured by fixed annuities were displaced by individual retirement accounts tethered to the fortunes of the stock market, and flex-time, part-time, and what we now call "gig work" would become the name of the game. For the so-called average American, these were the felt consequences of a productive regime that traded largely in finance capital, was dominated by multinational corporations, and extorted unprecedented profits from a new international division of labor.

By the 1980s, the prized principle US economists exploited to account for and rationalize Post-Fordism's impacts on everyday life was "the wisdom and efficiency of markets."[29] Neo-Keynesian macroeconomic theory had lost all favor in highly influential academic and political circles, their ranks turning as if on a dime to champion microeconomic theory and rational-actor models. Gone, too, then, were the once-powerful apologists for thinking about the economy in terms of aggregate demand and investment functions, and for conceiving economic stability as an informed exercise in conscientious social and institutional compromise. Indeed, by the time Reagan took office in 1981, a new neoliberal consensus—built by working up from the microeconomic foundations of individual choice—boldly rejected any measure that would attempt to steer the economy by intervening on the side of aggregate demand. As historian Daniel T. Rogers recounts, political economists' rediscovery of the naturalness and wisdom of the market, coupled with their confidence that the unencumbered "play of private interests might better promote maximum social well-being than could the active management of regulators,"[30] set the stage for Reaganomics, otherwise called supply-side economics. The Reagan administration moved aggressively to remove any and all perceived barriers to market efficiency, from cutting the marginal personal income tax rate, reducing government spending, and deregulating major industries to advocating flexible labor pools, free trade, and free-floating capitalism.

Neoliberalism—shorthand for a mode of rationality whose core principle is the wisdom and efficiency of free markets and whose twined values are calculation, competition, and enterprise—did not rule the economic domain alone. It also came to govern activity in the social, legal, and political spheres. As Foucault explained in his 1979 lectures published under the title *The Birth of Biopolitics*, twentieth-century American neoliberalism as a rationality materializes as the effort "to use the market economy and the typical analyses of the market economy to decipher non-market relationships and phenomena which are not strictly and specifically economic but what we call social phenomena."[31] The application of market analysis to government was, of course, the opening for the incessant demand that the social safety net be unraveled and departments and agencies—from the Department of Education to the Department of Energy, from the CDC to the NEA and NEH—be downsized or eliminated altogether. It also is the rationality by which the privatization of prisons, the paramilitary, and primary health care can make (good) sense. In *Undoing the Demos*, Wendy Brown examines additional entailments of the neoliberal recalibration of the state at length, calling out the regularity with which it offloads the responsibility and, of course, cost of human well-being and development onto individuals and private institutions. But in order to do this kind of "political" work in the United States, the neoliberal democratic state needs a political, public, and popular culture that more than nominally endorses it as well as a citizenry that subsidizes it. Enter WWII redux: it is my argument that between 1985 and 2005 WWII memory practices, texts, places, and events together provided the ethnonationalist state fantasy that transformed the neoliberal common sense into a new American creed that recalibrated accordingly the citizenry's desires.

Of course, another word for that common sense is "hegemony," which Antonio Gramsci used in the place of "ideology" in order to underscore the always already provisional and contested character of the collective status quo and, thus, the persistent effort that must be expended in every domain of life to sustain it.

What is less well-known is Gramsci's use of hegemony also to call attention to the complex processes by which any state formation procures and secures its provisional authority. Stuart Hall, a singularly committed and nuanced reader of Gramsci, insists on this dimension of hegemony, however daunting a challenge it poses for concrete analysis. Quoting directly from Gramsci's *Prison Notebooks*, Hall writes, "[Hegemony] is neither a functional condition of ruling-class power, nor a matter, exclusively, of 'ideological consent' or 'cultural influence.' What is in question, is the issue of the 'ethical state': the ceaseless work required to construct a social authority, throughout all the levels of social activity, such that a 'moment of economic, political, intellectual and moral unity' may be secured, sufficient to 'raise the level of the state to a more general plane.'"[32] Although, so far as I am able to tell, he did not ever use the term, Gramsci helps us to understand that modern state authority is predicated on a certain *kind* of fantasy that, for all its other historically contingent and singular features, always infuses every social relation with an overriding, dare I say transcendent, ethical imperative or desire. Hence, not "we will" (consent or influence) but "we must" (imperative) or "we cannot not want" (desire). Put a bit differently, in staging the "ethicalization" of everyday life, national state fantasies habituate their subjects to a process of abstraction that, I argue, is irreducibly rhetorical. More to the point, in this book I carefully track work that took place between 1985 and 2005 under the obfuscating rubric of WWII remembrance to fashion a "new" equilibrium in the United States whose authority and power is shown to be owed to the restoration of a certain *kind* of ethical state that I call ethnonationalist. Indeed, as I intend to demonstrate, the rhetorical evisceration of the historical and the political in the name of the ethical vis-à-vis the cultural has been one of the new hegemony's signature gestures. It is, then, a fundamental mistake to regard the memory practices, texts, places, and events to which I attend in detail—including but not limited to the controversy over the National Air and Space Museum's *Enola Gay* exhibit to Steven Spielberg's blockbuster film *Saving Private Ryan* and Tom Brokaw's best-selling book *The Greatest Generation* to the Women in Military Services for America Memorial—as "merely" cultural. In its articulation with a post-Fordist economy whose neoliberal rationality had already migrated into the private and civic spheres of life in the United States, WWII redux—with one important exception, the United States Holocaust Memorial Museum, that I discuss at length in the fourth chapter—delivered the ethnonational ethos requisite to the ethical elevation of the neoliberal state.

Archives and Popular Memory

Of the many presuppositions (which will, I hope, become clear as the analysis unfolds) grounding my effort to take political measure of WWII's return, two demand discussion at the outset. First, I take the archive to be a site of inscription from which ensues rhetorical inventions that have a distinct relation to power. This is, of course, a loaded sentence, the words "inscription," "rhetorical inventions," and "power" laden with theoretical and methodological implications. I use the word "inscription" to call attention to the archive's irreducible textuality. By that I mean simply to say that the archive, any archive, is a weave or tapestry of conspicuous or durable marks that, for better or worse, must be understood or read as traces—neither simply present nor simply absent, but both. For me the archive is not, then, a space of referential plentitude or presence whose stability, materiality or "givenness" positions it in advance to serve as arbiter of Truth. To put it otherwise, as trace structure, the archive alone cannot guarantee or anchor any Truth absolutely.[33] But I also use the word "inscription" to signal a principled interest in guarding the question of intention, of always keeping it open. To be sure, there is intention and there are intended marks and scripts. But just as surely, something may be inscribed without the intention to do so. And just as surely, a surface may be marked in such a way that it "says" something more or less than what was intended. In other words, to guard the question of intention is not to dispense with it altogether. Quite to the contrary, it is to vigilantly remain open to the possibility that in addition to whatever may be intended something else may (also) (have) take(n) place. The archive, then, as a site of inscription.

Now it is precisely because traces are what reside in the archive that archives can serve as resources of an indeterminate but not wholly undetermined number of rhetorical inventions. I use the word "rhetorical" at this point in a relatively simple sense, which is to say as a name for situated symbolic acts that, aggressively or subtly, by design or default, seek to move their audiences to action or to attitude. Hence, the range of rhetorical inventions that archives can subsidize include not only explicit attempts at persuasion but also everyday practices of identification. I also use the word "inventions" in the relatively simple sense of a new fabrication or forming of the symbolic resources at hand.

Of course, rhetorical invention is never free in the strong sense of the term since it always takes place within a field of constraints that is also its surface of emergence. Of the many constraints on rhetorical invention, one deserves special mention here: power. I suggested above that we understand the archive as a site of inscription from which ensue rhetorical inventions that have a distinct relation to power. My point in marking the relationship between those rhetorical inventions and power is to insist emphatically that the deconstruction of the sign (or, as the case may be in the archive, object) does not mean that out of the archive any fabrication whatsoever may emerge. Nor does the deconstruction of the sign imply that the effects or consequences of the rhetorical inventions the archive subsidizes are anyone's guess. That is because what is sayable—like what is seeable and doable—must abide by the rules of formation of discourse (or objects and practice) of the field in which the enunciation takes place.[34] That speech, to turn the phrase, is never free, is one of the lessons to be taken from Michel Foucault who, as early as *The Archaeology of Knowledge* and as late as *Fearless Speech*, implored us to attend carefully to the relations between different elements that together configure an enunciative field and the enunciative modalities proper to it.

That enunciative modalities are not to be confused with speaking beings is a point Foucault made time and again but, perhaps, never so clearly as in the important middle section of *The Archaeology* titled "The Formation of Enunciative Modalities": "I do not refer the various enunciative modalities to the unity of the subject—whether it concerns the subject regarded as the pure founding authority of rationality, or the subject regarded as an empirical function of synthesis. Neither the 'knowing' (*le 'connaître'*), nor the 'knowledge' (*les 'connaissances'*). In the proposed analysis, instead of referring back to *the* synthesis or *the* unifying function of *a* subject, the various enunciative modalities manifest his dispersion. To the various statuses, the various sites, the various positions that he can occupy or be given when making a discourse."[35] For these reasons, we are obliged to think not about Truth or "Truths" but, rather, about the "'general politics' of truth" or the "'political economy' of truth" operative at a given time. Again, Foucault: "Each society has its regime of truth . . . that is, the types of discourse it accepts and makes function as true; the mechanisms and instances that enable one to distinguish true and false statements; the means by which each is sanctioned; the techniques and procedures accorded value in the acquisition of truth; the status of those who are charged with saying what counts as true."[36] As I have put it in so many words elsewhere, from the historicity of the archive, rhetorics; wrought from the traces of the past are discourses that the archive cannot *authenticate* absolutely but can be made to *authorize* nonetheless.

As noted above, the return of WWII took many forms, from Senate hearings and presidential speeches to television talk shows, series, and prime time specials; from one blockbuster movie and a lot of lackluster films (several that were remakes) to best-selling print, audio, coffee-table, and pop-up books; and from video games for kids and cruises for adults to countless museum exhibits and one mammoth WWII memorial on the National Mall. Although the list could go on, the point is that WWII redux took aim at *popular* memory. Hence, the second presupposition meriting discussion at the relative start: popular memory is absolutely central to modern state authority and, more specifically, to the establishment of any fantasy whose primary purpose is to install and maintain a particular form of social equilibrium.[37] To begin unpacking this presupposition I first call attention to the two distinct senses in which, taking my cues from Foucault, I am using the word "popular."

One, recuperations of WWII are popular by virtue of their working to diminish people's historical knowledge about the war, putting a popularized version of that history in its place. For example, it was a well-known fact during the war and in its immediate aftermath that the United States did not put its soldiers on the ground, in the air, and onto the seas until December 1941, although the British and the French had been fighting the Germans since September 1939. The fact that the United States was not "all in" for a very, very long time simply is lost to WWII redux, an assemblage whose near singular focus on a retooled heroism that is at once ethnonationalist and neoliberal renders that fact unrepresentable in advance. To put it simply, war heroes keyed to the neoliberal state need battle scenes, and years of deliberations over getting in or staying out, of going in before or after the Russians, simply do not fall "naturally" within that frame.

Two, WWII redux also was an exercise in reshaping *popular* memory in the sense that it worked to abate the people's historical knowledge of themselves, glossing over struggles related to class, race, religion, gender, and sexuality before, during, and after the war. It did so not by willfully erasing them, but by deftly sublating them into an ethnonational fantasy keyed to a neoliberal state beleaguered by "multicultural" difference and division. Hence, a movie like *Windtalkers*, directed by Jon Woo and released in theaters in 2002. Based on "real events," the movie follows the heroic triumphs and travails of US marine corporal Joe Enders (played by Nicolas Cage) who is charged to protect Ben Yahzee (played by Adam Beach), a Navajo private trained in directing US artillery fire via coded messages. In order that the code not ever fall into enemy hands, Enders has been ordered to kill Yahzee if or when his capture is imminent. Following the invasion of Saipan, during which Yahzee engages in lethal combat for the first time and Enders kills another code talker to protect the code, the unit is again mobilized and ambushed. Sparing the mediocre details, it will suffice for my purpose here to note that, as the enemy closes in on the few surviving marines and a wounded Yahzee, Enders (who also has been hit by enemy fire) must decide whether he will protect the code by killing him. Enders refuses to do so; instead, he carries the code talker on his back to safety, dying just as friendly forces, having received Yahzee's earlier call for an airstrike, arrive on the scene. The movie ends with Yahzee, his wife, and his son George Washington Yahzee paying their respects to Enders atop Point Mesa in Arizona. The movie's epilogue is a brief ode to the Navajo soldiers whose code, never broken, was key to America's success in the Pacific theater. Overall, then, the movie rhetorically sublates the particular into the universal (ethnonational), a negation of the negation that preserves and protects on one level what it destroys at another: a shared vision of the greater good that overcomes by negation a still unresolved, protracted, and violent history of difference between white colonial settlers and the native North American peoples.[38]

These two senses of the popular also make it possible to newly appreciate the doubled significance of the National World War II Memorial that opened to the public in April 2004. Situated between memorials to Washington and Lincoln, the new World War II memorial functions rhetorically as the symbolic center of the national memorial landscape, retroactively reshaping collective national memory by peripheralizing all the other events recalled there. So, popular in the first sense. But it is not only the nation-state's history that is being recalibrated there. It is also the peoples' histories of themselves. Widely applauded for being the first war memorial or monument to break from the convention of honoring only those who served in the armed forces, the National World War II Memorial also pays homage to those on the home front: "Above all, the memorial stands as an important symbol of American national unity, a timeless reminder of the moral strength and awesome power that can flow when a free people are at once united and bonded together in a common and just cause." Sublation without remainder: WWII as new nodal point of an ethnonational neoliberal state fantasy.

But why, we might justifiably ask, is *popular* memory so central to the establishment of any modern state fantasy whose primary purpose is to install and maintain a particular form of social equilibrium? In an interview conducted in

1974 and published under the title "Film and Popular Memory," Foucault tenders an answer that is as provocative as it is enigmatic in response to a question about how history was at that time being rewritten by French cinema and television. I quote him at some length:

> There's a real fight going on. Over what? Over what we can roughly describe as *popular memory*. It's an actual fact that people—I'm talking about those who are barred from writing, from producing their books themselves, from drawing up their own historical accounts—that these people nevertheless do have a way of [living that] history and using it [*de la vivre et de l'utiliser*]. . . .
>
> Now, a whole number of apparatuses have been set up ("popular literature," cheap books and the stuff that's taught in school as well) to obstruct the flow of this popular memory. . . .
>
> Today, cheap books aren't enough. There are much more effective means like television and the cinema. And I believe this was one way of reprogramming popular memory, which existed but had no way of expressing itself. So people are shown not what they were, but what they must remember having been.
>
> Since memory is actually a very important factor in struggle (indeed, it is [in a kind of dynamic conscious of history] that struggles develop), if one controls [*tenir*: keep, convene, hold on to, put down] people's [the people's] memory, one controls their dynamism [*dynamisme*]. And one also controls their experience [experiment, expertise, practice, taste], their knowledge [*savoir*: awareness] of/about previous struggles.[39]

Allow me a restatement: if one controls the people's memory or popular memory, one control's the people's dynamism. For me it is significant that the French word *dynamisme* is left untranslated or barely translated in the English edition, since a number of alternatives present themselves: energy, vitality, drive, pulsion, enthusiasm, force. So what is this dynamism that the people have that is linked to a memory of themselves and that also has a relation to struggle?

I propose we read *dynamisme* as Foucault's name for the generic potentiality or incipient power (*pouvoir*, as in can-do-ness) of the governed or of the demos to lend form (*bíos*) to life (*zoë*). In other words, I am suggesting that *dynamisme* signifies power's collective mode of politicized existence as potentiality. As potentiality and not (yet) actuality, *dynamisme* is that which has collective existence but not substance. *Dynamisme,* in other words, is subject to a judgment of existence but not subject to a predicative judgment; it is an existence whose character or quality cannot be described. Much like Foucault has said that "'the' pleb, undoubtedly, does not exist; but there is 'plebness,'" there, too, is *dynamisme.*[40] Furthermore, in taking my interpretive clues from Giorgio Agamben's exegesis of Aristotle's metaphysics and physics, I noted above that *dynamisme* is a generic rather than an existing potentiality. By that I mean to say that the governed, the people, or the demos "must suffer an alteration (a becoming other) through learning," the last word taken in the broadest of possible senses and not only as formal instruction (for Foucault, *savoir* as well as *connaissance,* popular memory as well as the lessons handed down by the state).

Following Agamben a bit further, it is consequential for our thinking about hegemony, state fantasy, or the installation and maintenance of a particular form of social equilibrium to notice that *dynamisme,* like any other potentiality, also is impotentiality. If, according to Aristotle via Agamben, potentiality (*dynamis*) is to be rigorously distinguished from actuality (*energeia*), potentiality must be understood as that which "maintains itself in relation to its own privation, its own *sterësis,* its own nonbeing." If it were otherwise, if potentiality were to be conceptualized as a pure and positive presence, it would quite simply be an actuality. Hence, Agamben writes, "To be potential means: to be one's own lack, to *be in relation to one's own incapacity.*" Even more to the point, Agamben finds in Aristotle's fundamentally passive sense of potentiality—the human being's capacity to suffer its own non-being or impotentiality—what he identifies as the "origin of human power" and the "root of [human] freedom" that, because the human being is capable of its own impotentiality, may be for good or for evil.[41] In considerably less hyperbolic terms we might say, the potentiality or not for struggle or the status quo. All the above is intended to suggest that I take WWII redux as a decentralized and many-pronged effort to domesticate the *dynamisme* of the demos at a critical conjuncture in US history. It is in this way, then, that WWII redux is also a biopolitical enterprise whose object is the people, whose modality is the popular, and whose specific aims take cover under the rubric of the general welfare.

Strategy of Reading, Rhetoric, and Form

My use of the words "strategy of reading" rather than "method" is deliberate in the extreme and not, perhaps for all readers, for only the most obvious reasons.

First, I use "strategy of reading" to call attention to the irreducibly rhetorical character of my engagement with each element, primary or secondary, visual or linguistic, over the course of these pages. Much like before, here I use the word "rhetoric" to indicate that my readings are self-consciously situated, interested, and deliberately designed to persuade the reader of the ethico-political and pedagogical usefulness of critically engaging the popular in a particular way, at and for a particular time. This book operates, then, in a different key and at a measured distance from various modes of literary interpretation, aesthetic appreciation, and philosophical exegesis whose aspirations are self-consciously transversal maybe even transcendental. Again, situated, interested, and designed to persuade.[42]

Second, I use "strategy of reading" because the questions I ask about my archive and the theoretical and critical resources I recruit on the way toward answering them changes over the course of the book. Indeed, by this point the reader will have already discovered that I toggle among Derridean, Foucaultian, and psychoanalytic/Lacanian rhetorical readings, not only between but also within individual chapters. The question, of course, is why? I employ all three modes of inquiry because they radically question foundationalist premises, like reason, sovereignty, and self-presence, each one of them because the singular foci of their conceptual labor remind me that no question can be answered simply. To recall a metaphor from the great structural anthropologist Lévi-Strauss that Derrida puts under erasure in order to mark (without being able to nullify) its propensities toward presence (anthropology's empiricism) and sovereignty (method as clean start), I read critically like a *bricoleur*, aspiring always to adhere to a double intention: "to preserve as an instrument something whose truth-value [I] criticize."[43] The challenge is to put them to use but with "a readiness to abandon them, if necessary, should other instruments appear more useful"—and not only to put them to use, one by one, or one after one, but also "several of them at once, even if their form and their origin are heterogenous."[44] No one of them is the ticket to truth, and even their intellects combined will not stand in as a transcendental key. Given the lack of an overarching method or morphology of interpretation, I track the development of one of the book's leitmotifs to give the reader a sense of how things will move.

As noted at the outset, my primary aim is to take measure of the ethico-political entailments of the renovation and reintroduction of WWII at a particular moment in US history. That objective demands, it seems to me, that I carefully consider context, a task noticeably easier said than done. Indeed, for all kinds of scholars and all sorts of reasons, "context" has long been a fraught term, a bit like the word "infrastructure" in political policy talk today: What is included and what is excluded by it? According to whom and why? Rhetorical scholars have long focused on the context of symbolic acts. However, defining context has been a challenging problem, leading to different and sometimes conflicting theories of rhetoric.[45] While it is neither desirable nor necessary to detail the history of that conversation here, I do wish to recall my own attempt thirty-odd years ago to guard the question of context,[46] reissuing the caution in less-nuanced terms now: the lexical shift from, say, context to scene (Kenneth Burke's recoding), or from scene to situation (be it determined as rhetoric is situational or situations are rhetorical), or from situation to circulation, or from circulation to ecology, brooks no gain on the irreducible indeterminability of context as such. And *because* of that irreducible indeterminability whose condition of possibility is what Derrida dubbed the graphematics of iterability, no determination of context can be justified absolutely. Every determination of context is a violent inscription.[47]

As Derrida explained in *Limited Inc*, the entailments of understanding context as always already an exercise of force that cannot be attributed fully to the speaking, writing, working, or designing subject are highly consequential, and not only for the so-called human sciences:

> There is always something political "in the very project of attempting to fix the contexts of utterances." This is inevitable; one cannot do anything, least of all speak, without determining (in a matter that is not only theoretical, but practical and performative) a context. . . . Once this generality and this a priori structure have been recognized, the question can be raised, not whether a politics is implied (it always is), but which politics is implied in such practice of contextualization. This you can then go on to analyze, but you cannot suspect it, much less denounce it except on the basis of another contextual determination every bit as political.[48]

There is no meta-discourse or meta-position that will get us out of the fundamental fix that is contextualization.

With Foucault's help I begin to stake my ground in the next chapter, identifying in the *Enola Gay* controversy an important shift in US political and public discourse. That is to say, considered within the broader frame of the demise of the national Cold War state fantasy and ascendent neoliberalism, I decipher in the *Enola Gay* exhibition debate a disturbing change in how we talk about and tell the truth that transforms what it means to be a good citizen and to do things the so-called American Way. By the end of the book, I circle back to the complexities of context via a critique of the new ethnonationalism's political economy of sacrifice. I tap psychoanalysis to propose an alternative conceptualization of patriotism or "love of country" that sutures Foucault's enigmatic notion of *dynamisme* to a psychoanalytic notion of (the) drive(s) for an affirmative biopolitics that confounds the neoliberal ethnonational state fantasy.

Finally, some thoughts about rhetoric and form, beginning with a declaration. I have yet to change my mind that everything to do with signification and value gets its start in *différance*. As I put it some years ago, but rephrase ever so slightly now in the interest of clarity, *différance* is the name Derrida cautiously assigned to the condition of possibility for signification as such, "the non-full, non-simple, structured and differentiating origin of differences": presence-absence, active-passive, true-false, inside-outside, literal-figural, et cetera.[49] "Rhetoric," then, is the term I use to designate the requisite finessing (condensation and displacement) of *différance* that inaugurates every textualization—a production that must be understood as an effect-structure, albeit one without a simple cause in either the casual or metaphysical senses of the term. I understand all signification, including communication, as rhetorical in this general sense; therefore, like the determination of context discussed above, I operate on the presumption that no textualization can be justified absolutely. Rhetoric in the general sense, then, is the inexorable opening onto the ethico-political.[50]

If rhetoric in this general sense is theoretically and practically irreducible, rhetoric in its narrower senses is critically indispensable, and not only because it covers so much ground. From the study of figures and tropes to the analysis of modes of persuasion and forms of argument; from the Derridean deconstruction of Western metaphysics to the Foucaultian interrogation of the discursive operations by which a signifier is gelled into a referent to the psychoanalytic exploration of economies of enjoyment, rhetoric in one or more of its narrow senses will always have its place there and in these pages.

What must be emphasized, however, is that across all the chapters I pay particular attention to the ethico-political affordances, witting or not, of *rhetorical forms* in public and popular culture. With this emphasis, I add my voice to a growing chorus of scholars challenging the fetishization of formlessness and the consequent attenuation of formal analysis in the literary, critical, and theoretical humanities.[51] Unabashedly pointing the proverbial finger directly at the likes of Bruno Latour, Giorgio Agamben, and Jacques Rancière—while also calling out by association with key terms entire "schools" of contemporary thought, from the neo-Deleuzians and neo-Spinozians to affect theorists, object-oriented ontologists and new materialists—Anna Kornbluh challenges the now highly orthodox investment in formlessness: "Formlessness becomes the ideal uniting a variety of theories, from the mosh of the multitude to the localization of microstruggle and microaggression, from the voluntarist assembly of actors and networks to the flow of affects untethered from constructs, from the deification of irony and incompletion to the culminating conviction that life springs forth without form and thrives in form's absence. Noting its characteristic horizon of *an-arche*, the 'without of order,' we might deem this beatific fantasy of formless life 'anarcho-vitalism.'"[52] In direct opposition to all who embrace formlessness as a political virtue, Kornbluh advocates a new aesthetic, literary, and political formalism that productively supplements the old by grasping "collective social life not as an empirical referent, but as [an] ever-evolving, provisionally stable, improvised form."[53] Obviously, then, this is not our grandmother's formalism; indeed, it is not even the formalism my generation of English majors was schooled in. It is a formalism that is self-consciously (to the extent that is possible) made to function on the other side of the deconstruction of form and structure—a formalism, that is to say, that submits all formalization to what Derrida dubbed in his inaugural lecture in the United States the critique of "the structurality of structure."[54]

As readers are likely to surmise at this point, I not only enthusiastically support but wish to supplement the new formalism by positioning rhetorical forms front and center, taking them seriously even when, especially when, they appear to inhabit the margins. I do so by identifying numerous rhetorical forms that play a meaningful role in the formation of an ethnonationalist state fantasy keyed to the neoliberal state at the end of the twentieth century. For example, I emphasized earlier my keen interest in *popular forms* of memory—blockbuster films, best-selling books, beloved museums and memorials—whose function in the (re)*form*ation of a national state fantasy was both distinct and profound. But I also have a keen interest in an array of rhetorical forms whose impact is ignored altogether by the trivialization of textuality and the concomitant inflation of "reading-as-paraphrase" or "summary" into a critical art.[55] Those additional rhetorical forms include but are not limited to repetition, serialization, sequentialization, and amplification; metaphor, metonymy, synecdoche, and part-object (a psychoanalytic name for what I later suggest is a distinct rhetorical function); antithesis, synthesis, and hierarchy. Importantly, however, because mine is a rhetorical analysis of rhetorical forms, I take their political affordances to be irreducibly situated, which is to say, articulatory effects. Again, without guarantees: what any form, say a monument or memorial, "means" or "does" now may differ from what it "meant" or "did" in the past and what it "will mean" or "will do" in the future.

I bring this already extended introduction to a close with a highly schematic summary of the chapters to follow. As noted above, chapter 1, "The *Enola Gay* Controversy: The Politics of Experience and Truth Telling at the Turn of the Twenty-First Century," focuses on the successful assault on "The Last Act," the planned fiftieth-anniversary exhibit at the National Air and Space Museum documenting the historic flight of the *Enola Gay*, the dropping of atomic bombs on Hiroshima and Nagasaki, and the end of the war in the Pacific. I argue that this controversy's legacy is to have inaugurated a process by which WWII was discursively transformed from an event in the past about which we try to make sense into a mode of sense making or matrix of popular reasoning in the present.

Chapter 2, "Popular Memory and Civic Belonging at the End of the American Century," analyzes the monumental World War II Memorial on the National Mall, Steven Spielberg's blockbuster film *Saving Private Ryan*, Tom Brokaw's best-selling book *The Greatest Generation*, and the Women in Military Service for America Memorial, as well as the discourses circulating about them in the popular press and mass media. This chapter tracks the popular emergence of a powerful new "truth teller" who burst onto the national scene in 1998 with the release of *Saving Private Ryan*. This figure would speak with unassailable authority not only about the Good War but also, and more importantly, about what it means to be an American and to do things the American Way. In short, for a generation beset by fractious disagreements about the viability of US culture and identity, these reconstructions of WWII function rhetorically as civic lessons in ethnonational neoliberal fantasy.

The third chapter, "Remembering the 'Good War' / Refiguring Democracy: Ethico-Political Resubjectivation at the United States Holocaust Memorial Museum," explores the dangerous consequences of WWII redux. I argue that at the end of the twentieth century and the beginning of the next, the United States Holocaust Memorial Museum is a uniquely commendable commemorative text whose singular rhetorical virtue is that it, unlike all the others examined thus far, contests the premature ossification of WWII memory, its translation into a truth and a program of prudential conduct, and instead promotes the responsibilization of history. To recall what has already been foreshadowed above, in this chapter I return to the question of patriotism, tapping psychoanalysis for an alternative conceptualization of "love of country" that confounds rather than collaborates with the ethnonational neoliberal biopolitical order.

In chapter 4, "The Culture and History Wars of the Twenty-First Century, or, Can You Be WHITE and Look at This?" I examine today's US culture and history wars, paying warranted close rhetorical attention to *The 1619 Project* and *The 1776 Report*. Reading both as pedagogies of citizenship for the twenty-first century, I argue that the substantive and stylistic differences between them, as well as those between them and WWII redux, signify a potentially explosive mutation in political and public culture. Respectfully recalling Elizabeth Alexander's seminal essay written at the height of the early nineties culture and history wars, "The Culture and History Wars of the Twenty-First Century, or, Can You Be WHITE and Look at This?" uses several of the book's dominant analytics and motifs (e.g., popular memory, *dynamisme*, and desubjectivation) to soberly assess where our politics are currently headed.[56]

1

The *Enola Gay* Controversy | The Politics of Experience and Truth Telling at the Turn of the Twenty-First Century

On January 30, 1995, and at the behest of eighty-one members of Congress, the Air Force Association, and the American Legion, Smithsonian secretary I. Michael Heyman canceled the National Air and Space Museum's planned fiftieth anniversary exhibit of the *Enola Gay*'s historic flight. With the cancellation of "The Last Act: The Atomic Bomb and the End of World War II," conceptualized by National Air and Space Museum director Martin Harwit, Heyman promised a new exhibit would open in its place, the organizers of which surely learned a key rhetorical lesson from their deposed predecessor: exhibits need to be timely *and* appropriate. Heyman claimed that although the director and curators of the scrapped exhibit had rightly recognized that the Hiroshima bombing's fiftieth anniversary as an opportune moment to unveil the restored B-29 Superfortress, they unfortunately failed to do so in a manner befitting the occasion. As the secretary put it at his press conference that day:

> We made a basic error in attempting to couple an historical treatment of the use of atomic weapons with the 50th anniversary commemoration of the end of the war. Exhibitions have many purposes, equally worthwhile. But we need to know which of the many goals is paramount, and not to confuse them. In this important anniversary year, veterans and their families were expecting, and rightly so, that the nation would honor and commemorate their valor and sacrifice. They were not looking for analysis, and frankly, we did not give enough thought to the intense feelings such an analysis would evoke.[1]

Holding true to his word, Heyman's "minimalist" exhibit, titled simply "The *Enola Gay*," opened in June 1995.

There were, of course, dramatic differences between the two exhibits. According to the final script and exhibit drawings, Harwit's "The Last Act" was to have been a six-part installation "describ[ing] the war between Japan and the United States and its allies, the building of the atomic bomb, the decision to use it, the military effort to carry out that mission, the effects of the bombing, and the surrender of Japan." Heyman's surrogate exhibit had only two parts: a meticulous, step-by-step chronicle of the Superfortress's renovation, at the very center of which was the infamous B-29's gleaming forward fuselage, followed by a decisively less meticulous recounting of the production and deployment of the bomber that was capped off with a looped video in which members of the 509th reflected on their historic flight.

What are we to make of Heyman's surrogate exhibit that displaced a visual and verbal rhetoric of historical inquiry with one of technological progress, staged first as a magnificent renovation narrative and second as a success story commemorating a singular development in US scientific and technological innovation? From a historical standpoint, Heyman's exhibit is a watershed moment in a decade-long culture war against liberals who, conservatives like Rush Limbaugh claimed, had seized "control of our major cultural institutions... the arts, the press, the entertainment industry, the universities, the schools, the libraries, the foundations, etc." and begun to undermine the nation's most sacred narratives and traditional values.[2] As Marilyn B. Young noted in her stinging analysis of the controversy, for the conservatives the stakes had never been higher: safeguarding the untarnished legacy of the "Good War" meant the preservation of "one of the few remaining anchoring points of national mythology."[3] For conservative veterans and their relatives, members of the Congress, and the press, then, the successful assault on the *Enola Gay* exhibit was a crucial victory in a larger crusade to fend off the national fragmenting effects of what Homi Bhabha has called the "jargon of the minorities"—identity politics, ethnic particularism, and multiculturalism—and to reinstate a sense of the "common culture."[4] For museum professionals, liberal scholars, and liberal members of the press, on the other hand, Heyman's stand-in exhibit signified a devastating blow to the credibility and autonomy of the Smithsonian Institution. More important, by caving into mounting political pressure and threats of massive budget cuts by the Republican-controlled House and the Senate, the secretary of the single most powerful US cultural institution had sacrificed one of the most fundamental principles of American democracy—freedom of speech. As Brigadier General Roy K. Flint, president of the Society for Military History and a former dean of the faculty at West Point, wrote in a letter to the chairman of the Smithsonian's Board of Regents, Chief Justice William Rehnquist, only four days before Heyman aborted "The Last Act," "While our members possess varying views about the history of World War II, we share a passionate commitment to freedom of speech and to providing the best scholarship with integrity. Overwhelmingly we believe the past should be represented honestly, sensitively, and with verisimilitude. . . . Even more importantly, the Smithsonian must stand publicly against the politicizing of scholarship in public discourse, and it must resist all efforts to impose conformity in the rendering of history."[5] Having joined the ranks of photographers, performance artists, novelists, poets, and literary scholars whose battered reputations littered the cultural landscape, liberals understood the conservatives' "successful attempt to muzzle the Smithsonian" not as a sign of national reparation and democratic renewal but as a symptom of their slow but steady demise.

There was, however, one point on which all parties could agree: that certain differences between Harwit's "The Last Act" and Heyman's "The *Enola Gay*" mattered. Most significant for both detractors and enthusiasts of Heyman's display—albeit for different reasons—was its near-complete omission of the devastation at Ground Zero. When asked why, "apart from a twenty-second video snippet showing bomb effects (which may or may not have included an almost subliminal image of a corpse) and a label copy saying that the two bombs 'caused tens of thousands of deaths,'"[6] his exhibit did not address the bombs' destruction at Hiroshima and Nagasaki, Heyman stated, "I really decided to leave it more to the imagination."[7]

Without question, the exhibit's verbal silence on and visual erasure of what took place beneath the mushroom clouds was a deliberate act, Heyman's direct response to a vitriolic exchange over what, in curator Tom Crouch's words, was to have been "the emotional heart" of the canceled version. Indeed, from the moment representatives of the Air Force Association got their first glimpse of the sixteen-page exhibition planning document in 1993, the director's, designer's, and curators' intention to incorporate visual rem(a)inders of Ground Zero provoked heated debate. Although there was no question on any side that "melted roof tiles, testimony to the awesome heat generated by the explosion," and "bent steel girders, evidence of the magnitude of the blast" should be displayed, plans to document the impact on human beings and human bodies were vigorously challenged by opponents and persistently defended by its director, curators, and their advisers.[8]

As Harwit studiously documents in his published account, *An Exhibit Denied*, the team responsible for the display had worried the question of visual effects long before the controversy broke out. As early as the fall of 1987, Admiral Noel Gayler (Ret.), member of the museum's Research Advisory Committee, expressed concern "that a massive, gleaming *Enola Gay* would give the impression that the museum was celebrating raw power."[9] Similarly, correspondence with Japanese authorities about borrowing photographs and artifacts from the Hiroshima and Nagasaki Peace Memorial Museums, internal memoranda, and minutes from various planning sessions addressed strategies by which the National Air and Space Museum might avert the impression that it had callously erected a shrine for the Superfortress. As Harwit put it in a passage of his retrospective, which I quote at length:

> To avoid this perception we needed to show that the bomb had caused unimaginable damage and suffering. This would be done by emphasizing the thoughtful debates that had preceded the decision to drop the bomb (section 200) and by treating with understanding the effects of the bomb on the two cities and their populations (section 400).
>
> We could imagine that a visitor who had just seen the fifty-six-foot-long forward fuselage of the *Enola Gay* (in section 300) might come into section 400 and walk right past the small, modest-looking, everyday objects we could borrow from the museums at Hiroshima and Nagasaki—a wooden clog, a small watch with its hands frozen at the exact hour of the bombing, some scorched clothing, a child's lunch box with charred contents. Because of the very modesty of these objects, we felt we had to call our visitor's attention to them. To do that, we resorted to deliberately compassionate text and photographic images.[10]

For Harwit and his team who understood themselves to be "responsible for portraying [the historic flight of the *Enola Gay*] accurately and truthfully" photos of Hiroshima victims were crucial for striking a balance between the "awe-inspiring" Superfortress and its cost to human life.[11] Without them, there would be nothing to counter the *Enola Gay*'s sublime effects.

To the opposition the matter looked altogether different. According to veterans, military historians, members of Congress, and journalists who pushed for the cancellation of "The Last Act," the supposed "shock and awe" effect of the Superfortress—and, thus, the need to provide "balance" by incorporating photographs documenting the bomb's destruction—was a ruse. First, as Colonel Tibbets (the pilot of the mission who had named the plane after his mother) emphatically argued, the very manner in which the plane was to have been displayed would not leave viewers in awe of its power. Quite the contrary: because its size and weight prohibited display of the fully assembled B-29 in the National Air and Space Museum, the presentation of the forward fuselage—"without wings, engines and propellers, landing gear and tail assembly"—would enhance "the aura of evil in which [it was] being cast."[12] Second, in light of the literal and figurative mutilation of the plane that Tibbets and other veterans took as a sacrilege, the incorporation of photographic images taken of Ground Zero promised to deliver one thing only: a gross distortion of history that would inevitably provoke a crisis of national conscience and, thus, promote anti-American sentiment. As American Legion National commander Bruce Theisen wrote to President Clinton on August 12, 1994:

> Smithsonian officials have argued, not disingenuously, that nowhere does the exhibit explicitly state an anti-American bias. That is true. But the preponderance of visual material, personal perspectives and descriptive narrative, taken as whole, prompts the unmistakable conclusion that America's enemy in the latter days of World War II was defeated and demoralized, ultimately the victim of racism and revenge, rather than a ruthless aggressor whose expansionist aims and war fervor yielded more than a decade of horror and death for millions of the world's people.
>
> As a visual experience, the potential of the exhibit to engender a revised view of history will be even more powerful, and render a serious disservice to the post-World War II generations—of both sides.[13]

Unlike the director and the curators for whom the traumatic photographs were understood to lend "balance" to the exhibit, opponents were deeply troubled by their irreducibly obfuscating and ideological effects.[14] Indeed, as was emphatically noted in a letter signed by twenty-four members of the House, the incorporation into the exhibit of personal artifacts taken from Ground Zero along with images of dead and dying Japanese civilians would surely make Americans appear unlikable to themselves:

> We write to express our concern and dismay about the National Air and Space Museum's intended exhibit on the fiftieth anniversary of the bombings of Hiroshima and Nagasaki. . . .
>
> As you are aware, there has been much controversy about this exhibit based on the fact that many respected military historians and veterans' organizations found the original exhibit and accompanying script to be lacking in balance and context. It portrayed Japan more as an innocent victim than a ruthless aggressor, and cast Americans as being driven to drop the bomb out of revenge and for political reasons rather than out of concern for the hundreds of thousands of American lives that would have been lost during an invasion of Japan.
>
> Air and Space tried to quell criticism by revising the exhibit and script after consultation with veterans, historians, and representatives of the armed forces. However, after review we have found that the revised script is still biased, lacking in context, and therefore unacceptable. . . .
>
> There are 32 photographs of Japanese casualties during the war for the Pacific, but only 7 photographs of American casualties. Attention to the fact that the atomic bombs prevented an invasion of Japan and an estimated one million American casualties is limited to one small wall label at the end of the exhibit. There are 84 pages of text and 97 photographs relating to Japanese suffering, but less than one page and 8 photographs relating to the suffering caused by the fierce Japanese aggression between 1930 and 1945.[15]

After months of meetings with high-ranking officials of the Air Force Association and the Veteran's Association of America a thoroughgoing review of the exhibit's script by a "tiger team," chaired by a retired Air Force brigadier general, and extensive revisions—not the least of which were the addition of a four-thousand-square-foot introductory photo exhibit documenting Japanese aggression and brutality between 1930 and 1945 as well as the removal of two-thirds of the images and all but eight of the personal objects recovered from Ground Zero—public debate rose to an unprecedented pitch, negotiations reached an impasse, and the exhibit was scrapped.[16]

But exactly what made all those involved so certain that the truth of the exhibition hinged on the inclusion or exclusion of those traumatic images and objects? What guaranteed that those bodies or, more precisely, their material traces were, to turn Judith Butler's phrase, bodies that would always already matter to patrons of the exhibit? Counterintuitively, perhaps, I want to suggest that they were not. Indeed, I want to call into question the presumption on both sides that the incorporation of these "counter-monuments" would inevitably prompt patrons to question—rightly or wrongly—the official national narrative sanctioning the dropping of the bombs.[17] "If," as George Will put it in his usual pithy way on *This Week with David Brinkley* at the height of the controversy, "the question is, was the bomb necessary and moral?" it is not necessarily the case that exposure to those charred remains would always already move the viewing public to doubt "former president Harry S. Truman's and his advisors' decision to end the war quickly, avoid an invasion of Japan, and save thousands of American and Japanese lives" by dropping atomic bombs on Hiroshima and Nagasaki.[18]

That visual documentation of the human suffering caused by the dropping of the bombs need not *necessarily* produce a crisis of American collective conscience is borne out by US cultural history itself. On Memorial Day 2002, little more than ten years after the public controversy over "The Last Act: The Atomic Bomb and the End of World War II" began, NBC aired *Price for Peace*. Although the cultural cottage industry about WWII inspired by its golden anniversary had attended almost exclusively to the European campaigns, this prime-time special was not its singular focus on the Pacific theater. Even more remarkable was its unabashed inclusion of the kind of image that had caused so much trouble for Harwit and his team a decade before. Indeed, *Price for Peace*—directed by James Moll, produced by Steven Spielberg and Stephen Ambrose, and hosted by Tom Brokaw—did not "leave [the human cost of the blasts at Hiroshima and Nagasaki] to the imagination" of its viewers but brought it squarely into the living room of thousands of US households (figs. 1 and 2).[19] In a full segment of the program on the atomic bomb and "the end of the war," audiences not only saw iconic footage of the mushroom clouds rising over both cities from above (not incidentally, with corresponding text at the bottom of the screen indicating the date of the drop and approximate casualty figures, 140,000 for the former and 74,000 for the latter), they also got a graphic look at what took place on the ground.

Following sustained panoramic footage of the leveled landscape come five vivid close-ups of Japanese civilians maimed by the blast: the forehead of a young girl, the right torso of one young boy and the shoulder and face of another, the hands of one woman and the entire back of another are severely burned or melted away. Moreover, the presentation of the five women and children whose

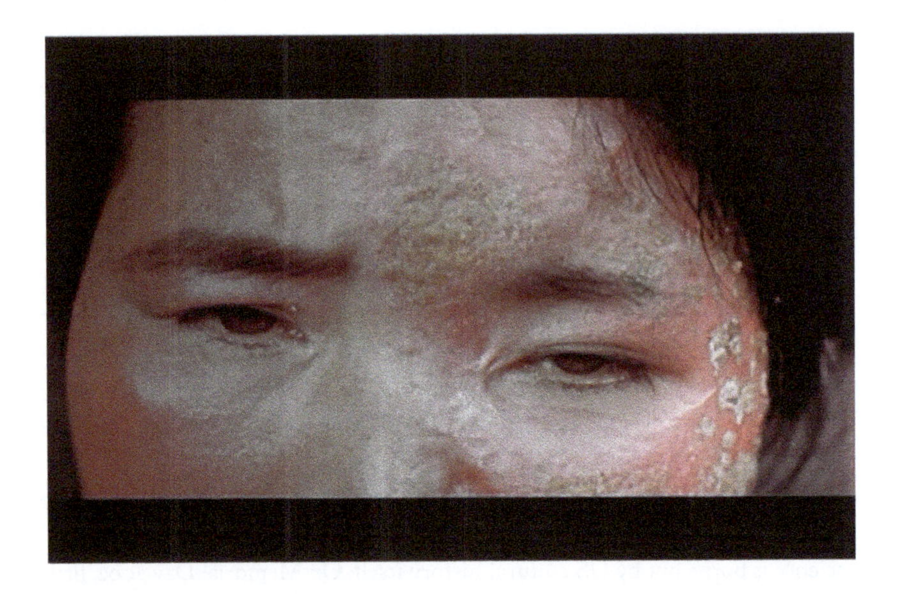

Fig. 1 | Film still from *Price for Peace: From Pearl Harbor to Nagasaki*, directed by James Moll. National D-Day Museum, 2002.

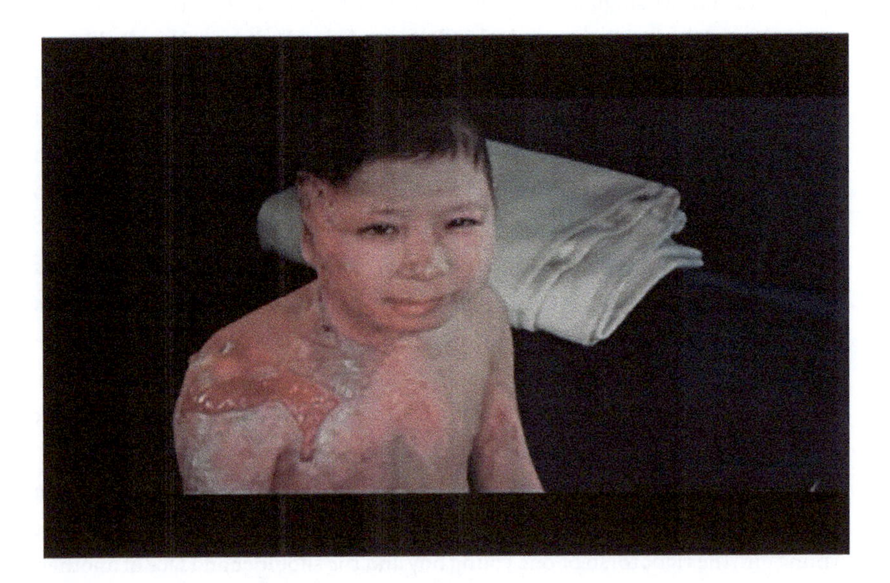

Fig. 2 | Film still from *Price for Peace: From Pearl Harbor to Nagasaki*, directed by James Moll. National D-Day Museum, 2002.

mutilated bodies metonymically stand in for thousands is prefaced by the inclusion of yet another civilian, a Japanese eyewitness and survivor of the drop on Nagasaki, who gives voice to human suffering as the mushroom cloud takes shape on the screen:

> Mr. Sakita: (*Japanese spoken, translated on screen*) I could hear the distant hum of planes.
>
> (Footage of blast and emerging mushroom cloud with script "Nagasaki August 9, 1945 Approximately 74,000 killed)
>
> Mr. Sakita: (*Japanese spoken, translation on screen*) About 500 meters above, I saw a large red fireball as large as the sun. And from this fireball, multicolored sparkles flashed everywhere. And these sparkles came down like rainfall. This light pierced my face and I immediately felt pain and heat. I touched my face with my left hand and slid it down my face. The skin on my face peeled off and was hanging down to here (*gestures with hand to upper torso*).
>
> (Panoramic view of devastation at Nagasaki)
>
> Mr. Sakita: (*Japanese spoken, translation on screen*) For as far as I could see, houses and other buildings were destroyed. The town was in ruins.[20]

More might be said about Mr. Sakita's return in the next and final segment, wherein he speaks passionately about his suffering from radiation poisoning, multiple surgeries, and a compulsion toward suicide that is checked only by a commitment "to abolish nuclear weapons," a "cause" that "gives [him] a reason to live." And more might also be said about the inclusion of competing views—albeit strictly bifurcated along American and Japanese lines—on whether a Japanese surrender would have come sooner or later had the bombs never been dropped or dropped in an unpopulated area so as to issue a warning without killing tens of thousands of Japanese civilians. And even more might be said about how this film, in striking contrast to Harwit's canceled exhibit, never raised the ire of veterans despite its failure to address Japanese aggression and brutality between 1930 and 1945 at length and mentioning the Bataan Death March only once. Indeed, despite candid admissions by WWII vets who testify over the course of the film that "the only thing that we wanted to see the Japanese was dead," that "it was very easy to shoot a Jap, believe me," that "I don't care if it had been a woman, child, baby, I could shoot," that "we didn't mind shooting them in the back either," *Price for Peace* is never charged with having sought, wittingly or otherwise, to produce anti-American sentiment. Indeed, if the popular press reviews are any indication, not even Paul Tibbet's reflections on the *Enola Gay*'s historic fight seems to have compromised the clarity of the documentary's pro-American message:

> Mr. Paul Tibbets: I put out of my mind anything that had to do with morality, religion, or anything like that. War is hell, and I wanted to get the killing over with as fast as I could. The airplane was quiet. Normally, you'd fly with the crews, they were telling dirty jokes and all that. There was none of that this time. There was dead silence, because they were all determined, just as I was, to get that bomb on the target for what good we thought it might do. And I thought the first day that I heard there was that weapon that if we could do that we'd certainly help the war effort along. I could see over the instrument panel the island. It was Hiroshima.
>
> (Footage of blast and emerging mushroom cloud with script "Hiroshima August 3, 1945 Approximately 140,000 killed")
>
> Mr. Tibbets: I didn't see it. All's I saw was the sky lit up in front of me; beautiful pink and red colors, and in the end there was three and a half square miles of Hiroshima devastated in one blow. That—that's how terrific it was. Rest of the trip, going back, everybody was relaxed, tension was over with. I told Bob Lewis, my copilot, I said, "You take it over, let the autopilot fly it. I'm going to get a couple hours' sleep." And that's what I did. . . .
>
> I've been asked time and again, "Don't you feel terrible about killing all those people?" No, I don't feel terrible. I'm sorry that they were there and had to be killed, but what had to be done was bigger than those people, bigger than me.[21]

That the visual and verbal representation of the Ground Zero carnage will not necessarily cast a dark shadow on the national self-image finds additional support in the use to which *Price for Peace* has been put. On the fifty-sixth anniversary of the Normandy invasion (June 6, 2000), the 70,500-square-foot D-Day Museum (later renamed the National World War II Museum) opened its doors to the public. Founded by Stephen Ambrose in 1991 and located in New Orleans, the museum was named in honor of Andrew Higgins, who designed and built the landing craft that made possible the amphibious invasions to which

Eisenhower credited the Allied victory in Europe. The exhibit is split in two: one half covers the war in Europe, the other half addresses the war in Asia. Two films, *D-Day Remembered* and *Price for Peace,* introduce each exhibit, both played several times a day in the Forbes Theatre next to the main hall. Of course, seeing the introductory films is not required to explore the exhibits, and since no one tracks who watches them, it is impossible to know how many patrons do. However, what is significant here is that the forty-five-minute version of *Price for Peace,* which includes the graphic segment on the bomb, is understood by the museum's design team as fitting easily within the parameters of its uncompromisingly patriotic mission: "The National D-Day Museum is designated by Congress as 'America's national World War II Museum.' It interprets the American Experience during the World War II years and celebrates the American spirit, the teamwork, optimism, courage and sacrifice of the men and women who won World War II and promotes the exploration and expression of these values by future generations."[22] Furthermore, graphic footage of the bombs' human toll reappears at the exhibit's end as part of a substantial installation titled "'Shatterer of Worlds': The Atomic Bomb," whose first panel consists of an illustrated time line documenting the development and deployment of the bomb. The opening text reads as follows:

> The Final Act
>
> In July 1945, as planning for the invasion of Japan continued, an event occurred that altered the course of the war—and global history. On July 16, scientists exploded the world's first atomic bomb near Alamogordo, New Mexico. As the bomb lit up the sky, Robert Oppenheimer, director of the scientific team, recalled words from the Bhagavad Gita: "If the radiance of a thousand suns, were to burst at once in the sky, that would be like the splendor of the Mighty One . . . I am become death, The shatterer of worlds." A terrifying new weapon had entered America's arsenal.
>
> The new weapon had taken more than three years and $2 billion to develop. America's largest and costliest weapons project to that date, it had employed more than 100,000 people. President Truman was at the Potsdam Conference in Germany when he learned of the test. He authorized use of the new weapon. Truman always maintained that he used the bomb to shorten the war and save lives. But his action became the subject of a controversy that persists to this day. Were atomic weapons needed to bring about Japan's surrender? Did they save more lives than they cost?

> Were there alternatives for ending the war? Over half a century later, the debate continues.

The time line in the main gallery directs visitors to the exhibit. Along the way, patrons pass through a standing-room-only theater. There, another short documentary film, simply titled *The Bomb*, plays continuously. In contrast to *Price for Peace*, this final and silent—excepting the haunting a cappella soundtrack—film relies exclusively on black-and-white archival footage. Five or so minutes in length, *The Bomb* chronologically sutures together a series of images, events, and scenes to dramatic effect: from the loading of Little Boy into the bomb bay of the *Enola Gay* to its drop, from the loading of the Fat Man bomb in a second Superfortress to the mushroom cloud over Nagasaki. Notably, the film once again gives patrons an unblinking, gritty, and relatively sustained (in relation to the overall length of the film) look at the devastation caused by the blasts: panoramic aerial footage of Hiroshima and Nagasaki documents mile upon mile of cities destroyed by the bomb; now and then an individual or two, face masks covering the mouth and nose, walk a path or sift through the rubble; a small team of official investigators examines three corpses that are charred from head to toe; and finally a young mother whose face and exposed leg have been turned to ash lies next to her dead infant child whose face has been face seared by the blast.

Admittedly neither *Price for Peace* nor the National World War II Museum Pacific exhibit are cultural texts that, to borrow Jacques Derrida's turn of phrase, even "guard the question" of the decision to the drop the bombs. The film gives the last word on the matter to a veteran who speaks of a natural regime of justice and common sense: "It ended the war, and it brought us home. What was left of us. Yeah." By its end, the somber, even pensive, tone of the installation on the dropping of the bombs is displaced by a vast assemblage of celebratory V-J Day photos that afford patrons much needed comic relief .

The point of tracking this intertextual chain is not only to document the extent to which things changed between July 23, 1992, when WWII veteran W. Burr Bennett Jr. began his letter-writing campaign on behalf of "the proud display of the *Enola Gay*," and May 27, 2002, when Tom Brokaw hosted the Memorial Day prime-time network presentation of *Price for Peace*, which Glenn Garvin of the *Miami Herald* called "a sweeping tale of heroism and torment," Joe Rubi of the *New York Post* characterized as "life affirming," and the *Tampa Tribune* deemed a "tribute to the approximately 120,000 US service people who died in the Pacific."[23] More important is to understand why. What happened over the course of a single decade such that the images which had provoked a public controversy of near epic proportion appear to have lost their power of counter-hegemonic address? To what do we attribute the waning of their affect? As Susan Sontag and others have argued about the traumatic image or atrocity photograph more generally, is it simply the case that the regular mass-media diet of horrors has deadened us to their shock?

To begin to formulate an answer, I want to return to the *Enola Gay* controversy and steal it momentarily away from the historians, provisionally positioning it as a kind of "origin" rather than "end."[24] My purpose in doing so is to specify and take measure of its *constitutive* rhetorical effects. That is to say, by putting this story into explicit contact with the larger cultural formation to which it contributes and of which it is a part, I want to suggest that its legacy is to have inaugurated a process by which WWII is discursively transformed from an event in the past about which we (continue to) try to make sense into a mode of sense making or matrix of popular reasoning in the present. More specifically, I argue that what is of lasting political significance is that this controversy laid the epistemological groundwork for the emergence of a powerful new "truth teller" for the twenty-first century; this figure, who broke onto the scene in 1998 with the release of Steven Spielberg's *Saving Private Ryan*, would soon begin to speak with unassailable authority about what it means to be an American and to do things the American way.

My primary aim in this chapter is not to challenge the liberal historians' scholarly account of the *Enola Gay* controversy. However, I do want to supplement their interpretation of the controversy as the story of the demise of the freedom of speech at the end of the twentieth century with another reading: the story of the discursive installation of a singularly commanding new speaking subject on the eve of the next. Not coincidentally, this truth-teller for the twenty-first century on whose ethos is predicated his authority to tell the truth has a determined relation to those visual remainders and reminders of Ground Zero whose own truth effects are, along the way, being remade.

Doubling Down on Identity

In his otherwise bold and illuminating analysis of the *Enola Gay* controversy, it is precisely the question of truth effects that historian Mike Wallace leaves unanswered. Perhaps this is because the question of truth effects is not about history but about rhetoric, not about truth in its narrowest sense but about truth in its general sense, as an activity and effect of power. Taking exception to Secretary Heyman's claim that in his 1995 "minimalist exhibit" the "aircraft speaks for itself," thereby presenting a nonpartisan or objective account with which no party to the debate could reasonably disagree, Wallace writes:

> In fact, it is the *Enola Gay*'s pilot and crew who speak on its behalf, in a sixteen-minute concluding video presentation. It is certainly appropriate to include the crew's reminiscences as part of the story. But why should their ringing retroactive justification of their mission (and that of their colleagues over Nagasaki) be privileged, and the troubling post-war reflections of men like Eisenhower, Leahy and even Truman himself be proscribed? It is as if the plane that dropped that atomic bomb were an artifact akin to a kettle or a wedding dress, which required only some donor-provided information about its original usage.[25]

Indeed, why? What play of forces made it possible for this singular authoritative voice to emerge? What were the conditions of possibility for producing and privileging, in the case of the exhibit, the truth of the *Enola Gay*'s pilot and crew—and, in the case of the larger controversy, that of the veterans and their allies? By what processes were these truth effects made so secure that by the turn of the century the graphic representation of death and destruction at Ground Zero could be comfortably incorporated within the conservative regime's cultural fold?

Of course, without assistance, no interpretation of the past, however patriotic, will (take) hold. Thus, let it be said that a good deal more than narrative reframing or a semiotic sleight of hand within a willfully circumscribed textual frame had to have been in operation here. It is therefore necessary to look to a certain beyond, to a discourse that, although at one time anterior and strictly opposed to the conservatives' own, would soon be made to work within, indeed function as, its authorizing center: identity politics.

The identity politics that came of age in the eighties has an intimate, albeit vexed, relation to poststructuralism, which migrated from France to the United States in the late 1960s. Both "movements"—the former liked to "the streets," the latter to "the ivory tower"—were outgrowths of the exacerbated and exhausted New Left's stubborn focus on class at the expense of race, ethnicity, gender, and sexuality. This prompted new single-issue social movements whose residual enlightenment and universalist predilections became the target of acute theoretical critique. Seeking a political alternative to Marxism's failed logics of revolt, the new social movements looked with deep suspicion, even hostility, on the theoretical anti-humanism that interrogated one of its own most prized premises: the self-willed and rational subject. Is it a mere coincidence, activists asked, that at the very moment when women of color and other minorities had begun to take up their rightful place as subjects, the subject as such is dismantled?[26] For groups fighting for rights and recognition, the deconstruction of identity, agency, intentionality, and reason seemed, at first, little more than another version of "white [male] mythology."[27]

At least in retrospect, however, it is possible to see a relation of another kind taking shape between these two discourses over time. Although never developing into a full-throttled alliance (for reasons that will be addressed below), the poststructuralist critique of universalism, self-presence, and essentialisms—including the biologism that subtended racist and sexist constellations of power—could be seen to be at work within the new social movements. Tackling identity's rigid designators from the other end, so to speak, the doubly and triply disenfranchised—those constituencies marked and marginalized not simply, for example, by gender or race but by both gender *and* race or by gender *and* race *and* sexuality—began to agitate on behalf of differences *within* as well as between less than thoroughly politicized categories of identity. Notably, concomitant with arguments made on behalf of the pluralization of identity differences was the proliferation of appeals to experience. In the wake of anti-foundationalism, it was experience—particular, local, concrete, and painful—that functioned as ground. Having the force and status of a material fact, the lived experience of different and often conflicting modes of oppression, exclusion, injury, and victimage proved to be rhetorically powerful. They served as the primary lever by which subordinated groups pried open homogenizing identity categories that had been too easily applied and also launched rights claims that resonated powerfully within the political public sphere.

"Politicized identity . . . enunciates itself, makes claims for itself, only by entrenching, restating, dramatizing, and inscribing its pain in politics; it can hold out no future—for itself or others—that triumphs over this pain. The loss of historical direction, and with it the loss of futurity characteristic of the late modern age, is thus homologically refigured in the structure of desire of the dominant political expression of the age: identity politics."[28] So argued Wendy Brown in *States of Injury: Power and Freedom in Late Modernity*, whose

Nietzschean-inflected analysis of late twentieth-century identity politics boldly queried its dangerous complicity with the liberal-democratic formation from which pain's redress is sought and worried its susceptibility to "a politics of recrimination and rancor, of culturally dispersed paralyses and suffering, a tendency to reproach power rather than aspire to it, to disdain freedom rather than practice it."[29] Insofar as any subordinated group's political identity is derived from the experience of domination—and to the extent that its political power is predicated on the recognition of that wounded identity by those positioned to do something about it—purportedly emancipatory projects will be inclined toward fetishizing rather than overcoming the experience of pain. It is this sense, according to Brown, that identity politics is a politics of self-subversion.

Brown's central concern was to discern how identity politics' internal logic of desire begets a self-negating resentment and "politics of unfreedom" on the part of subordinated groups seeking progressive change. Meanwhile, Lauren Berlant's concern had been to show how the minoritarian politics of painful experience sometimes works insidiously against its own interests and aggressively on domination's behalf. Particularly in a context such as ours, where talk of political struggle and systemic change has been drowned out by national sentimentality and a "rhetoric of true feeling," the price to be paid for any relief from pain may be the long-term perpetuation of the hegemonic status quo:

> For one thing, it may be that the aura of sudden piercing injury implied by the traumatic model of pain implicitly mischaracterizes what a person is as what a person becomes in the experience of concrete social negation, thus potentially oversimplifying the historical field; this model also falsely promises a sharp picture of structural violence's source and scope, in turn promoting a dubious optimism that the law and other conspicuous regimes of inequality can be made accountable (the way persons are) to remedy their own taxonomizing harms. It is also possible that counterhegemonic deployments of pain as the measure of structural injustice actually sustain the utopian image of a homogeneous national metaculture, which can look like a healed or healthy body in contrast to the divergently scarred and exhausted ones. Finally, it might be that the tactical use of trauma to describe the effects of social inequality so overidentifies the eradication of pain with the achievement of justice that it enables various confusions: for instance, the equation of pleasure with freedom, or the sense that changes in feeling, even on a mass scale, amount to substantial social change.

> Sentimental politics makes these confusions credible and these violences bearable, as its cultural power asserts the priority of interpersonal identification and empathy for the vitality and viability of collective life.[30]

Although pain's publicity may secure the benevolence of the powerful and even on occasion deliver the letter of the law, neither one nor both is a substitute for systemic change. For Berlant and Brown, a change in idiom—for the former from "trauma" to "suffering" and for the latter from "being" to "wanting"—is the order of the day.[31]

It would be a mistake to ignore these astute warnings of the limitations to identity politics. But the question of how to overcome them or what rhetorical idiom will most effectively work in place of "identity" cannot be answered in advance of a sober(ing) analysis of the particular situation within which the new idiom is to be deployed—a context that, despite its genealogical ties to and abiding affinities with a long-standing liberal discourse of national sentimentality, has changed significantly. Indeed, for me the most troubling feature of both Brown's and Berlant's otherwise keen analyses is that both are written *as if* the politics of identity and rhetoric of painful experience belongs only to the so-called Left, *as if* it is *still* exclusively the discourse of the disenfranchised and dispossessed.

I want to insist that this is no longer the case. But I also want to suggest that the *Enola Gay* controversy served as the opportune moment for political and cultural conservatives to *expropriate* the rhetoric of painful experience, to *transform* identity or victim politics from the inside out and, in so doing, to renegotiate the operative terms of the "parresiastic contract" itself—that more or less explicit agreement that Michel Foucault explains in *Fearless Speech*, determines "who is able to tell the truth, about what, with what consequences, and with what relation to power."[32] In other words, conservatives noticed that by the eighties talk of "diversity" or "multiculturalism" had so pluralized social identities and relations that it had effectively leveled the political field. They also recognized that the experience of injury was taken by those pluralized populations to speak for itself. Hence, they saw in the fiftieth anniversary display of the *Enola Gay*—an exhibit that parties on both sides *anticipated* would be controversial—the rhetorical occasion to move into that already established and powerful space of speech and retool it to their own political advantage.[33] How so, exactly?

First, let us not pass over the obvious: the key to stepping into and reconstituting that site or space for authoritative speech whose master term is "painful experience" is the repeated invocation of the "I." Without exception, utterances formed in objection to Harwit's "The Last Act"—from letters written to the president to articles published in the popular press, from statements made on *Nightline* to testimony delivered during hearings on the Hill—are founded on the personal pronoun "I." The overwhelming majority issue directly from that position: for example, "In 1945, I was a POW in Japan"; "In April 1942, I was captured by the Japanese forces"; "In 1945, I was wearing the uniform of the US Army Air Forces"; "I was there, I am a veteran of World War II."[34] In a few others, they appeal directly to it. For our purposes, one example will suffice: "For the majority of Americans now alive, . . . World War II is old history. For veterans like Grayford C. Payne, 74, of Annandale, who survived the Bataan death march in the war's earliest days plus 'three years, five months and 20 days' of starvation and slave labor in five Japanese prison camps, it was something else. . . . 'I hadn't been a prisoner for 15 minutes before.'"[35] As was the case before, which is to say during the heyday of identity or victim politics, painful experience is posited as an irrefutable or absolute ground. As Republican Senator Wendell Ford, a member of the US Senate Committee on Rules and Administration, put the matter during hearings which, according to an article in *Air Force Magazine*, revealed that "the museum's failure to consult individuals who had actually been there and seen the war firsthand"[36] was the primary reason why Harwit's exhibit utterly missed its mark: "Before me is history, personal, real, you can put your hand on it. I think our responsibility is to be sure that this real reflection on what actually happened—and I underscore real and personal—is projected into the future and not sanitized. . . . I was there, I am a veteran of World War II, not as active as some, more active than others maybe. . . . So somehow or other I want the institutional memory to stay."[37] What could be more certain or more true than a veteran's own account of what he has lived through and seen with his own eyes? As Ford elaborates, "I do not mind having different opinions and different interpretations. But it is awfully hard to refute General Sweeney. It is awfully hard because he was there, and he seems to be of sound mind and all that here today. I feel comfortable with his testimony."[38] The "personally" lived and felt, suffered and seen, is taken to be foundational. That is to say, it functions as a pre-discursive fact that neither requires explanation nor warrants inquiry but, to the contrary, serves as "the bedrock of evidence upon which [an inquiry] and explanation are built."[39] Indeed over the entire course of the public controversy and the hearings that followed, a uniquely clarifying effect is repeatedly attributed to the personal and painful experience of war. In the words of Major General Charles W. Sweeney (Ret.), who flew the instrument plane on the Hiroshima mission, commanded the second atomic mission over Nagasaki, and was the first to testify during the hearings before the Senate Committee on Rules and Administration whose members repeatedly invoked their own wartime experience, "My fellow veterans and I were impelled to ask how could the Smithsonian have been so terribly wrong about the true nature and meaning of the war in the Pacific and the atomic missions? Fortunately, this threat . . . was aired out in the open because the proposed exhibit of the *Enola Gay* was so devoid of factual support. Other historic events may be too subtle to be seen as clearly. Certainly the country was fortunate that millions of veterans of the war . . . were still alive to report on what really happened."[40] Like the "I's" of identity politics who proceeded it, this "I" poses its intimate, firsthand encounter with a painful real as a corrective to an ostensibly hegemonic construction of history. Its direct, unmediated, and embodied experience on the battlefield challenges the "establishment's" conventional wisdom whose inaccuracy is a consequence of inadequate vision. Its close proximity to, indeed, direct participation in, the brutal experience of war in the Pacific theater not only lends distinction to this enunciative "I" but positions it to call Harwit's exhibit into question. The experience of having endured and having seen—up close and with one's very own eyes—the human suffering of war lends to this speaking subject's words their particular character, credibility, and prestige.

But the cunning expropriation of the rhetoric of experience should not be viewed only in terms of its relation to the cancellation of Harwit's exhibit. As I noted at the outset of this chapter, progressive scholars and public spokespersons typically have read the *Enola Gay* controversy as the concluding episode in the story of freedom of speech's erosion at the near turn of the century. In the final analysis, they argue, the cancellation of "The Last Act" is best understood as nothing more nor less than a barely concealed act of bald "governmental censorship":[41] a powerful alliance of institutionally supported and well-funded conservative forces was able to reproduce and promote the "patriotic orthodoxy" by suppressing documents, visual images, and artifacts that, together, constituted a compelling and competing historical account.

In sum, the silence imposed on one version guaranteed the legitimacy of the other. As far as it goes, there is more than a grain of truth to the charge. Pages from President Truman's diary and letters penned by his hand expressing reservations about dropping the bomb, without warning, on anything other than a "purely military" target a never saw the light of day. Not one personal artifact from Ground Zero and not a single photograph taken beneath either of the mushroom clouds was displayed in the surrogate exhibit. And at the insistence of the American Legion and US Representative Sam Johnson, "The Last Act" companion exhibition catalog that had been prepared for and already advertised by the Smithsonian Institution Press in the spring of 1995 was never published.[42]

There is also a sense, however, that this principled reading of the controversy, whose singular focus on Power forecloses an analysis of power, misses the forest for the trees. The conservative campaign for "the proud display of the *Enola Gay*" needs to be examined in terms of something else it was seeking to not merely conceal but thoroughly debunk: namely, historical inquiry herein understood as a competing mode of knowledge production that identifies and analyzes the structures and principles on which primary experience depends but which it cannot directly comprehend. That is, the ultimate political aim of the conservative alliance was not merely to stifle a truth but, even more important, to deauthorize a competing mode of truth telling that it doggedly described as audacious, radical, revisionary, un-American, and above all out of touch.[43]

"Now, on what basis do you justify an interpretation of the history of this event so different from those of us who lived through it? On the basis of scholarly enterprise?"[44] Inscribed in this disparaging accusation of irrelevance—thinly disguised as a question—are the shadowy outlines of the strategy by which conservatives mounted their successful assault on History, a mode of knowledge production that, as the controversy moved along, would come to stand in for learned knowledge as such.[45] Notably, the conservative alliance did not strictly oppose the academic historians' analytics of truth by challenging directly its norms of research and argument. Instead, they rhetorically outflanked "the enterprise" altogether by discursively positioning intellectual work at an irreducible remove from the material real.[46] Indeed it was not without consequence that the veterans' "practical knowledge of history" was pitted with stunning redundancy against "academic understanding" in the popular press, by the mass media, and over the course of the Senate hearings themselves.[47] For example, on *Nightline* Deborah Amos's opening report framed the controversy as "a struggle between those who study history and those who experienced it";[48] for the *Washington Times* Donald Irwin wrote, it "takes real chutzpah for scholars who have not faced the life-or-death immediacy of the situation to second-guess decisions made earlier";[49] and in his prepared testimony, Major General

Sweeney (Ret.) wrote to the Senate Committee, "We cannot allow armchair second guessers to frame the debate by hiding the facts from the American public and the world."[50]

Notably to this vigilant exercise in disarticulating intellectual work from the world corresponds the dematerialization of the "evidence" on which the veracity or force of the "scholarly enterprise" depends. In other words, the imposition of a sharp divide between intellectual work and the world, which underlies the conservatives' attempt to secure a monopoly on knowledge production or truth telling, is the key to transforming the referents of historical inquiry into the mere signifiers of an overzealous and politically motivated textualism. "Especially now," wrote *Washington Post* columnist Jonathan Yardley, "when the rank odor of deconstruction hangs over the scholarly community, it is easy for people to fabricate intellectual arguments for the triviality of facts and then to find whatever 'meaning' they choose in such facts, or non-facts, as they are willing to 'deconstruct' for their ideological convenience."[51] Or, in the words of Major General Sweeney's prepared statement before the Senate committee, "To support such distortion, one must conveniently ignore the real facts or fabricate new realities to fit the theories. It is no less egregious than those who today deny the Holocaust occurred. How could this have happened? The answer may lie in examining some recent events. The current debate about why President Truman ordered these missions, in some cases, has devolved into a numbers game. The Smithsonian in its proposed exhibit of the *Enola Gay* revealed the creeping revisionism which seems the rage in certain historical circles."[52]

Here, again, the usefulness of the expropriated rhetoric of personal experience and the uninterrogated and interanimating logics of proximity, presence, and authenticity that underwrite it can be keenly felt. To recall the worlds of Ken Ringle once more, "Scholarly abstraction[s] composed of archival records, argumentative books, and . . . fading images on black and white film" could not compete with the "powerful flesh-and-blood stuff" offered up by veterans.[53] By virtue of its newly determined distance from "lived history," historical inquiry and analysis would be perceived to be speculative at best. Indeed, it is to this line of reasoning that Secretary Heyman ultimately concedes in his own testimony before the Senate committee: "I have observed here today what I observed during this whole controversy, that people, especially those who were participants in the Second World War, remembered with vividness and with emotion their participation and their sacrifice, what happened to their lives in relationship to that. I think when you are dealing with a subject matter of this sort, where those who have in fact experienced have to be look to, and you have to . . . you have to organize it consistently with those remembrances and those recollections."[54] "You have to": simple way of describing the positive effects of the rules of formation of the discourse that determine what can and cannot be said, represented, or done.

I have tried to track how, at a particularly opportune moment, the rhetoric of experience was expropriated by conservatives in order to lay the epistemological ground for the emergence of a singularly powerful truth teller for the twenty-first century. To this point, I have focused on the redeployment of "identity" or "victim" politics as a powerful technology of truth whose effects of veridiction—not just what is to be known or what is to count or register as "true" but also who is uniquely qualified to tell the "truth"—are nothing short of profound. But as the above-cited words of Secretary Heyman make clear, the social and political importance of this discourse extends beyond the reconfiguration of the rules by which certain subjects, to the exclusion of others, are recognized as "within the true" and therefore positioned to tell the "truth."[55] This expropriated rhetoric of experience, to put it summarily, functions not only as a regime of veridiction but also as a regime of jurisdiction; tied to the recalibrated rules of the production of "truth" are "programmes of conduct which have . . . prescriptive effects regarding what is to be done."[56] Thus, to close, I want to sketch the manner by which a *transformed* politics of identity and rhetoric of experience functions as a technology of power—or, more specifically, governance—that, as subsequent chapters will suggest, undermines the interests of the multiply fractured populations who, only ten years before, had been its primary beneficiaries.

Sacrifice as Political Rationality

In *The Body in Pain: The Making and Unmaking of the World*, Elaine Scarry wrote, "At particular moments when there is within a society a crisis of belief—that is, when some central idea or ideology or cultural construct has ceased to elicit a population's belief either because it is manifestly fictitious or because it has for some reason been divested of ordinary forms of substantiation—the sheer material factualness of the human body will be borrowed to lend that cultural construct the aura of 'realness' and 'certainty.'"[57] To be sure, the *Enola Gay* controversy surfaced at precisely the kind of moment Scarry describes. Attributed largely to the splintering force of an identity politics that put our imagined sense of community to every possible test, it was widely believed that American national identity itself was in serious distress. Indeed, throughout the eighties and well into the nineties there was the ordinary understanding that nothing was more urgent than the need to produce a sense of oneness among populations in the United States that had become increasingly heterogeneous. "There is no 'higher' social formation than the local group, no historically necessary universalism beyond the newly articulated universe of difference," wrote political theorist Michael Walzer.[58] "For the second time in the nation's history," Stanley Renshon noted, "there [was] a real question of how to maintain a stable and effective relationship between America's *unum* and *pluribus*."[59] Enter the veteran of WWII who, having risked life and limb, suffered and seen, is uniquely positioned on the eve of a new century to, in the words of Todd Gitlin, "cultivate the spirit of solidarity across the lines of difference—solidarity with 'anyone who suffers.'"[60]

Of course, at this point a rather obvious question imposes itself: How is this speaking subject able to do anything other than aid and abet the fracturing effects of identity politics and its injury-based claims by insisting that the truth, which is his particular pain and suffering, be collectively recognized? What mechanism makes it possible for his speech to fight off rather than feed the culture of divisiveness and the pathos of ressentiment? In other words, what sets this discourse apart from the others to which, as I have argued thus far, it owes much of its force? I already have pointed to how, in its expropriation, identity politics and the rhetoric of painful experience that underwrites it has been made to relate to a different domain of reference—WWII or, more precisely, a version thereof. What I want to consider at this point is that a very different political rationality has been articulated to this new organized field of objects: "sacrifice." That is, sacrifice displaces victimage as a privileged form of practical and political reason that, by the end of the century, will stand in as "common sense." I should stress that the claim that sacrifice is a political rationality is not simply another way of saying that it is a dominant thread, theme, or motif that uniquely inflects an interested or ideological stance. Rather, I wish to contemplate sacrifice as a materialized—indeed, in this instance, literally embodied—system of distinction that classifies and distributes objects and serves as the basis for political judgments. Through sacrifice, programs, policies, and institutions are newly linked, lines of force are redrawn, and norms of conduct are transformed. Sacrifice, in other words, is the name given by this speaking subject to a different economy of power that, ultimately, would incite a citizenry to evaluate and reform itself in accordance with its norms.

Although, to this point, I have deliberately refused to attend to it, sacrifice had been a salient feature of the *Enola Gay* controversy from the very beginning to its embittered end. The entire affair was in the interest of insuring that "the valor and individual sacrifices of individual Americans in combat" would not be lost on the American public that veterans groups mounted their assault on Harwit's planned exhibit.[61] But even at the start it was not the case that those sacrifices were simply to be duly remembered, acknowledged, or revered; they were to be emulated in practices that, of necessity, would be different in kind. As Herbert Molloy Mason Jr., writing for the *Veterans of Foreign Wars* magazine, put it, "The valor and the motives of Americans who were willing to give their lives on coral atolls, in jungles, and in the depths of the Pacific ocean" should serve as "inspiration to the present and future generations."[62]

By the mid to late nineties and into the new century, however, sacrifice as a principle by which Americans were to conduct themselves extended well beyond the relatively limited frame of the public controversy as such. It figured prominently in a vast assemblage of popular culture texts, a virtual cottage industry dedicated to the remembrance of WWII. Here, five examples will have to do.

First: on May 25, 1993, President Clinton signed the law that allowed the sacred ground between the Washington Monument and the Lincoln Memorial be broken for the raising of a $100 million World War II Memorial that would pay just tribute to the sixteen million WWII veterans and offer homage to all Americans who supported the war effort on the home front. The memorial opened on Memorial Day 2004. At its ceremonial entrance, the purpose of the memorial is inscribed on an announcement stone: "Here in the presence of Washington and Lincoln, one the eighteenth century father and the other the nineteenth century preserver of our nation, we honor those twentieth century Americans who took up the struggle during the Second World War and made the sacrifices to perpetuate the gift our forefathers entrusted to us: a nation conceived in liberty and justice." In the base of that stone, the following words have been etched: "They fought together as brothers-in-arms. They died together and now they sleep side by side. To them we have a solemn obligation. Admiral Chester A. Nimitz." And on one of the plaza's rampart walls can be read these words of President Harry S. Truman: "Our debt to the heroic men and valiant women in the service of our country can never be repaid. They have earned our undying gratitude. America will never forget their sacrifices."

Second: late in the summer of 1998, Steven Spielberg's Academy Award–winning blockbuster *Saving Private Ryan* opened in theaters across the country. The film closes with the gray-haired and teary-eyed Ryan's soliloquy at the gravesite of Captain John Miller: "My family is with me today. They wanted to come with me. To be honest with you, I wasn't sure how I would feel coming back here. Every day I think about what you said to me that day on the bridge. I have tried to live my life the best I could. I hope that was enough. I hope at least in your eyes I have earned what all of you have done for me."[63]

Third: by March 1998, only two months after its release, Tom Brokaw's *The Greatest Generation* hit the *New York Times* bestseller list for nonfiction. Therein Brokaw writes, "[This] is a generation that, by and large, made no demands of homage from those who followed and prospered economically, politically, and culturally because of its sacrifices. It is a generation of towering achievement and modest demeanor, a legacy of their formative years when they were participants in and witness to sacrifices of the highest order. They know how many of the best of their generation didn't make it to their early twenties, how many brilliant scientists, teachers, spiritual and business leaders, politicians and artists were lost in the ravages of the greatest war the world has seen."[64] And the book closes with the following words: "They will have their World War II memorial and their place in the ledgers of history, but no block of marble or elaborate edifice can equal their lives of sacrifice and achievement, duty and honor, as monuments to their time."[65] Sales kept it on the bestseller list for well over two years and it was soon reissued in paperback and audio forms. Due to its unprecedented popularity, two spinoff books were published as well.

Fourth: in September 2001 thousands of viewers watched the HBO miniseries *Band of Brothers*. In the words of Mike McDaniel, TV editor for the *Houston Chronicle*, "*Band of Brothers* tells the real-life stories of the ordinary men of Easy Company. . . . The arc is their World War II tour of duty, from boot camp in Georgia to D-Day in Normandy, from the Battle of the Bulge to the capture of Hitler's 'Eagle's Nest.' . . . Based on the book of the same name by best-selling author and historian Stephen Ambrose, *Band of Brothers* matter-of-factly unfolds. This isn't a story to pump up this particular group of soldiers, but to illustrate plainly their sacrifices, and the sacrifices of hundreds of thousands like them."[66]

Fifth: on September 25, 2003, Congress officially designated the National D-Day Museum as "America's National World War II Museum." As noted above, its mission statement reads as follows: "It interprets the American Experience during the World War II years and celebrates the American spirit, the teamwork, optimism, courage and sacrifice of the men and women who won World War II and promotes the exploration and expression of these values by future generations."

In each of these examples a code of national conduct is at play that works within and against identity politics' political rationality of "victimage." Now as Wendy Brown has amply demonstrated, the identity politics from which, I have argued, this new discourse takes its rhetorical cues is animated by "an economy of avenging." Albeit internally contradictory since "it cannot cease to be invested in [avenging its pain] without giving up its identity as such," it wants nothing more than to have the social wound recognized and redressed.[67] Herein resides a logic of symmetrical social and political exchange figured as a closed circle and expressed as the due restitution of a recognizable and recognized truth: damages paid, reparations made, parity reinstated or, perhaps, made real for the first time. In any case, an exchange, a circulation, and a rightful return.

What about "sacrifice"? Here, again, a notion of debt is invoked. But this time it is intimately tethered to "sacrifice," indeed to the "ultimate sacrifice" that, by way of the mechanics of efficient recoding, is represented as the gift of the felled soldier figured as *philanthropos*—the subject whose altruistic concern for the general welfare or common good expresses itself in an act that transcends partisan conflicts and is utterly devoid of selfishness. And therein lies the crucial difference: the "ultimate sacrifice" that has been made on our behalf can never be fully repaid. It is always already exorbitant to any gesture of recompense. This sacrifice that, by virtue of history's passing, has been laid at our feet is beyond calculation and, thus, redress becomes for us at once a persistent and impossible project. This, then, is an economy that radically suspends the logic of the closed circuit or rightful return; what operates in its place is what Jacques Derrida has called the *aneconomics* of the gift:

> Now the gift, *if there is any*, would no doubt be related to economy. One cannot treat the gift, this goes without saying, without relating this relation to economy, even to the money economy. But is not the gift, if there is any, also that which interrupts economy? That which, in suspending economic calculation, no longer gives rise to exchange? That which opens the circle so as to defy reciprocity or symmetry, the common measure, and so as to turn aside the return in view of the no-return. If there is gift, the *given* of the gift (*that which* one gives, *that which* is given, the gift as given

> thing or as act of donation) must not come back to the giving (let us not already say to the subject, to the donor). It must not circulate, it must not be exchanged, it must not in any case be exhausted, as a gift, by the process of exchange, by the movement of circulation of the circle in the form of return to the point of departure. . . . It is perhaps in this sense that the gift is the impossible.

Not impossible but *the* impossible. The very figure of the impossible.[68]

"Sacrifice" is thus the name for a political rationality and national code of conduct that productively exploits the aporetic structure of the gift, of the impossible gift, of the gift of time and the gift of death. Precisely because time—from one's "formative years" to an entire lifetime or lifetime cut short—neither can be given back nor has a general equivalent (there is no substitute for time that has been lost, taken, or given away), sacrifice imposes an obligation on all those who are its beneficiaries that is at once absolutely determining and irreducibly indeterminate. Put somewhat differently, if, as Harry S. Truman, a president celebrated for his plain speaking, put it, "Our debt to the heroic men and valiant women in the service of our country can never be repaid," that is not because we don't have enough time. Rather, it is because time is the one thing that cannot be inserted into the closed circuit of exchange, in itself or by proxy. Indeed, not even the sacrifice of another life will settle our debt.

It is, then, in the interval between the sacrifice that has been made and the indefinitely postponed moment of its full redress that citizen-subjects are positioned by this discourse. And it is in the space of the irreducible nonfit between the sacrifice and any gesture of recompense that a vast—indeed, theoretically indeterminate—field of practices opens up. How, then, are citizens to choose between one act and another? By what standards or set of criteria are citizens to conduct themselves? For an answer to that question, we may begin by going to the movies.

2

Popular Memory and Civic Belonging at the End of the American Century

Paregoric: . . . [1675–85; LL *paregoricus* <Gk *paregorikós* soothing = paregor(os) pertaining to consolatory speech (par-PAR + -egoros, adj. Der. of *agorá* public speaking, assembly, AGORA) + ikos—ic]
—*Oxford English Dictionary*

This chapter is about the body, the construction of a corpus, and US nation building at the turn of the millennium. Specifically, it is an inquiry into the way the body was being conscripted and a certain event rescripted to newly anchor national life. This is, then, an examination into how the body's and history's (re)inscription into the popular was deployed to inspire a new esprit de corps, a new common sense or national sensibility. Another way of putting it: over the course of this chapter I critically dissect the emergence of a paregoric rhetoric, a wildly popular verbal and visual consolatory speech whose dialectically paired and organizing tropes are the pained body of WWII and the contemporary crippled nation. Its hegemonizing power came from its simultaneous production and exploitation of a growing public intolerance for wounded attachments and so-called victim politics. This analysis tracks how, as the United States entered what Ronald Takaki called "the multicultural millennium," that pained body trumps the historically and socially disenfranchised subject in the national imaginary.[1]

I begin by taking notice of one the most recent and successful attempts to enter the national "given-to-be-seen": the World War II Memorial.[2] Proposed to Congress at the same time that accounts in the popular press expressed concern that the Washington Mall's "satisfying geometry" was being threatened by "irritable factions" vying for national visibility and recognition,[3] I read the memorial's speedy approval as symptomatic of a fierce desire on neo-liberals' part to reconfigure the terms of national identification and belonging. Taking formal leave of the memorial but following the lines drawn by its salient images and motifs, I then turn my attention to two of the most widely disseminated and wildly popular of all paregoric rhetorics, Steven Spielberg's *Saving Private Ryan* and Tom Brokaw's *The Greatest Generation*, and close with a studied tour of the less familiar Women in Military Service for America Memorial. By looking closely at these popular memory texts as well as the discourses that circulated about them in the mass media, I draw out a kind of cultural map of the conjuncture and identify some of its deeply troubling implications for the politics of national life.

National Geo-Graphy

In "Subaltern Studies: Deconstructing Historiography" Gayatri Chakravorty Spivak recalls the intractable relation of words and worlds:

> A functional change in a sign-system is a violent event. Even when it is perceived as "gradual," or "failed," or yet "reversing itself," that change itself can only be operated by the force of a crisis.[4]

A profound—indeed violent—event has taken place on the Washington Mall and in the national symbolic: the construction of the World War II Memorial on the sacred ground between the Washington Monument and the Lincoln Memorial. First proposed in December 1987, signed into law by President Clinton on May 25, 1993, and promoted by former senator, disabled veteran, and Viagra spokesperson Bob Dole, as well as the exorbitantly popular cultural icon Tom Hanks (who was not a WWII vet but played one on the big screen), the projected $100 million memorial opened on April 29, 2004. As described on its fundraising campaign's home page, the memorial's neoclassical design, whose final revision passed the notoriously tough hurdle of approval by the US Commission of Fine Arts without objection, delivered a structure that at once bestows just tribute to the sixteen million WWII veterans, pays appropriate homage to all Americans who supported the war effort on the home front, and grants due respect to "its magnificent site on the National Mall."[5]

Although first proposed at a time when more than eighty new monuments were warring for position in the nation's capital, the World War II Memorial progressed with relative ease. In this case, unlike so many others, there simply was no debate over whether "there [were] any other existing memorials that pay tribute to like or similar subjects" and no doubt about its "preeminent historical and lasting significance to the nation."[6] Indeed, the only serious reservation aired was that its monumental significance to the nation would require an edifice whose proper magnitude would overwhelm the mall's democratically sublime symmetry.[7] As John Graves, speaking on behalf of a minority of WWII veterans opposing the initiative, put it on the day the memorial won resounding approval from the commission, "We want a memorial but not on that particular spot."[8] Given that six other sites had been considered for placement of the memorial (the Capitol Reflecting Pool area, the Tidal Basin, West Potomac Park, the Washington Monument grounds, Freedom Plaza, and Henderson Hall), it is no minor detail that nearly five years *prior to* final design selection, the Commission of Fine Arts, the National Capital Planning Commission, and the National Park Service swiftly and unanimously settled on the east end of Constitution Gardens, between Constitution Avenue and the Rainbow Pool. They attempted to calm opposition by ceding that the design "not interrupt the vista between the Capitol, the Washington Monument and the Lincoln Memorial."[9]

Why was priority granted to pride of place? The strong answer came from President Bill Clinton on Veteran's Day 1995 in a speech that officially closed the fiftieth commemoration of WWII:

> Let me urge all of us to summon the spirit that joined that generation, that stood together and cared for one another. The ideas they fought for are now ours to sustain. The dreams they defended are now ours to guarantee. In war they crossed racial and religious, sectional and social divisions to become one force for freedom.
>
> Now, in a world where lives are literally being torn apart all over the globe by those very divisions, let us again lead by the power of example. Let us remember their example. Let us live our motto, *E pluribus Unum*—from many, one. Let us grow strong together, not be divided and weakened. Let us find that common ground for which so many have fought and died.[10]

Like that of the memorial's fundraising campaign, the theme of Clinton's panegyric to WWII was the urgent need for national reunification.[11] As he put it again later that afternoon during the site dedication ceremony, the memorial "will be a permanent reminder of just how much we Americans can do when we work together instead of fighting among ourselves."[12]

Like Clinton's, numerous other public statements argued that the projected memorial's capacity to resuscitate a waning sense of the "People" warranted its construction at the heart of the Mall:[13] "There is no other spot. The memorial should be right there, in the center of things, because World War II is central to our history, central to our view of our role in the world, central to our values. A World War II memorial at the foot of the Rainbow Pool would do to our nation's capital just what World War II did to our country. It changed the landscape. It changed the way we look at things. Build it. They will come around."[14] Or, "An event as momentous in American and world history as World War II deserved this prominent site. . . . When it is finally completed, all Americans will be proud of a World War II Memorial that epitomizes what can happen in our country when its citizens mobilize and become united in a just and common cause."[15] A prime piece of property parceled out for posterity, for the repair of a nation crippled by "division and resentment": a small price to pay for the recognition of what the president, on yet another occasion addressing the matter of "responsible citizenship," referred to as the "common ground" requisite to the forging of a "New [American] Covenant."[16]

Given the memorial's singular location on the mall and the authorizing logic invoked on its behalf, there is more at stake here than establishing an eternal repository of the heroic accomplishments of a generation past. Indeed, over the course of this chapter I will argue that the historic decision to place the World War II Memorial at the center of the Mall—flanked on one side by the memorial to the veterans of the traumatic Vietnam War and on the other by the memorial to the "forgotten" or Korean War—signals the reemergence of WWII as a new nodal point that promised to secure the national future against the vicissitudes of its multicultural present.[17] Traversing different forms and operating across multiple domains of discourse and practice, a certain vision/version of WWII was (re)materializing as the central coordinate of national life, reshaping social relations by reconfiguring the category of US citizenship. In other words, the privileged positioning of the World War II Memorial on the National Mall was symptomatic of an ongoing effort to rearticulate the relation of the citizen to the nation, thereby newly determining what differently positioned—by class, race, gender, and ethnicity—citizen-subjects could and could not claim or expect from the state.[18] That it will continue to operate in such fashion is certainly one of the effects of—if it was not the intent behind—the restriction drafted in September 1999 by the National Capital Planning Commission, the National Capital Memorial Commission, and the Commission of Fine Arts that "bann[ed] the building of any other memorials in a cross shaped area reaching from the Capitol to the Lincoln Memorial and from the White House to the Jefferson Memorial."[19] Hence, to alter only slightly a phrase taken from the memorial's promotional materials, WWII will have been "the defining event of the [early twenty-first] century in American history."

Fictioning the Common "Ground" of Citizenship

It is only in the wake of the deconstruction of truth that the real effects of politics may begin to be grasped. As Michel Foucault explains it:

> Truth is of the world; it is produced there by virtue of multiple constraints. And it induces there the regulated effects of power. Each society has its regime of truth, its "general politics" of truth: that is, the types of discourse it harbours and causes to function as true; the mechanisms and instances which enable one to distinguish true from false statements, the way in which each is sanctioned; the techniques and procedures which are valorised for obtaining truth; the status of those who are charged with saying what counts as true.[20]

Nearing the turn of the century, it was looking like the great melting pot was melting down; we were in desperate need of a way to feel national again, and, as always, the mainstream media lent a helping hand. Like clockwork, each evening our national news anchors would tell us two stories, one on the front end and one on the back: first, a report of yet another instance of acute sexual, racial, ethnic, and religious tension and conflict on our streets or in our schools, at the workplace or in our home; last, a so-called human interest story about one or another benevolent corporation, nonprofit group, neighborhood association, or charitable individual taking up the Good Samaritan challenge to feed the hungry, house the homeless, adopt the abandoned, or retrain the "old economy" workers whose skills had been swiftly outflanked by a high-tech revolution.[21] Out of these narratives—which also became headlines in our newspapers, received prime-time play on our radios, and mutated into "special issues" in our popular periodicals—emerged images of citizenship and incivility as well as a moving moral frame by which we might make sense of them. Indeed, by way of the media whose silences spoke volumes, we were rhetorically induced to believe that the nation was being brought to its knees by all those "mutually suspicious and antagonistic subgroups" whose overinvestment in their own wounded attachments was causing us to lose touch with "our common ground" and sight of our most precious national resource—"values."[22] Never mind that despite unprecedented national prosperity, a stubborn standard-of-living gap between rich and poor was growing ever wider; the nation's social safety net was continuing to unravel as funds for dramatically downsized federal entitlement programs were increasingly being channeled into private, voluntary, and "faith-based" organizations; anti-affirmative action initiatives were fast becoming common sense and common law; and fetal rights were slowly but surely upending women's rights. The country, we were encouraged to believe, could be brought back to its feet by little more than a healthy dose of old-fashioned American moral fiber.

With the release of *Saving Private Ryan* in the summer of 1998, the commonweal got a fabulously timely shot of homegrown goodness right between the eyes. Set against the backdrop of the epic invasion of Normandy and delivered from the point of view of the men in the trenches, this celluloid fanfare for the common man tells the guardedly triumphant tale of James Francis Ryan who, dropped deep behind enemy lines, is discovered to be the last surviving son of a mother of four whose three older boys had recently been felled by enemy fire. Having only narrowly escaped the slaughter on Omaha Beach, Captain John Miller (played by Tom Hanks) receives new orders from no less a figure US Army Chief of Staff George C. Marshall: he is to patch together a small Ranger unit and bring Ryan home to his mother, alive. For the remaining two and a half hours we watch a "public relations" mission for the home front morph into an eight-man moral pilgrimage that leads the "multicultural" squad—Sergeant Horvath (Miller's righthand man and confidant), Corporal Upham (the bookish, feminized translator), Wade (the merciful medic), Private Reiben (the Brooklyn bad boy), Private Jackson (the Scripture-citing sharpshooter), Private Caparzo (the Italian), and Private Mellish (the Jew)—into greater and greater peril. With them we set out on the journey asking, "Can [anyone] explain the math in this to me? Where's the sense to risk the eight of [them] to save one guy?" And at the end, like the young Ryan, we are left standing on an Allied-held bridge in the fictitious town of Romelle, with Miller's last, barely whispered command echoing in our ears: "Earn this." Therein lie the simple contours of a story about doing the decent, patriotic thing even when "the whole world has taken a turn for the surreal," even when, on their face, the numbers just don't add up.

Of course, the numbers do add up in *Saving Private Ryan* at an astonishing rate. Much of the unbridled enthusiasm for the movie was attributed to what is typically, albeit mistakenly, referred to by reviewers as its "opening scene," Spielberg's recreation of the US D-Day invasion of Nazi-occupied France. Repeatedly, those twenty-five unrelenting minutes of meticulously chronicled mass slaughter are credited with setting new standards for realistic filmmaking. In *Newsweek*, for example, Jon Meacham heralded *Saving Private Ryan* for being the first war film to represent "battle as it really was, in all its bloodshed and brutality, terror and tedium";[23] Jay Carr of the *Boston Globe* called it "the war movie to end all war movies";[24] writing for the *New York Times*, Martin Arnold imputed the film with "introducing a whole new generation to the spilled-guts school of war storytelling."[25] What Norman Mailer's *Naked and the Dead* did for literature, he argued, Steven Spielberg's *Saving Private Ryan* did for film: it exposed audiences to "the same brutal, sudden, absurd death—but in this case concentrated carnage—that is, the chaos and reality of combat."[26] It may be tempting, to this day, to see the film, in James Wolcott's words, as "an overture of pure cinema" that wholly rejects the "ideals of both patriotism and patriarchy" characteristic of nearly all previous Hollywood renditions of WWII.[27] However, I want to argue that *Saving Private Ryan* functioned rhetorically less as a medium for the demystification of the Good War than it worked as a vehicle for the production of a new national sensibility predicated on retooling the category of citizenship.[28]

The first thing that deserves critical attention is the particular way the film deploys the white male body in pain. Almost from the start, Spielberg gives moviegoers what he calls an "unblinking look" at the chaos and carnage that is real war (fig. 3). As the Higgins landing craft, crowded with American soldiers, approaches Omaha Beach, the ocean breaking over its sides, orders are issued and raw fear takes its most humble, human form: one GI's hand trembles as it reaches for a canteen and another's vacant eyes look toward the beach; two soldiers vomit and others are barely able to draw in what may be one of their last breaths. Within thirty seconds the ramp is released. Most of the GIs are cut down by merciless rapid German gunfire before they even step off the craft. Those who manage to clamber over the side of the vessel are plunged into a sea of streaming bullets. Some drown from the weight of their gear; others are struck by what appears to be wandering gunshot. Blood billows. As scores of boys and

Fig. 3 | Film still from *Saving Private Ryan*, directed by Steven Spielberg. DreamWorks Pictures, Paramount Pictures, Amblin Entertainment, 1998.

men scramble to get out of the bloody surf, onto the beach, and over to the seawall, bodies are blown in half, legs and arms are torn off, faces are ripped away. Others die more slowly, clutching their wounds, crying out for their mothers, receiving their last rites as they look with horror on their own entrails poured out on the sand.

What sets Spielberg's rendition of war's human carnage apart from all the others is not merely, as reviewers have noted, the rate at which it confronts us with those pained male bodies. Nor is it simply a matter that for the first time "we [get to] see, thanks to advances in technology, precisely what happens to the soft-shelled human body when it encounters explosives, projectiles, fuel, flame, and sword."[29] The real "sneak punch" of Spielberg's film, as Wolcott correctly points out, "is that it bypasses the usual introductions to its characters" and goes straight into war.[30] What difference does it make that our contact with a battlefield soon to be littered with the pained bodies of war precedes our knowing anything about its many victims and few survivors other than that they are all American? Without a doubt there is more than artistry in Spielberg's inversion: there is rhetoric. In exposing us to countless trembling bodies, perspiring bodies, gagging bodies, punctured bodies, drowning bodies, bleeding bodies, bodies with missing arms, legs, eyes, and faces, before informing us of their individual histories, Spielberg's Omaha Beach scene promotes our patriotic identification with *all* of them while blocking our subjective identification with any *one* of them. In literally bombarding the audience with these *not quite* empty signifiers, we become witnesses to a mass execution in which the pained white male body of war begins to function as ground or warrant for knowledge and judgment. In all its positivity, our collective, albeit mediated, experience of mass American slaughter functions as a great leveler of sorts; bearing witness to material, corporeal, sensual pain stands in for the pre-ideological, apolitical, universal, and, thus, universalizing experience out of which truth ("what really counts") and prudential wisdom ("what should be done") may emerge.

That bearing witness to the sheer factualness of the American GI in pain—its "realness," "density," and "certainty"—may be the foundation for a new rationality from which can be derived a vision of "the life worth living" is, of course, the story *Saving Private Ryan* ultimately tells. Having made the trek back to Normandy and standing over Captain John Miller's grave, the aged Ryan with generations in tow closes the film with the following words: "Tell me I have lived a good life. . . . Tell me I'm a good man." If Ryan is positioned *in* the film as someone scripted to gauge the value of his life in relation to those soldiers who—despite differences in age, race, education, class, religion, and ethnicity—collectively sacrificed their own to save it, we are positioned *by* the film to do so as well. Having brought the viewers "as close to combat as most of us will ever get,"[31] those dead American men, to turn only slightly the well-known phrase from Protagoras, become for us the measure of all things. It is in this way that the moral message of the film bleeds well beyond its diegetic frame and is infused with modern rhetorical force: the pained white male body of WWII displaces the traumatized psyche as origin, end, and arbitrator of individual and collective national life. As Matt Damon, who played young Ryan in the film, put it for the *Buffalo News*, "You can see us on Sally Jessy Raphael talking about how tough our lives are because we weren't breast-fed long enough. Try taking a *beach*."[32]

The second thing to notice about *Saving Private Ryan* is its heavy reliance on verbal and visual paramnesias, images that, as Lauren Berlant has put it, "organize consciousness, not by way of explicit propaganda, but by replacing and simplifying memories people actually have with image traces of political experience about which people can have political feelings that link them to other citizens and to patriotism."[33] Without a doubt, the pained body of war is one such image;

"home" is another. It is no accident that the two-and-a-half-hour-long rescue of Ryan is punctuated by real as well as remembered scenes of home. Indeed, when the men in Miller's Ranger unit are not fighting to survive the battles to eventually get home, they incessantly talk about it. With them we visit, visually or imaginatively, sanitized and sentimentalized images of "home," from the country kitchen and pristine porch of the Ryan family farm in Iowa, to a dressing room in a small women's shop on a side street in Brooklyn, from a young boy's bedroom visited by a mother who has just returned from the second shift, to the hammock and rosebushes in Miller's backyard. Decisively juxtaposed against the gritty and grainy chaos of war on foreign territory, "home" is transformed over the course of the movie into a fantastical space utterly bereft of the complexities, ambivalences, and incoherence of daily US life both in those war-torn years and today. Such an idealized vision/version of "home" is the nation's humble, homely, utopian aspiration, its version of "the good life."[34]

Having attended critically to these two typically underacknowledged elements of the film, it becomes possible to appreciate the rhetorical import of another more fully: the frame narrative. Contrary to what reviews in the popular press would lead us to believe, *Saving Private Ryan* neither opens on the surf of Normandy Beach nor closes on a bombed-out bridge in a French village; instead, it begins and ends with a multigenerational journey to the gravesite of Captain John Miller in a US cemetery in France at which the present-day Ryan delivers his long-awaited soliloquy: "My family is with me today. They wanted to come with me. To be honest with you, I wasn't sure how I would feel coming back here. Every day I think about what you said to me that day on the bridge. I have tried to live my life the best I could. I hope that was enough. I hope at least in your eyes I have earned what all of you have done for me." It is hardly a surprise that nearly all critics failed to mention this scenario that frames the story of Ryan's rescue: the deliberate not noticing of this highly sentimental, even saccharine scene is requisite to saving *Saving Private Ryan* as progenitor to a new generation of American realist cinema. However, something else was at stake. In refusing to attend to the truncated narrative that frames the tale of Ryan's rescue, critics disavowed what may be one of the film's most disturbing consequences for contemporary US collective life: its domestication of civic responsibility.[35]

It is obvious that the drama of the core narrative hinges on the almost infinitely suspended and anxiously anticipated encounter with the real James Francis Ryan. For Miller and his Rangers, progress on this mission is neither steady nor swift. The journey is repeatedly interrupted by unexpected and costly encounters with hostile German forces, rerouted because of a mistaken middle name,

Fig. 4 | Film still from *Saving Private Ryan*, directed by Steven Spielberg. DreamWorks Pictures, Paramount Pictures, Amblin Entertainment, 1998.

and nearly aborted by a one-man mutiny. With each calamity and casualty, the investment in Ryan goes up to the point at which even Miller, the captain whose steadfast determination to find Ryan and thus "earn [him] the right to get back to [his] wife," is given pause to question the "mission [that] is a man": "This Ryan better be worth it. He better go home and cure some disease or invent the longer lasting light bulb or something." Of course, by the film's end, audiences know that Ryan went home, and they may surmise on the basis of his mild demeanor and modest dress that he neither developed a vaccine nor "brought good things to life."

Here the motif of counting that played such a central role in the film's core narrative makes itself felt in—and beyond—the frame. Did Ryan earn it? Is he a good man? The film ends with the assurance that its audience has learned to count the ways: a wife, a son and daughter-in-law, a grandson and granddaughters (see fig. 4). A solid body count; a fruitful and productive life; a closing portrait of the multigenerational, white, iconic citizen-subject who embodies the becoming-national of home and the becoming-private of citizenship. For all its blood and guts, *Saving Private Ryan* is a paregoric rhetoric that expresses, justifies, and induces nostalgia for a national future in which everyone's debt to the republic may be paid in minor acts of "privatize[d] patriotism."[36]

The Civic Art of Personal Abstraction

"It is not enough," Jean-Jacques Rousseau famously quipped in *A Discourse on Political Economy*, "to say to the citizens, *be good*; they must be taught to be so." No less than four months after the release of *Saving Private Ryan* and on the eve of the Jasper dragging-death trial, the Center for Individual Rights' anti-affirmative action lawsuit against the University of Washington Law School, and a landmark settlement of $3.1 million to underpaid female employees of the Texaco oil company, Tom Brokaw's *The Greatest Generation* appeared on bookstore shelves across the nation. Within two months this collection of the life stories of forty-seven US men and women—whom Brokaw began interviewing on the fortieth anniversary of D-Day and who in one way or another played a part in the Allied war effort—topped the *New York Times* nonfiction bestseller list. By mid-January 1999 NBC's *Dateline* had already aired its own prime-time special documentary on the book and, owing to its remarkable popularity, *The Greatest Generation* was soon reissued in paperback, large print, and audio editions.[37] Given their substantive and stylistic similarities, Spielberg's and Brokaw's popular odes to the Americans who came of age during the Great Depression and the WWII years prompted columnists to proclaim the emergence of "World War II chic" or "retro patriotism," a new popular culture form whose "purpose . . . is to represent a world where all the tensions of the present are subsumed by the mission and the men."[38]

But to read *The Greatest Generation* as inducing readers to escape the social conflicts of the present by imaginatively transporting themselves to the past is to grossly oversimplify the rhetoricity of Brokaw's text. It not only invokes explicitly the social injustices that vexed the country during and after the war (in order to heap praise on the individuals who overcame them), but it also persistently calls up the disparities of social power in the 1990s and lays all blame for citizens' failures at their own feet. Indeed, by strategically juxtaposing an imperfect past and a troubled present, Brokaw's trip down memory lane leverages the past for a vicious attack on the identity politics of the day. In other words, history serves as Brokaw's alibi for a civics lesson in turning a blind eye to the social differences that still make a difference. Indeed, *The Greatest Generation* is a particularly robust contemporary paregoric rhetoric whose war on "victim politics" was symbolically subsidized by the "sacrifices" of an entire generation and discursively rationalized by their homespun wisdom.

Much like Spielberg's cinematic account, Brokaw's treatment of WWII delivers to its readership the experience of "ordinary" Americans. In the main, it tells the story of the little people's war, of their unsung struggles and unacknowledged sacrifices: of Lloyd Kilmer who, after spending ten months in German prison camps, returned home to marry, raise a family, sell real estate, and serve as county clerk; of Daphne Cavin, a newlywed who, after learning her twenty-two-year-old husband had been killed by enemy fire in France, made her way as a beautician in Lebanon, Indiana; of Martha Settle Putnea who, as a young black member of the Women's Auxiliary Corps, contended daily with institutional racism but later earned her doctorate and became a professor of history; of Wesley Ko, who, upon his return to the States after serving in the Eighty-Second Airborne, joined forces with a friend and opened a printing business, married, and raised a son and two daughters. As has already been hinted, for all their striking similarities there is something significant that sets *The Greatest Generation* apart from *Saving Private Ryan*: Brokaw's work has as much to tell us about the lives of these Americans after the war as during it. Indeed, it is significant that most of the ink in this book is spent on describing—in meticulous, sometimes tedious detail—the US postwar era, those decades during which "more than twelve million men and women put their uniforms aside," "returned to civilian life," and, along with those who had worked on behalf of the Allied victory on the home front, "immediately began the task of rebuilding their lives and the world they wanted."[39]

What is the significance of Brokaw's treating our "rendezvous with destiny" as the point of departure for forty-seven tales of personal triumph that take place when all is again quiet on the European and Pacific fronts? It facilitates the transmogrification of WWII from a sign that has the status of an event into what Michel Foucault has called a technology, what rhetoricians have long called *doxa*, and what I, following others, have termed a new esprit de corps that has the status of a structure. In *The Greatest Generation* WWII shifts from being an event in the past, about which we might still try to make sense, to a mode of sense making in the present. Under Brokaw's pen "World War II" becomes shorthand for a retroactive common sense or "matrix of popular reason" through which we are able to comprehend and negotiate the challenges of contemporary life, not the least of which, in his view, is the ideological unity of the US polity itself. As Brokaw opines in the closing pages, "There is no world war to fight today nor any prospect of one anytime soon, but racial discrimination remains an American cancer. There is no Great Depression, but economic opportunity is an unending challenge, especially in a high-tech world where education is more important than ever. Most of all, there is the need to reinstate the concept of common welfare in America, so that the nation doesn't squander the legacy of this remarkable generation by becoming a collection of well-defined, narrowly cast special-interest fiefdoms, each concerned only with its own place in the mosaic."[40] As he reports over the course of his sympathetically spun stories, a citizenry that has become ever more heterogeneous and contentious has left its demoralizing and devastating mark on the nation. Here the news anchor joins with other like-minded public figures in bemoaning the new "identity" or "victim" politics, holding it accountable for an impending crisis of national character and national culture. Whereas "the women and members of ethnic groups who were the objects of acute discrimination" during and immediately after the war "have not allowed it to cripple them, nor have they invoked it as a claim for special treatment now," subsequent generations of socially injured Americans, according to Brokaw, are disproportionately invested in their own putative subjection. How, then, might we arrest this attitudinal erosion?[41] How might we reverse the national course, "transcend partisan considerations," and cultivate a sense of oneness? By training, to use Brokaw's words, "a new kind of army" of citizen-subjects schooled in three classic American virtues—self-reliance, self-discipline, and self-sacrifice—that have been retooled to suit the demands of the multicultural, late-capitalist neoliberal state.[42] Notably, *The Greatest Generation* is that new army's field handbook. Here, what Toby Miller identified as the call for "the well-tempered self"—which first rang out in mid-sixteenth-century Europe with the mass dissemination of Erasmus's *De civilitate morum puerilium* (On civility in children)—reaches a new pitch.[43] To have read *The Greatest Generation* is to have completed a tutorial in the kind of radical subjective re-formation requisite to national renewal.

It is hard to imagine a popular text more adroit at using history for the purpose of US nation (re)building. *The Greatest Generation*'s success in doing so lies in the precise way it strategically invokes and foregrounds the social and cultural differences of the past—economic, racial, sexual, and ethnic—to prompt its readers to discount them in the present. That is, *The Greatest Generation* engineered a singular version of "then" to induce its readers to disavow their own primary and political passionate attachments "now"; allegiance to the nation or interpellation into the national was to be secured by a willed disregard of certain particularities of self that readers, in their reading, will have already begun to enact.

By the book's end readers will be well versed in the art of personal abstraction that for Brokaw is the sine qua non of national consubstantiality. His assemblage of tales, both thematically and formally, is an exercise in disincorporation.[44] Again and again readers encounter yet another variation on the same theme: thanks to the qualities of character developed during the war—self-reliance, self-discipline, and self-sacrifice—scores of Americans were able to beat the odds that mitigated against their success, be it physical disability, economic privation, gender oppression, or racial and ethnic discrimination. In every case, becoming part of "the greatest generation" is accomplished through the self-conscious dismissal of the body's particular and potentially disabling material attributes. One representative example is the profile of Sergeant Johnnie Holmes. Indeed, the life story of this black American who, in his early years, served in the 761st Tank Battalion and later in life "specialized" in "low-income rental apartment in buildings in black neighborhoods," supplies Brokaw with an exemplary illustration of how the racially marked and stigmatized can succeed by reimagining themselves as unmarked: "For all of his combative ways, Johnnie decided he wouldn't personally bow to the inherent frustration of discrimination. As he puts it today, 'If I let all of the negatives intervene, I would have never achieved anything. I kept focused on what I wanted to do, which was to make money, provide for my family.' . . . It was as a landlord and as a black man who had overcome so much on his own that he came to hate the welfare system that grew so fast in the fifties, sixties, and seventies. 'It just killed ambition,' according to Holmes. 'I had all of these [black] tenants who in their late twenties had never worked a day in their life. They just waited around for that government check. No incentive.'"[45] Obviously there is a lot going on here: the unabashed celebration of the individuated, self-making, liberal subject as well as a bourgeois norm of relative material comfort; the discursive obliteration of the politics—as effects of power—of the asymmetrical distribution of opportunity and resources in the nation; and the privatization of civic responsibility and social virtue.[46] Notably, what underwrites all the above is the persistent self-repudiation of the materiality or particularities of embodiment. Requisite to success and, thus, national belonging is what Sergeant Johnnie Holmes, in his "twilight years," calls keeping one's "focus on what one wants to do."[47]

Second, by virtue of the book's serial structure, the social and cultural particularities of American bodies—physical ability, class, gender, race, and ethnicity—are rendered merely paratactic. That is, in this assemblage asymmetries of embodiment become differences to which readers learn to be indifferent, markings to which readers are taught to disregard. It is hardly fortuitous, then, that the first of the forty-seven vignettes recounts the travails and triumphs of Thomas

Broderick, who lost his sight to a German bullet in the head. "*What's a handicap?*" asks Brokaw's blind bard in an epigraph at the very start of the book. "*I don't have a handicap.*"[48] Here the pained male body of WWII, which in *Saving Private Ryan* was the pre-ideological ground for prudential wisdom and judgment, reaches its apogee.

If *The Greatest Generation* is a pedagogy of prosthetic citizenship in the multicultural age that induces readers to enact the fantasy of the undifferentiated "We" of "We the People," what is to be made of the photographs throughout the book of "those men and women who have given us the lives we have today"?[49] Might these visual displays of the particular block the reader's translation into disincorporated subjectivity? When, in his preface, Brokaw meta-critically reflects on his book and declares that he does not understand it to be "the defining history of [the WWII] generation" but "instead, think[s] of [it] as like a family portrait," he is not speaking only figuratively.[50] Indeed, Brokaw, his research assistants, and his publishers went to considerable lengths to recover and reproduce 130 amateurish snapshots, stock family photos, and studio portraits that lend the volume the appearance and feel of a family photo album whose images relate a tale yet to be determined. As Annette Kuhn has written in *Family Secrets: Acts of Memory and Imagination*, in family albums "pictures get displayed one after another, their selection and ordering as meaningful as the pictures themselves. The whole, the series, constructs a family story in some respects like a classical narrative: linear, chronological; though its cyclical repetitions of climactic moments—births, christenings, weddings, holidays . . . —is more characteristic of the open-ended narrative form of the soap opera than of the closure of classical narrative. In the process of using—producing, selecting, ordering, displaying—photographs, the family is actually in the process of making itself."[51] What sort of national family story, then, is being made as we read Brokaw's ensemble of inscriptions of shadow and light?

Contrary to what we might first suspect, this visual archive poses no threat to the text. It encourages the self-violating interpellation of individuals into abstract citizen-subjects. Significantly, like its verbal counterpart, Brokaw's collection of images is structured as a series of discrete but intimately related vignettes, each of which comprises at least two photos, a "before the return from the war" shot followed by a "long after the return from the war" shot. Obviously, the strategic sequencing has one primary function—to visually authenticate the verbal text.[52] But if each pair of photos works alone to certify the verisimilitude of the verbal tale told, taken together they produce a different truth effect.

When viewed as a group, the visual, as Lisa Cartwright has argued at length, is anti-visual.[53] As an album or archive, serialization displaces sequence, and the negation of difference is effected through pluralization. On the visual plane, then, a paratactical logic reduces the asymmetries of embodiment to equivalence, interchangeability, and invisibility. Indeed, by the time readers near the end of Brokaw's tutorial, they will have been trained to disregard that the concluding seventeen vignettes, notably grouped into sections titled "Famous People" and "The Arena," feature the life stories of fourteen white men, two white women, and one "model minority," Daniel Inouye, whose closing words in this context encapsulate, to use Wendy Brown's terms, "liberalism's universal moment" for the multicultural state in late capitalism:[54] "The one time the nation got together was World War II. We stood as one. We spoke as one. We clenched our fists as one, and that was a rare moment for all of us."[55]

All in all, *The Greatest Generation* is a particularly robust paregoric rhetoric, and a particularly insidious one: an antipolitical political image text that, in claiming to be merely representing what it is helping to produce and promote, advances a highly normative, indeed exclusionary, notion of the citizen-subject, the *sensus communitatis*, and the national family.

(Wo)men and War

History is what happened. We then go about making it make a (certain kind of) sense. Or, as Foucault explains in *The Order of Things*:

> Order is, at one and the same time, that which is given in things as their inner law, the hidden network that determines the way they confront one another, and also that which has no existence except in the grid created by a glance, an examination, a language; and it is only in the blank spaces of this grid that order manifests itself in depth as though already there, waiting in silence for the moment of its expression.[56]

With the opening of its doors in the fall of 1997, the Women in Military Service for America Memorial (WIMS), a thirty-three-thousand-square-foot structure situated at the ceremonial gateway to Arlington National Cemetery, would appear to have dealt a decisive blow to (largely white) masculine presumption on the Washington Mall and in the national symbolic. For the first time, the United

States acknowledged the accomplishments of the more than two million women who had served in times of domestic and international crisis since the Revolutionary War. They were understood to be worth their symbolic weight, if not in gold then in granite, steel, and glass. Thus, on the eve of the new millennium and in the wake of Tailhook, Aberdeen, and Citadel investigations, it seemed we were a nation finally prepared to get our history right. As Rep. Mary Rose Oakar (D-OH), who introduced Resolution 36 to authorize the establishment of the memorial, put it on dedication day, "This Memorial will change the teaching of American history. . . . We will know that in every war, contrary to past popular belief, women have been killed, disabled and injured physically and psychologically. We will know of women's bravery, courage, their love, dedication and sacrifice for their country and their strong desire for world peace."[57] But the memorial does much more than call attention to the systematic exclusion of women from the annals of US military history and, thus, implicitly call for its revision. Rather than leave that job to posterity, the memorial takes on itself the compensatory task. "This memorial," as the mission statement on one of the central interior walls boldly declares, not only "honors the women who have served in and with the US Armed Forces from the time of the American Revolution to the present. . . . The Education Center within this memorial tells the stories of these forerunners and then focuses on women of the 20th century who have served both in and with the military in ever-expanding roles."

Because of its educational function, WIMS is more akin to a museum than a memorial or monument. To step into the memorial is to leave the minimalist rhetoric and aesthetic of national commemoration and to move into a system of representation in which an assemblage of image texts is engineered for pedagogical effect.[58] Upon crossing the memorial's threshold, patrons find themselves in a centrally located exhibit gallery. Various objects—from reproductions of photographs, paintings, drawings, and posters to flight logbooks, dog tags, handmade clothespins, undergarments, and uniforms—are consolidated within exhibit alcoves that track the numerous roles women have played in the nation's military history. The memorial uses explanatory plates, a guidebook and a thirteen-minute video presentation, "In Defense of a Nation: The History of Women in the Military" (shown at regular intervals in the memorial's state-of-the-art theater) to show visitors that women have been *agents* of US history even if their contributions have been systematically ignored.

The memorial's declared pedagogical purpose is advanced in other ways as well. From the renovated hemicycle wall "representing the barriers to greater opportunity and recognition that women have encountered in their efforts to serve our country" to the four new stairways "carved through the existing stone and concrete, symboliz[ing] women's efforts to break through these barriers," the memorial challenges the conventional wisdom by making women visible as vital participants in military history, not just its passive beneficiaries.[59] Indeed, nowhere is the memorial's repudiation of majoritarian male culture made more explicit than on its roof, a literalization—indeed materialization—of the "glass ceiling," this one constructed out of 138 rectangular transparent glass tablets, eleven of which have etched on them words such as the following:

> From the storm-lashed decks of the Mayflower . . . to the present hour, woman has stood like a rock for the welfare of the history of the country, and one might well add . . . unwritten, unrewarded, and almost unrecognized (Clara Barton, founder of the American Red Cross, 1911); Let the generations know that women in uniform also guaranteed their freedom. That our resolve was just as great as the brave men who stood among us and with victory our hearts were just as full and beat just as fast—that the tears fell just as hard for those we left behind (Unknown US Army nurse, WWII); The ground they broke was hard soil indeed. But with great heart and true grit, they plowed right through the prejudice and presumption, cutting a path for their daughters and granddaughters to serve their country in uniform (Secretary of Defense William J. Perry, groundbreaking, June 22, 1995).

An unguarded, dare we say militant, feminist stance against the received history?

For the rhetorical critic of US culture poised to appreciate the memorial's contestatory force, a seemingly abstract lesson of so-called elite or high theory—that a discontinuous relation always already obtains between origins and ends—makes itself felt as a productive practical caution: to guard vigilantly the question of ideological effects or, in this instance, to refuse the presumption that, as Peggy Phelan has put it, "increased visibility equals increased power."[60] Not necessarily, not always, not only, because at this particular conjuncture, it may not. In this instance, as Lacan once put it, visibility may be a trap.[61] Indeed, a critical analysis of the memorial makes it possible to discern how this lesson in revisionary history may be pressed into the service of another ideological agenda.[62]

As noted, the heart or center of the memorial is an exhibit gallery housing sixteen alcoves that by virtue of running the length of the renovated hemicycle may be accessed from double doors on either end. Upon entering, visitors to the memorial inescapably encounter seven glass-enclosed display cases, four of which house exhibits devoted to women's role in WWII; the other three hold displays documenting women's service in the eighteenth and nineteenth centuries, between 1901 and 1945, and since 1946. Although the exhibits use photographs, drawings, and paintings to show the growing importance of women in the military, the displays' impact is enhanced considerably by a massive collection of paraphernalia related to women and war. Indeed, these WWII displays are loaded from floor to ceiling with an array of objects that, notably, do not record the fantastic feats of singular individuals but instead metonymically mark the regular rhythms and daily practices of our nation's servicewomen. Among scores of others are a pair of mosquito boots that protected one army nurse in Africa from contracting malaria, a sample identification card issued to all Women's Army Auxiliary Corps recruits, one of the hundreds of summer uniforms issued to Women Accepted for Volunteer Emergency Service inductees, the helmet and calculation instruments used by an unidentified air force service pilot, one anonymous student's handwritten notes on how to repair guns and pack parachutes, and another's army-issued underwear and pajamas. From the first installment to the last, what the WWII collection features are ordinary, commonplace objects; typicality rather than rarity subtends the order of things here. The principle of typicality also underwrites the photographs that have been incorporated into the permanent exhibits. Instead of bearing witness to striking moments of uncommon valor, these archived images make visible the collective or cooperative, anonymous and even monotonous or generic, character of servicewomen's daily life: here a sea of telephone operators, there a secretarial pool, here the US Cadet Nurse Corps in formation, there a mass of women working on a factory line to "free our men to fight." Although rare, when formal portraits and snapshots of individual women in particular situations do appear, they are reconfigured into a collage, thereby reconstituting them as members of a larger whole and those events as part of a broader-based effort. When amassed, arranged, and placed behind glass, the artifacts presented in the exhibit alcoves are invested with new significance, are infused with new force, with "representativeness." In this way a seemingly complete, unabridged history of women in the US armed services begins metonymically to be made visible and present.

All the objects brought together at WIMS are placed in individual exhibit alcoves that have been clearly labeled and chronologically arranged: "Serving with the Military: 18th and 19th Centuries," "Serving in the Military: 1901–1945,"

"Women Go to War: World War II," "Servicewomen in World War II: Recruiting, Training and on the Job," "Volunteering on the Homefront: World War II," "Overseas with the Military: World War II," and "Serving in the Military Since 1946." Thus, although each individual window into the past is made to represent a distinct period of US military history and women's place in it, the passage from the first to the last reveals, step by step, women's *ever-evolving* role in the armed services, their *natural* ascension over time from handmaiden to helicopter pilot, from battlefield nurse to brigadier general. The sequential display of periodized artifacts has been supplemented by two complementary narratives—a relatively elaborate *Self-Guided Tour* manual that visitors may pick up at the entrance to the memorial and a much-abbreviated version thereof that appears in installments over the course of the exhibit.

The handheld script works rhetorically as a mechanism to normalize and naturalize women's integration into the armed services by making it appear as the always already determined outcome of a process whose reasonableness has been made legible over time. First of all, its repeated deployment of the constative utterance helps conceal the discursive status of the display, thereby leaving patrons with the impression that rather than having been authored by someone, the written supplement has been dictated by the objects and movement of American history itself.[63] The impact of this exhibition rhetoric that accentuates the objects as it effaces itself is augmented by two strategic silences that together conceal the artistry at work.[64] Not once does the name of a photographer appear on the legend that accompanies each display case (in every case, however, the collection or archive from which the object has been extracted or donated is clearly identified), and nowhere in the memorial or in any of its PR materials are the curators of the exhibits acknowledged. Second, the script's adroit inclusion of directives to patrons on how they are to read crucial elements of the visual text controls to a considerable degree the images' signifying effects. Indeed, when pictures alone may fail, words step in: "The individuals pictured here are representative rather than famous"; "Again, the majority of photos are not of famous women but show the variety of ways in which women have served with the military since WWII"; "The increased number of photographs in this panel reflects the increasing numbers of women in the services during peacetime and times of conflict." Third, the handheld script disavows how social differences and power dynamics have influenced women's roles in the military. Although it purports to reveal the *historicity* of women's enfranchisement, the memorial effectively elides it by representing women's progress as the inevitable outcome of a rational historical unfolding and not a consequence of political struggle. Indeed, this is sensationally demonstrated in the decision to mark the Women's Armed Services Integration Act of 1948.[65] Presented as a singular, even watershed, moment in the exhibit gallery, the memorialization of the act neatly buries gender inequality within US military history, thereby constituting the present as post-feminist, post-political.

To represent history in evolutionary terms is often to privilege a conservative model of social transformation, which promotes tolerance of the status quo because it assumes change is the consequence of some greater force (e.g., History or biology). Nonetheless, the exhibit gallery invites a certain kind of collective action, one that is given palpable expression through the memorial's computerized registry and its engraved glass ceiling. Next to the exhibits, a room with twelve computers allows visitors to access "the photographs, military histories and memorable experiences" of "women veterans, active duty, reserve, and guard women, and women who have served in direct support of the military throughout history." Additionally, three larger-than-life screens have been placed above the entrance to the registry; there the name, record of service, and photographic image of every registered servicewoman serially appears by way of a computer-generated, around-the-clock roll call. Operating in tandem with the exhibit gallery, the computerized registry deftly deploys new information technologies, linking the abstract national to the situated local; in their engagement with the official image archive, visitors literally perform acts of national identification that provide them with embodied models of normative national character. Finally, the pilgrimage to the upper terrace caps off the "self-guided" tour. For patrons already party to the complex rationalization displayed below, the words etched on the roof not only grant official public voice to the women who have served but also function rhetorically as injunctions to serve the national cause:

> You have a debt and a date. A debt to democracy, a date with destiny (Oveta Culp Hobby, Colonel, Director of the Women's Army Corps, World War II); All of us must work at patriotism not just believe in it. For only by our young women offering their services to our country as working patriots in the armed forces can our defense be adequate (Helen Hayes, Defense Advisory Committee on Women in the Services, 1951); The qualities that are most important in all military jobs—things like integrity, moral courage, and determination—have nothing to do with

gender (Rhonda Cornum, Major, US Army Medical Corps, Operation Desert Storm).

Hence, beyond recognizing women's contributions to US military history, the Women in Military Service for America Memorial scripts a new version of normative US identity: service to the nation is the arche and telos of what it means for any American—man or woman—in the words of the *Self-Guided Tour* manual, to "exercise full citizenship." Thus, from a memorial "dedicated to the women who have served" figures forth an abstract category of civic agency that folds feminine subjectivity into universal (masculine) virtues. As Major Marie Rossi, killed in a helicopter crash the day after the close of the Gulf War, stoically noted in a nationally televised interview, a portion of which is woven into the memorial's video presentation, "It's our jobs. There was nothing peculiar about our being women. We were just the people called upon to do it."

The Power of Popular Memory

Over the course of this chapter, I have argued that late twentieth-century remembrance of WWII played a decisive role in reshaping the social imaginary. It did so not by willfully erasing race, gender, and class differences, but by rhetorically sublating them into an ethnonational fantasy keyed to a neoliberal state. Indeed, I have tried to demonstrate how a popular film, *Saving Private Ryan,* and a best-selling book, *The Greatest Generation,* redefine in highly restrictive and distinctly centrist terms what it means to be a "good American." Although both the film and book advocate the domestication and privatization of civic responsibility, the latter goes further by cultivating in its readers the civic art of personal abstraction. I have also tried to show how the potentially innovative or progressive political force of the Women in Military Service for America Memorial is colonized by its articulation into this broader popular culture frame or formation. Taken together, then, these popular memory texts assist in the reconsolidation and naturalization of highly traditional logics and matrices of white patriarchal privilege that continue to traverse the various arenas of collective life from the political to juridical, the economic to the social. The general lesson to be drawn from this reading of the contemporary WWII formation is unmistakably Foucaultian: "There *is* power, it *is* productive, and it works through the production and dissemination of truth, disciplining the citizen through a pursuit of the popular."[66] But by inflecting the constitutive and not merely mimetic role of these popular culture memory texts, this chapter also implicitly suggests that it is possible to remember otherwise; that not only what we remember but how we remember it could be different; and that popular memory could be pressed into the service of a very different politics. It is to that other kind of popular memory and politics that I now turn.

3

Remembering the "Good War" / Refiguring Democracy | Ethico-Political Resubjectivation at the United States Holocaust Memorial Museum

In a 1987 Gallup Poll, Americans were asked to identify "which major events most affected their political views." Only Watergate was mentioned fewer times than WWII. The Vietnam War, the Great Depression, the Reagan presidency, the Kennedy presidency, the assassinations of the 1960s, and the civil rights movement were reported to have more influence, in that order.[1] Hence, it is extraordinary that, in little more than a decade, a version of WWII tailored to the neoliberal political agenda resonated so strongly for the people. I have so far tried to show how the discursive renovation of WWII into a mode of popular reason was key to the Right's success. I also have argued that one of the more dangerous entailments of this rhetorical coup is its domestication of citizenship and civic life. In this mode of popular reason, situation-specific analysis and systemic critique are displaced by abstract moral arguments about rights and responsibilities founded on the ostensibly pre-political body of war, pain, and sacrifice.

In this chapter I want to examine yet another—and, for me, deeply troubling—rhetorical dimension of this late twentieth-century retooling of WWII that, admittedly, has made me uneasy from the start: its insistence that WWII be remembered as the moment when America became proper to itself, identical to its democratic aspirations. In its purposeful rehabilitation and strategic redeployment, WWII America was the democratic spirit made flesh. It is represented as the unprecedented and—to this day—singular occasion on which, to use Richard Rorty's phrase, we had "achieved our country."[2] To cite once again the WWII memorial's mission statement, WWII will "stand for all time as an important symbol of American national unity, a timeless reminder of the moral strength and awesome power that can flow when a free people are at once united and bonded together in a common and just cause." Hence, the "Good War": not simply a moment in the past in which an entire nation was "compel[led] by an event to decide a *new* way of being" together, but also an event in Alain Badiou's sense of the term to whose truth we are obliged to be faithful, even when doing so contravenes what appear to be our own particular interests.[3]

The broader problem framing this chapter thus concerns the consequences of imagining WWII as a unique truth event and, more specifically, as the singular instance of democracy's realization. What, I ask, are its implications for historically conscious and ethically minded political practice today, tomorrow, and thereafter? What could be worrisome about urging all Americans to "summon the spirit that joined" that greatest of generations and to once again "find that common ground for which so many have fought and died"?[4] Why not allow its truth to orient our passions and practices? Why not let it serve as our guide? When democracy's future is configured as a return, as an exercise in collectively grasping and simulating the democratic sensibility of that singular age, what is opened up, closed down, or foreclosed in the present? Indeed, how might the attempt to fashion our democratic future by holding ourselves accountable to that past be mistaken from the outset?

There is a general answer to all these questions that, in the interest of producing suspense, I might have saved for the very end. It first appeared in abbreviated form in a 1990 newspaper article in which Jacques Derrida meditated on how European identity had traditionally been defined and needed to be rethought, and it has since been translated into English and published in a small volume titled *The Other Heading: Reflections on Today's Europe.* Responding to a crisis of national identity that continues to this day and is not wholly unlike our own, Derrida explains why taking recourse to the past, however venerable, will not suffice:

> When the path is clear and given, when a certain knowledge opens up the way in advance, the decision is already made, it might as well be said that there is none to make: irresponsibly, and in good conscience, one simply applies or implements a program. Perhaps, and this would be the objection, one never escapes the program. In that case, one must acknowledge this and stop talking with authority about moral or political responsibility. The condition of possibility of this thing called responsibility is a certain *experience and experiment of the possibility of the impossible; the testing of the aporia* from which one may invent the only *possible invention, the impossible invention.*[5]

Here Derrida posits the irreducible necessity of proceeding without "a certain knowledge" that would set the course in advance, steering us toward a determined shore. Does this mean that we are obliged to have nothing to do with history? Should collective memory be wiped clean so that we may be freed to fabricate a democratic future ex nihilo?

Rather than continue in this relatively abstract way, I leave Derrida's ruminations on Europe's responsibility and return to the United States, albeit with his philosophical indictment of the programmed decision in hand. My specific task is to demonstrate how all the popular remembrances of WWII I have examined thus far promote a notion of political responsibility *to* the past and *for* the future that is irresponsible in the Derridean sense. I do so, however, not by revisiting them one more time but, instead, by examining another WWII memory text that seems to be an exception to the rule: the United States Holocaust Memorial Museum. There is, then, a significant sense that this chapter is a considered answer to a reviewer's question some time ago about a piece of this project previously published in my field's flagship journal: "There is literally no positive moment in the essay. Would *any* commemoration of the WWII dead satisfy this critic? This was a war in which for example, Raymond Williams proudly served as a tank commander and, so far as I can tell, only Patrick Buchanan currently wishes we hadn't fought. Silly me—I still carry my father's WWII dog-tags as a sign of pride and remembrance. I guess I am hopelessly unhip . . . well, whatever. I cannot imagine the author of this essay being attached enough to any value to wish to die for it. Too bad." Let it be said that this is moralism at its finest. Nearly all the rhetorical maneuvers that magically render any commemoration of WWII "untouchable" in the public and popular domains are at work here, not the least of which is the reviewer's substituting a swift indictment of the author's presumed flawed moral character for a substantive engagement with the essay's arguments. Having said that much and without wanting in any way to excuse the use of a mode of discourse that is particularly noxious in the context of academic exchange and debate, the basic question, albeit rekeyed in the present tense and fine-tuned in accordance to the project's avowed rhetorical approach, deserves an answer: does any *existing* commemoration of WWII satisfy this *rhetorical* critic?

I have argued all along that such a determination must be made with a view to the rhetorical situation as well as the national state fantasy to which any given commemorative structure contributes and of which it is a part. Because its rhetorical force is an articulatory effect, even "the permanence promised by a monument in stone," as Andreas Huyssen has put it, "is always built on quicksand."[6] Hence, although we certainly must attend to it, form cannot serve as the sole or final court of appeal. The rhetorical assessment of commemorative culture must refuse by definition the security and serenity of a detemporalized and detemporalizing aesthetic. However, I will also say this: at the end of the twentieth century and the beginning of the next, the United States Holocaust Memorial Museum is a uniquely commendable commemorative text whose singular rhetorical virtue is that it, unlike all the others examined thus far, contests the premature ossification of WWII memory, its translation into a truth and a program of prudential conduct, and instead promotes the responsibilization of history.

Hindsight Is Not Twenty-Twenty

The United States Holocaust Memorial Museum (USHMM) opened on April 22, 1993.[7] Over the course of the first week, the institution attracted twenty thousand patrons. Seventy thousand people had visited by the end of the first month, and roughly two million had toured the permanent exhibit by the close of the first year. At present, approximately five thousand people—the overwhelming majority of which are non-Jewish US citizens—go to the establishment on the National Mall each day. Eight months after the United States Holocaust Memorial Museum's opening, Steven Spielberg's *Schindler's List* was released in theaters across the country. President Clinton, who had officiated the opening of the USHMM, "implored" the public to see Spielberg's cinematic encomium of the German businessman who, going to Nazi-occupied Poland in search of economic prosperity, leaves it having rescued more than 1,100 Jews. The film was an immediate box office hit and took the 1993 Oscars by storm, winning seven Academy Awards, including Best Picture and Best Director. Between January 1993 and November 1994 hundreds of articles about the film appeared in the popular press; for months on end it served as the leading topic of conversation on morning, daytime, and primetime talk shows and news hours; and free screenings of the film were arranged for high school students across the nation.

Thanks in part to the extraordinary visibility and popularity of the memorial museum and Spielberg's film, by the mid-1990s there was no doubting that "America [had] embraced the 'Holocaust.'"[8] But what exactly were the terms and consequences of that embrace? In a piece written for the *Washington Post* that ultimately indicts the USHMM for being "one more American theme park," journalist Philip Gourevitch correctly noted that, "with a few rare exceptions, critics have hailed the museum and the movie as windfalls for the moral education of the nation."[9] Indeed, according to Oprah Winfrey, our encounter with Spielberg's Holocaust will make "better persons" of us all; a sober tour through the Holocaust memorial museum will prompt, in the words of its commission, a "deepening of [the] quality of American civil and political life and a strengthening and enrichment of the moral fiber of this country."[10] Like the graphic novel *Maus: A Survivor's Tale* and the films *Schindler's List* and *The Pianist,* the memorial museum "can teach ethical thinking, generate empathy, and thereby [progressively] reconfigure a person's worldview," argues American cultural historian Alison Landsberg.[11] And why not? Humanities education has long understood culture as something invested with subjectivizing force, with the power to transform consciousness and cultivate judgment.[12] If, to borrow the words of Kenneth Burke, literature may be best understood as "equipment for living," why not film and the new experiential museum? On Landsberg's and other like-minded cultural theorists' and critics' view, the time has come for academics and journalists to embrace the mass cultural age, appreciate the humanizing potential of the new cultural technologies of simulation, and understand their power to remake selves by engaging both body and mind.

I certainly am prepared to agree that the United States Holocaust Memorial Museum has played a part in the (re)formation of US citizen-subjects. Like the memorial museum's commission, Landsberg, Winfrey, and others, I believe a crucial relation obtains between culture and subjectivation, and I have argued as much over the course of this book. There is no question that the subjects human beings perceive themselves to be—and, therefore, the very manner in which they relate to others and lead their lives—is shaped by the films and television programs they watch, the books, periodicals, and advertisements they consume, the museums, monuments, and memorials they tour. But what, exactly, is required of representational practices so that the ethical approach sense in any given case? What position can and must be occupied by individuals if they are to be the subjects of the ethical statement at any particular instant? Even more specifically, how has the Holocaust been configured so that patrons leave the USHMM changed?

Critics who applaud the subjectivizing force of the exhibit, its capacity to "make better persons of us all," typically attribute its success to having situated patrons in stunningly close proximity to the Holocaust victims. Indeed, according to most critics the memorial museum's primary technique is repeatedly putting visitors into intimate contact with the tragically truncated life stories of countless individuals—Jews and non-Jews, young and old, capable and infirm—made to suffer the brutality of the Nazi regime. Three elements are noted most often. First is the exhibit's incorporation and strategic placement of hundreds of video monitors that oblige visitors to bear visual and audio witness to survivors' personal testimonies. Second is its "Tower of Faces." This stunning three-story enclosure surrounds the patron with the prewar photographic images of Jewish inhabitants from the Lithuanian town of Eiszyski whose entire community—3,500 adults and children—was slaughtered by the Germans in two days. And third is its extraordinarily successful ID Project, a booklet visitors receive upon entering and carry with them over the course of the exhibit. Resembling a passport, each of the ID cards bears the photographic image and recounts the brief biography of an actual Holocaust victim or survivor in stages that correspond to the exhibit's periodized structure.

In *Prosthetic Memory: The Transformation of American Remembrance in the Age of Mass Culture*, Landsberg productively supplements this commonly held account of the memorial museum's power to humanize its patrons. Taking as her cue Nietzsche's suggestion that effective memory is a sensuous phenomenon and, hence, "if something is to stay in memory it must be burned in," Landsburg explores how the Holocaust "become[s] a bodily memory for those who did not live through it," induces what she calls "a prosthetic relationship" to it, and thereby promotes "an empathetic relationship with the Holocaust victims" that "may inspire" ethically oriented action.[13] Although Landsberg does not dismiss as insignificant patrons' encounters with the photographed and video recorded face of victims, she does not regard them as key to the memorial museum's success. On her view, of more import is its deployment of what she calls "the logic of the corporeal experiential."[14] From the permanent exhibit's beginning to its end, she keenly notes, visitors are made to inhabit a dramatically atypical kind of exhibitionary space. Here I quote at some length:

> The permanent exhibit covers three floors: The Nazi Assault, 1933–39, The Final Solution, 1940–45, and The Last Chapter. A large elevator transports visitors to the top floor, from which they work their way down. While its layout may not sound radically different from that of other such museums, some structural differences are noteworthy. First, visitors are at

> the mercy of the museum and must submit themselves to its pace and its logic as there is no way out short of traversing the entire exhibit. . . . The architecture and exhibition design conspire to force visitors to confront images and objects that in other museums they might ignore. . . . Second, there are only five places in the entire exhibit where visitors may sit down. The museum is physically and emotionally exhausting and yet insists that one persevere in the face of discomfort. . . .
>
> Card in hand, you, the visitor, enter the ominous black elevator; the guards lead you in but leave before the doors close. Unlike most elevators, this one has no buttons and no controls. . . . The elevator doors open on a dark room. . . . Although several of the exhibits and showcases are optional—which means that they are not in the path you must follow to move through the exhibit—your mobility is largely directed.[15]

Noticeably, the display cases that were ubiquitous on the fourth-floor are missing on the third. Visitors find themselves in what feels like a wholly unmediated scene that renders palpable the brutality of Hitler's regime. As Landsberg deftly depicts it, again at some length,

> On the next floor, entitled "The Final Solution," . . . the traditional museum space is disconcertingly ruptured. On this floor your freedom of movement is much more restricted. You find yourself on a boardwalk-like walkway. The ground under your feet is uneven. You are walking on cobblestones—cobblestones, you learn, which came from the Warsaw Ghetto. . . . On this floor there is no longer a clear distinction between your space and the exhibit, your body and the history of the objects all around you. . . .
>
> Perhaps the most radical eradication of the dichotomy between your space and museum or object space occurs when you pass *through* a boxcar that was used to transport Jews from the Warsaw ghetto to Treblinka in 1942/43. Inside it is dark and small and empty, and yet the thought that one hundred bodies filled that car haunts the space. Its emptiness produces a kind of cognitive dissonance as you attempt to reconcile its present emptiness with the fact that people were at one time crammed into its interior. . . . When you emerge from the freight car, you enter the world of the death camps.[16]

Here Landsberg astutely describes the unique journey through the memorial museum as staging what a rhetorician might call the patrons' passage from alethia to ethos—that is, from a mediated experience that teaches critical thought by way of a documentary-historical rhetoric to training in a real situation, albeit artificially induced. The "truth" of the Holocaust is to be derived from its being experienced in a personal and, indeed, embodied way. The exhibit moves its visitors not by appeal to ideas, reason, or argument alone but also, and more importantly, by enveloping them in a scene that renders them vulnerable and, thus, receptive to its message.

For Landsberg, then, what is crucial to the ethical subjectivation of the patrons is they remain keenly, indeed disconcertingly, aware of themselves while experiencing the "profound absence" of others by way of objects that carry their sensuous trace. In this way patrons are situated—literally, materially—in an empathic relation to the victims that she defines in the following way:

> Whereas sympathy presupposes an initial likeness between subjects, empathy starts from the position of difference. Empathy is "the power of entering into the experience of or understanding objects or emotions outside ourselves." We might say that empathy depends less on "natural" affinity than sympathy does, less on some kind of essential underlying connection between the two subjects. Whereas sympathy relies on an essentialism of identification, empathy recognizes the alterity of identification. Empathy, then, pertains to the lack of identity between subjects, to negotiating distances. Empathy, especially as it is constructed out of mimesis, is not an emotional self-pitying identification with victims but a way of both feeling for and feeling different from the subject of inquiry.[17]

It is in setting the stage for a "transferential" exchange in which patrons are induced to identify with an absent, victimized Other without subsuming that Other into the same that the museum's value—its "ability to teach ethical thinking"—resides.[18]

I think Landsberg is right to draw our attention to the vital role played by what I call the memorial museum's technologies of comportment. Her emphatically nonassimilationist take on the patron-victim relation offers an important—albeit ultimately insufficient—corrective to other accounts that ground ethics on identification or the idea that understanding and goodwill depend on recognizing our shared humanity and "fundamental" similarities. Nevertheless, I am ultimately unsatisfied by Landsberg's analysis. Indeed, I have argued repeatedly over the course of this book that we should evaluate the impact of any discourse in the context of the cultural and political formation to which it contributes and of which it is a part. Notably, Landsberg's analysis of the ethical import for patrons of the technologies of comportment *in* the memorial museum is not coupled with a studied consideration of the larger scene in which they are embedded. Instead, the memorial museum is read as a complex but autonomous text.

There are, of course, consequences to Landsberg's severing the ties between any experience of the exhibit and the larger context in which it occurs. For one, she simplifies rather than explains the process of resubjectivation taking place at the turn of the century. Indeed, only by hermetically sealing off the experience of the exhibit from its cultural and political context can the possibility of ethical thought and conduct be seen to depend on this singular and staged relationship between visitor and victim. By virtue of having reduced the depth of field of the analysis to the internal dynamics of the permanent exhibit, Landsberg attributes its power to humanize to a thoroughly idealized relation of patron and victim. In other words, Landsberg's concept of empathy and its "humanizing" force, like the ethics of proximity that governs the present-day politics of human rights, is predicated on the presumption—or, in her case, the configuration by decontextualization—of what Robert Meister has identified as "a pre-political relationship between the victim of evil . . . and the spectator capable of discerning evil and willing to respond."[19]

As I have already noted, by the mid-1990s there was no doubting that "America [had] embraced the 'Holocaust.'" In fact, it would not be far from the truth to say that the opening of the USHMM was late in coming, since by the early nineties Holocaust memory had already saturated public and popular culture. As Peter Novic correctly reminds us, it was in April 1978 that Americans began to be schooled en masse in Nazi atrocity, as nearly one hundred million viewers tuned in to NBC's four-part miniseries *Holocaust.*[20] Over the course of the next decade, we witnessed the Holocaust with increasing frequency in our movie theaters (the popularity of Alan J. Pakula's 1982 adaptation of the William Styron's bestseller *Sophie's Choice* rose dramatically after having been nominated for multiple Oscars and Golden Globes), in our classrooms (stories and photographic depictions of Nazi atrocity were integrated into secondary and higher education curricula), and in our living rooms (prime-time viewers by the droves watched made-for-television films and miniseries such as ABC's *Anne Frank: The Whole Story* and *Playing for Time*); moreover, graphic photographic depictions of Nazi brutality became regular fare in newspapers, magazines and picture-books, many of which were published by Time Life.[21] And, of course, prior to breaking ground in Washington, DC, almost every major American city had at least one memorial or museum dedicated to remembering the Holocaust.[22]

In striking contrast to the claims made by Landsberg and others regarding the USHMM, what is particularly disconcerting for some about our collective obsession with the Holocaust is its tendency to induce ethical *in*difference and *in*action. That is to say, a number of prominent scholars worry that the act of bearing witness to the atrocities of the past may no longer compel but, instead, hinder response. James Edward Young worries that "in this age of mass memory production and consumption, in fact, there appears to be an inverse proportion between the memorialization of the past and its contemplation and study." He elaborates: "Under the illusion that our memorial edifices will always be there to remind us, we take leave of them and return only at our convenience. To the extent that we encourage monuments to do our memory-work for us, we become that much more forgetful. In effect, the initial impulse to memorialize events like the Holocaust may actually spring from an opposite and equal desire to forget them."[23] Andreas Huyssen, too, fears that current modes of remembering like those to which Landsberg directs her attention have begun to function as "stumbling block[s] to the needs of the present rather than [as] an opening in the continuum of history."[24] And in a book-length study that lays the groundwork for a critical genealogy of looking at atrocity, Barbie Zelizer mournfully concludes that we are "remembering to forget." Indeed, in *Remembering to Forget: Holocaust Memory Through the Camera's Eye* Zelizer argues that bearing witness to the Holocaust has metamorphosized into a set of habituated practices of representation and looking that drain from the images their power to move audiences to action. Analyzing how the presentation of WWII atrocity images has shifted, particularly the elevation of the images' "symbolic value" at the expense of their "denotative" or "referential force," she argues that picturing atrocity "may function most directly to achieve what it ought to have stifled—atrocity's normalization. It may be that the act of making people see is beginning to take the place of making people do, and that witnessing—even if it involves a narrowed representation of atrocity and little real response—is becoming the *acte imaginaire* of the twentieth century."[25]

If it is the case that by the turn of the century, in looking at Holocaust atrocity, we become witnesses to our own vanishing as ethical agents, how might this destructive trend be reversed? In light of the focus, movement, and referential theory of representation subtending her overall argument,[26] Zelizer argues that our empathy for those suffering and our willingness to redress contemporary atrocities may be heightened by encountering a different *kind* of image of atrocity, one that avoids the morally numbing and politically paralyzing effects of what she aptly terms the "Holocaust aesthetic." For her, this shift entails the mass dissemination of visual depictions resembling those of the 1940s. First would be a renewed commitment on the part of the media and culture industries to "referential detailing through captions and texts," full accreditation of images, and "a thrust to accommodate the broad story of atrocity rather than the contingent details of the photo." Second, the publication or display of images capturing "the [full] extent of horror," a "variety in the targets of witnessing, types of witnesses, and types of witnessing activity" as well as fewer images of individuals bearing witness to atrocity and more images of collectivities doing same, since "implicit" in the latter is "the insistence on collective action."[27] And third, because "our helplessness toward . . . contemporary atrocities may . . . derive from our sense that we already know what they look like," the principled refusal to recycle images of or associated with the Holocaust when addressing the brutalities of the present.[28]

With Zelizer's claim that "as memory proliferates in the public imagination, the act of bearing witness is growing thin, and our often empty claims to memory work render us capable of little more than remembering so that we may forget in its shadow," I could not be more sympathetic.[29] But much like I argued with respect to the controversy over whether the truth of the *Enola Gay* exhibition hinged on the inclusion or exclusion of traumatic images and objects of Ground Zero, here I am less inclined to agree that a change, however dramatic, in the way we represent the victimization of the Other will produce the desired effect. It has been my view from the beginning that the act of looking cannot be grasped so easily. Thus, for me her account of *habituated* looking lacks a working notion of ideology and subjectivation that would call into question the adequacy of conceptualizing "bearing witness" in such positivistic and instrumental terms. Indeed, what a theory of ideology "as larger than the concepts of individual consciousness and will"[30] can teach us about looking is, as Jacques Derrida put it long ago, that "there is no perception."[31] Seeing, in a manner of speaking, is always already a certain kind of blindness. By this I do not mean only that wholly adequate or total representation is impossible, that things "in themselves" are inaccessible in advance and, hence, seeing or looking is not merely perspectival but constitutive. Nor do I mean only that the relation of the seer and the seen is always discursively constituted and therefore provisional and contingent. I also mean that looking always has a relation to power; indeed, it is one of power's most significant articulatory effects. Because ideology intervenes between the (visual) sign and the subject who sees, the advent of seeing otherwise requires much more than the strategic manipulation of the object within the terms set by the national given to be seen. What is necessary is striking a blow to—by making visible the historicity and limits of—the key relations that lend coherence to the hegemony of vision itself.

Subjective Destitution

In "Nietzsche, Genealogy, History," Foucault meditates at length on the conditions of possibility for and the subjective entailments of history crafted in a resistive rather than consolatory key:

> History becomes "effective" to the degree that it introduces discontinuity into our very being—as it divides our emotions, dramatizes our instincts, multiplies our body and sets it against itself. "Effective" history deprives the self of the reassuring stability of life and nature, and it will not permit itself to be transported by a voiceless obstinacy toward a millennial ending.[32]

The case to be made here is the USHMM delivers effective history.

It will have surprised none who are familiar with modern rhetorical theory that one of the aims of this book has been to specify how both overt persuasion and subtle forms of identification have transformed imaginatively the heterogeneity of the social into a relatively homogeneous space. Thus, it may seem odd that I want to take strong exception to analyses of the USHMM that attribute its power to humanize its patrons (or the very possibility thereof) to its visual, material or "experiential," and verbal rhetorics of identification. Indeed, modern rhetorical theorists, whose task since Aristotle has been to identify the available means of persuasion in any given case, must resist "finding" what they have been trained to expect and instead focus on what is actually delivered. And in the case of the USHMM at the turn of the century, I want to argue, identification is not the key. To the contrary, even more crucial to the ethical resubjectivation of patrons *at this particular conjuncture* is the presence in the memorial museum of another rhetoric that, rather than promoting the patrons' positive attachment to the Other, induces a negative relation to the self. More specifically, also at work here is a rhetoric that throws into crisis the very way citizens perceive themselves by undermining the symbolic structure that currently fixes the coordinates of their national identity and existence: not only or even primarily, the visual and verbal production of identification between but also, and more importantly, the violent introduction of difference within. By making visible certain gaps, voids, or breaks in the symbolic order of national being and belonging that patrons have been taught to embrace, this relatively minor and episodic but salient rhetoric precipitates a certain destruction of self on the occasion of which a new citizen subject may be formed.

I have said it already, but it bears repeating here: in contrast to all the others, the USHMM is a singular WWII memory text that contests the premature ossification of WWII memory, its translation into a truth and a program of prudential conduct, and instead promotes the responsibilization of history. At this point I will put my thesis in simpler terms: the USHMM is an exemplary WWII memory site because it positioned Americans to question radically their nation's and, thus, their own presumed exemplarity. How so? Before moving into an answer, I issue a theoretical caution in advance: a thoroughgoing answer will oblige me to think about the subject of "effective history" in other than strictly Foucaultian terms.

Not fortuitously, the USHMM "experience" begins before visitors step foot into the exhibition space as such. After the doors of the large elevator that will lift them to the start of the permanent exhibit on the fourth floor close, patrons view on a small video monitor black-and-white documentary film footage of US troops discovering the death and work camps. The moving images are accompanied by the nonsynchronous testimony of a single US serviceman attempting to capture in speech that to which patrons are bearing visual witness. Upon the elevator stopping and its doors opening, patrons find themselves in the presence of a massive—indeed, large as life—black-and-white photomural of US troops looking at a heap of burned corpses (fig. 5). It is after this point that the permanent exhibit begins, dramatically, with a return to 1933 and a historical account of the emergence of National Socialism in Germany.

Fig. 5 | The "Liberation Mural" and "The Holocaust" wall on the fourth floor. Photo: Edward Owen. © United States Holocaust Memorial Museum.

What are we to make of the video montage, its voiceover, and the colossal image? How do they function rhetorically in relation to an elaborate exhibit that, albeit by atypical and innovative means, retells the Holocaust story in largely chronological, which is also to say conventional, terms? In one of the few scholarly analyses of the memorial museum that attends to this question, historian Tim Cole argues that, from the start, the visual is a vicious trap, not of the gaze, as Lacan would have it, but of the patrons' look. More specifically, he claims that this initial sequence is absolutely determining of the patrons' understanding of the exhibit. More than merely presenting them with something to be seen, it situates them squarely within a hegemonic, indeed patriotic, point of view from which they will then make sense out of everything to come: "The US troops stand on the far side of the pyre, and we find ourselves—shuffling out of the elevator—standing this side of the pyre. It is as though we form a ring around this pile of half-burnt corpses. We join the 'liberators' and so become like them: 'Americans [who] encounter the camps.'"[33] It is Cole's argument that, in triggering an imaginary identification between patrons and an idealized national image, that of the liberator, which is then set in stark contrast to the German perpetrators throughout the exhibit, the initial sequence sets the stage for "a stars and stripes 'Holocaust'" that cultivates national self-assurance, superiority, and conceit. "Liberation" functions rhetorically as a totalizing perspective, point of view, or interpretative frame that bolsters a spurious and blinding sense of national pride that gives license to ethico-political passivity. As Cole puts it, "There is a sense in which the United States Holocaust Memorial Museum is essentially established as an un-American museum, telling the story of an un-American crime to Americans. As we walk through this anti-museum, we reaffirm who we are in opposition to the historical 'them.' . . . Rather than learning from the past, we can leave comforting ourselves in the present that we are not like that."[34] The primary lesson taken away is not, despite the content committee's and design team's intent, "never again" but rather "not us."

Cole indicts the initial sequence's hegemonic and, thus, self-conserving effects, but his argument finds no support in an analysis that refuses to empty both the sequence and its hegemonic context of their positive and particular rhetorical content. To put it summarily, the initial sequence bears little, if any, resemblance to the visual and verbal hegemonic assemblage to which, according to Cole, it refers and from which it derives its subjectivizing force. First, everything about the photomural conspires against reading it as a photographic ode to the heroic American "liberation" of the camps. In this image there are no survivors, no brutalized Others to save; there are only victims or, more precisely, their ashen remains. In this image there likewise are no saviors or heroes; the troops have arrived too late to the scene. In the top left corner is the large-type panel title, "Americans Encounter the Camps." What is painfully obvious to patrons is that the troops' encounter with this camp is a missed encounter with those who should have, perhaps could have, been spared.

Furthermore, the initial sequence refracts as much as it reflects. But the point of refraction for the patron at the end of the twentieth century and beginning of the next, I submit, was not the blurred figures in the photomural that introduce time and movement into an otherwise static scene. Nor, thanks to the patrons' habituated practice of looking, was it the multitude of *Muselmann* on the video monitor or the corpses—those abject remainders and irrevocable reminders that good things do not always come to those who must wait—set in the foreground of the magnified image. What is altered, indeed nearly beyond recognition, is the American GI himself, that prized amalgam of visual and verbal signifiers that—by virtue of its reiteration ad nauseum in popular and political culture—had been transformed rhetorically over the past decade into the truth teller for the twenty-first century. This GI is not that GI. That singularly commanding speaking subject on whose ethos has been predicated an unassailable authority to speak the truth—not only about the Good War but also, and more importantly, about what it means to be an American and to do things the American Way—has gone missing from this scene. Indeed, a quite different figuration of that subject, one that makes its first "appearance" in the voiceover to the video montage, inhabits that space: "The patrol leader called in by radio and said that we have come across something that we are not sure what it is. It's a big prison of some kind, and there are people running all over. Sick, dying, starved people. And you take to an American, uh, such a sight as that, you . . . you can't imagine it. You, you just . . . things like that don't happen." Both semantically ("we are not sure what it is") and syntactically (the discourse stumbles and stalls) the utterance conjures a speaking subject who, in striking contrast to its prior iterations, apprehends but does not comprehend. Patrons encounter this subject for a second time in the photomural, a colossal representation of a moment in which what one sees makes no sense. Here, again, the sensible does not give way to the intelligible, neither for the GIs in the image nor for the patrons looking at it. Hence, Cole is correct to notice "it is as though [the patrons and the GIs] form a ring around this pile of half-burnt corpses." However, he is wrong when he thereby concludes, "We [the patrons] join the 'liberators' and so become like them."[35] The obverse is, in fact, the case: they become like us.

This reading suggests, of course, that the initial sequence rhetorically demotes the idealized and esteemed subject of truth whose cultural prestige and political power has long been attributed to the singular experience of having seen—up close and with one's very own eyes—the human suffering that is war. In other words, this delegate of the "true" and the "good" is laid low as that "experience" that reputedly served as the pre-political ground for his moral authority makes itself felt as an abyss. In this instance at least, "immediate experience" does not serve as the point of stability from which anything approaching truth may be derived. Hence, we encounter a faltering of the late twentieth-century parresiastic contract that determined "who is able to tell the truth" to the exclusion of others, and a bottoming out of the symbolic capital in accordance with which a relation of verticality had been established between US citizen-subjects and the GI. The downfall of this prized subject, in whose terms they have learned to live their own lives, unsettles the patrons' self-assured (national) identity.[36]

At this point we can appreciate the rhetorical force of other moments in the permanent exhibit that neither Cole's nor Landsberg's totalizing readings take into account. These moments also may be understood as missed encounters in so far as "good reasons" for them are either missing altogether or have been withheld. One: the guest book from the luxurious Hôtel Royal in Evian, France, which contains the names of conference delegates, including those from the United States, and corresponding text on the wall that has been titled "No Help No Haven, 1938." Here patrons are told that "of the thirty-three nations invited to the Evian conference to discuss the growing refugee crisis in Europe, only the tiny Dominican Republic offered to receive substantial numbers of Jews. Despite mounting pressure, the US maintained strict immigration quotas."[37] Two: the cap of commander Gustav Schröder, displayed against an enlarged black-and-white photograph of the MS *St. Louis* and her passengers. Accompanying text informs patrons that after having sought refuge in Havana for his nine hundred Jewish refugees in 1939, the German captain sailed for Miami but was again turned away, and "though the passengers found refuge in Belgium, England, France, and Holland, about half of them eventually ended up in Nazi death camps."[38] Three: documentation of the Allies' knowledge of the extermination of Jews at the Auschwitz-Birkenau camp, as well as evidence of Jewish leaders' unsuccessful attempts to persuade the US government to bomb the gas chambers and railways leading to it, juxtaposed against photographs documenting the sustained US air campaign that targeted the Auschwitz-Monowitz industrial complex, less than five miles from Birkenau.

Included within but not belonging to the USHMM permanent exhibit is a series of encounters that, without offering any explanation or extending an excuse (indeed, no narrative structure ties any of these encounters to one another or to the permanent exhibit as a whole), give the lie to America's democratic exemplarity during WWII.[39] Because this hermeneutic circle—which once secured the US citizen-subject's being by assigning knowing to the exemplary subject of that exemplary truth etched into a granite wall near the Hall of Witness: "The government of the United States . . . gives to bigotry no sanction, to persecution no assistance"—cannot be closed, the patron is left in an indeterminate state. Herein lies, I submit, an occasion in which history is effective, which is to say disruptively and productively rhetorical in the strongest sense of the term: mere image fragments from the past "introduce discontinuity into the patrons' very being," "divid[ing their] emotions, dramat[izing their] instincts, multipl[ying their] body and set[ting] it against itself."[40] Certainly, this is the sort of encounter with an image-text that not only Foucault but also Walter Benjamin had in mind when, in his most celebrated and notoriously dense passage, he advances the distinction between "genuinely historical" and archaic history:

> The historical index of images does not simply say that they belong to a specific time, it says above all that they come to legibility only at a specific time. And indeed, this "coming to legibility" constitutes a specific critical point of movement inside them. Every now is the now of a specific recognizability. In it, truth is loaded with time to the bursting point. (This point is nothing other than the death of intention, which accordingly coincides with the birth of authentic historical time, the time of truth.) It is not that the past casts its light on the present or that the present casts its light on the past; rather, an image is that in which the Then and the Now come together in a constellation like a flash of lightening.[41]

Included within but not belonging to, and not present as such: such is the power and resubjectivizing force of this irreducibly episodic, provisionally salient and, now I will add by working within and against Alain Badiou's philosophical lexicon, *excrescent* rhetoric that, although in and of history, exceeds its hegemonic totalization by "lend[ing] a latent figure to the void."[42]

The void as democracy, American democracy as a void: in the case of the Holocaust memorial museum at the turn of the century, democracy not as the power of the people but power given over to the people—*demos* and *kratos*, or *kratein* (which also means "to prevail," "to bring off," "to govern")—as something that remains collectively to be done: *dynamisme*. Hence, the patrons who enter the USHMM with Captain John Miller's command, "Earn this," echoing in their ears, exit onto the National Mall with a desire that, crucially, has no object. But, perhaps, this is precisely that of which the responsibility to democracy consists "in making of the name recalled, of the memory of the name, of the idiomatic limit, a chance, that is, an opening of identity to its very future."[43]

Love and Country

I have so far argued that at the turn of the century the USHMM functions rhetorically, to use Kenneth Burke's term, as a strong counterstatement whose power of resubjectivation *in the given ideological conjuncture* was attributable to a series of traumatic encounters in the exhibit that together radically unsettled or disrupted US citizens' ethnonational patriotic self-recognition. Indeed, contrary to critics who locate the humanizing force of the exhibit in its capacity to promote Americans' empathic identification with the victimized Other, I suggest that for US citizens steeped in the self-congratulatory commemorative culture of the Good War and schooled by the "greatest generation," the USHMM obliged a bearing witness to a constitutive lack of self. At this point one might well ask: but what, then, of patriotism? Is this a term that should be abandoned altogether, considering its history of rhetorical abuse? More than fifteen years ago and in the immediate aftermath of the first Gulf War, Judith Butler wrote, "If a deconstruction . . . suspends and problematizes the traditional ontological referent of [a] term, it does not freeze, banish, render useless, or deplete of meaning the usage of the term; on the contrary, it provides the conditions to *mobilize* the signifier in the service of an alternative production."[44] In other words, what is needed is not to shelve "patriotism" altogether but to rethink and use it otherwise.

According to the received wisdom, patriotism, or love of country, finds its most intimate homology in the amorous relation between the sexes.[45] Patriotism is taken to be most evident, indeed most true, when citizens wholly surrender their will or hand their agency over to the Other. Like real love, genuine patriotism is understood to entail the complete abandonment of self on behalf of the Other, its absolute measure being the willingness to lay down one's life. Here, then, no sacrifice of self is too small, none too great. Indeed, even the ultimate sacrifice of self cannot be understood as a net loss, since it is precisely by virtue of the absolute self-negation that is death that the patriot becomes part of the One. Now obviously it is from this formulation of patriotism that late twentieth-century commemorations of WWII took their moral bearing and, having been elaborated into a code of civic conduct, were thus able to exercise a uniquely persuasive and "principled" power. What may be less obvious is not only that patriotism had come to serve as shorthand for a specific regime of enunciation that, in Mary Poovey's words, "allows for the production of what counts for knowledge at any given moment, and which accords salience to particular categories, divisions, classifications, relations and identities,"[46] thereby helping to constitute the positive conditions of the late neoliberal order. Less obvious is the fact that love of country, like the amorous relation between the sexes from which this patriotism takes its significant cues, need not be thought as a nihilistic enterprise—a giving up or annihilation of self to enter into the count. To the contrary, I want to propose an alternative elaboration of patriotism that forsakes the mistaken conceptualization of love that currently lends it its figure, thereby breaking with a biopolitics that grounds—both in the sense of based on or anchored in and to prevent from taking flight or to restrict—all democratic aspirations in what Alain Badiou has called a "bio-materialism" which, in "recogniz[ing] the objective existence of individual bodies alone," tethers us to the deadening "dogma of finitude."[47]

It is in the interest of shaking off our modern and morbid obsession with a notion of bodily finitude whose imperfectly veiled investment in transcendence impedes the ethical act that Joan Copjec tenders a fresh account of the death drive, sublimation and, ultimately, love in her book *Imagine There's No Woman: Ethics and Sublimation*. Copjec readily grants the veracity of Giorgio Agamben's dismal diagnosis of our present biopolitical condition. He is quite right, she acknowledges, to have identified the collapse or conflation of *zoë* into *bíos*, of political existence into bare or naked life, as the key to modern biopower's success. As Agamben put it in a passage I quote at some length:

> We are animals in whose politics our very life as living beings is at stake. Living in the state of exception that has now become the rule has meant also this: our private biological body has become indistinguishable from our body politic, experiences that once used to be called political suddenly were confined to our biological body, and private experiences present themselves all of a sudden outside us as body politic. We have had to grow used to thinking and writing in such a confusion of body and places, of outside and inside, of what is speechless and what has words with which to speak, of what is enslaved and what is free, of what is need and what is desire. This has meant—why not admit it?—experiencing absolute impotence, bumping against solitude and speechlessness over and over again precisely there where we were expecting company and words.[48]

But more disquieting for Copjec than Agamben's cunning analysis, which makes it "almost impossible to imagine . . . a model that would *not* risk perpetuating this politics," is that even the most sophisticated of theorists among us us—and one can be sure that Agamben himself is to be included in this count—are themselves confused. That is to say, they "remain dupes of the dogma that death is imbedded in life"[49] in so far as their notions of and investments in the body or bodily finitude do not confound but, in fact, reinscribe the claim to transcendence by "maintain[ing] infinity at a distance that's both evanescent and sacred."[50]

Since "death becomes immanentized in the body only on condition that we presuppose a beyond," the impasse that is "the modern sanctification of bestial life" may be averted, Copjec argues, by (re)turning to another way of thinking the body that Agamben's attentiveness to historical continuities causes him completely to elide.[51] That other thinking of the body has its beginning, of course, in the work of Sigmund Freud. Copjec writes, "This rethinking [will] not . . . entail a radical reinvention, for, in truth, another notion of the body has already been proposed, precisely as a challenge to the one offered by the (bare) life sciences. The notion to which I refer is the one suggested by psychoanalysis, where the body is conceived not 'biopolitically' as the seat of *death* but, rather, as the seat of *sex*. Contrary to what Foucault has claimed, the sexualization of the body by psychoanalysis does not participate in the regime of biopolitics; it opposes it."[52] Copjec thus advances the strong and seemingly counterintuitive argument that psychoanalysis alone yields a conception of the body that, thanks to the drives, is able to extricate itself from its immanent conditions, thereby restoring power to life.

That hers is a proposition that appears to fly in the face of Freud's own conclusion in *Beyond the Pleasure Principle*, that "the aim of life is death," does not escape Copjec's notice. Instead, the seeming contrary claim functions as the lever by which she begins to rectify—in a brilliant gloss on the death drive that stretches from Freud to his radicalization by Lacan—several prevalent misunderstandings, not the least of which are: "(1) that there is no single, complete drive, only partial drives, and thus *no realizable will to destruction*; and (2) . . . that the drive inhibits, as part of its very activity, the achievement of its aim. Some inherent obstacle—the *object* of the drive—simultaneously *brakes* the drive and *breaks it up*, curbs it, thus preventing it from reaching its aim, and divides it into partial drives."[53] So, only partial drives and thwarted aims. Although the tendency may be to think otherwise, this, according to Copjec, is good news for the subject since "rather than pursuing the Nothing of annihilating dissatisfaction, the now partial drives content themselves with these small nothings, these objects that satisfy them."[54]

Attention needs to be paid to a decisive step in Copjec's argument: the drive's diversion from its aim is not caused by some entity other than the subject, say, the social, such that the subject "substitutes a more socially respectable or refined pleasure for a cruder, carnal one." To the contrary, the inhibition that prevents the drive from achieving its aim is "part of the very *activity* of the drive itself," inhibition being, in fact, the "*proper and positive activity*" of the drive. Herein, then, is established the isomorphic relation of the drive's activity and sublimation: "while the *aim* (*Ziel*) of the drive is death, the *proper and positive activity* of the drive is to inhibit the attainment of its aim; the drive, *as such*, is *zielgehemnt*, that is, it is inhibited as to its aim, or sublimated, 'the satisfaction of the drive through the inhibition of its aim' being the very definition of sublimation."[55] But what is the significance of the coincidence of the satisfaction of the partial drive and sublimation? What is riding on it? Nothing less, Copjec argues, than the *jouissance* "that opens a new dimension of infinity, immortality" that is radically inadmissible to—in fact, must be disavowed by—bio-logical thought and politics.[56] Indeed, on this thinking of the drive, the body is not, as Foucault would have it, merely one of the primary points of the application of power; instead, it is the site of a jouissance or satisfaction that is attainable and which bears witness to the irreducible but typically repressed autonomy of the subject, which is to say, the subject's noncoincidence with itself and/or the order of historical being.[57]

But given my overall purpose—to generate an alternative conceptualization of "love of country" that confounds rather than collaborates with the biopolitical order—at least two obvious questions impose themselves here. First, if, as was noted above, the complete abandonment of self on behalf of the other is the sine qua non of being in the state of love, isn't love the exemplary instance of the subject's capture rather than autonomy? And second, if, as the everyday expression has it, love is something that subjects *fall into*, isn't love illustrative of the subject's passivity rather than activity? Copjec's answer to both of these questions could not be more decisive or clear: absolutely not, since "love, any love, is always and fundamentally narcissistic," and "we are not passively affected by the object of love, we actively affect ourselves by loving it."[58]

Given the common understanding of narcissism, one would be hard pressed to divine a proposition stranger than this: loving is a narcissistic act of self-negation that secures the subject's release from her passive subjection to power. But Copjec explains:

> To love is to want to be loved; love is always narcissistic. One must remember that these statements do not issue from a phenomenological approach to the question of love; therefore, they do not mean either "I love you so that you may be induced to love me back" or "I love you because you remind

> me of myself." One cannot . . . love oneself directly because one cannot take oneself as an object. The "I" of the subject is a hole in being. How then can one love oneself; whence comes the experience of "oneself" on which narcissism depends? From the shattering jouissance one experiences in loving another. The "I" is a "passionate inference," as Bersani correctly says, an experience of the body, that comes from the libidinal cathexis of objects. What looks like an impatiently passive stance at first—wanting to be loved—is in fact the return curve of the drive to love.[59]

Copjec's crucial point is not that loving obliterates the subject but, rather, that it subverts the ego. In other words, out of "the feeling of pleasure taken in the feeling of pleasure" begins to emerge an "I" that exceeds its imaginary and symbolic interpolations. Hence, it is to this internal tension or noncoincidence of the self with itself—and, thus, the opening for something radically Other—which loving affords, that Copjec attributes love's revolutionary force. Because it "accords the subject the status not of an imaginary identity, nor even a fixed symbolic one, but of a hypothesis," love threatens the bio-polity with the autonomy of the subject, its independence from the Other.[60]

When Copjec posits love as the exemplary enactment of the sublimation of the drive whose consequence is a jouissance or satisfaction marking the subject's capacity to avoid "being a mere symptom of its historical conditions," the usefulness of her work for a reconceptualization of patriotism that outstrips both the spirit and the letter of biopolitical law comes into view.[61] That is, her radically corporealized account of love gestures toward a patriotism that, in opposition to its orthodox formulation, would identify "love of county" with the sacrifice of "the ultimate sacrifice."

I am acutely aware that recommending the sacrifice of the ultimate sacrifice be taken as the bearing point for the emotional substructure of the political is risky business, fraught with danger from nearly all sides. First, let it be said that in an age where the individualized mortal body functions as the basic unit of national pride and remembrance—indeed is that which now organizes the national count[62]—a call to sacrifice the ultimate sacrifice sounds a uniquely heretical note. Indeed, we are repeatedly warned that it is at our own peril that we not honor the exorbitant sacrifice made by the many who are "monuments to their time"[63] and "heroes" in our own.[64] But of course—and since I have discussed this at length in chapter 2, I can be brief here—precisely because every life lost on our behalf is always already exorbitant to any gesture of recompense, a patriotism that insists on fidelity to the ultimate sacrifice delivers us over to a cruel system of moral accounting. Since the gift of death is absolutely beyond redress, the numbers will never, to invoke again one of *Saving Private Ryan's* dominant motifs, "add up." A fateful dissymmetry: for this is a patriotism whose *aneconomics* of "the gift of death" renders our "making good" on that inheritance a persistent but already failed project. To be sure, this is a civic morality to which even Immanuel Kant would object, as it dooms the living to a kind of slow death or assimilation to "our failure ever wholly to be what we have in mind to become" since any act is deficient, defective, never quite (good) enough in advance.[65]

Second, in our time, readiness to die for one's country is championed as true patriotism *and* that on which our democratic life is said to depend; however, this call to sacrifice the ultimate sacrifice also sounds a particularly opportunistic, indeed self-preserving, note. But here I want to do more than simply counter such a charge with what I hope by now is the obvious retort: the sacrifice of the ultimate sacrifice is self-serving in this way *only* if one is already surrendered to biopolitical common sense. In truth, it is the idealization of the ultimate sacrifice or the ultimate sacrifice as ideal—rather than the sacrifice thereof—that jealously protects or safeguards the self. It demands from patriots nothing less than their detachment from or decathexis of the world. In other words, what "love of country" coded as the ultimate sacrifice prohibits is, paradoxically enough, loving itself—and, thus, the political life worth living that only loving will forge. As Copjec put it in another investigation into love wherein she returns to the opposition set up by Freud in *Group Psychology* between artificial groups and love:

> The members of a group, by identifying with the ego ideal or fragmentary idea that alienates them from their happiness, surrender their freedom and become fettered with regard to love and the invention it implies. In doing so, they become alienated from their happiness or happy only in their unhappiness. This alienation serves to protect them from chance. Focused on the ideal, they reject everything that happens to come along, every opportunity, every satisfaction, because none are "it," that is, each falls short of the ideal. If love poses a threat to the group, this is because it turns us from our hypnotic fascination with the ideal and thus from our contempt for or dissatisfaction with the contingencies of life. Love brings us not the satisfaction of deferral, of never getting what we want, but the satisfaction of obtainment, of which we can never get enough.[66]

Hence, if the sacrifice of the ultimate sacrifice becomes our civic morality's organizing principle, patriotism's litmus test changes. It would no longer, as the referee I cited near the start of this chapter insists, be one's "willing[ness] to die for any value," an ideal which colludes structurally, on the one side, with the fantasy of infinite postponement and, on the other, with the fantasy of transcendence. Instead, they would be patriots who, having "surrender[ed] . . . the *pedestal* that allows one to raise oneself above the battleground of decision and action," act *in* political time and *beyond* it.[67] Beyond it not because some transcendental Other (be it Reason, History, Justice, even God) guarantees the act's essential meaning, but beyond it in the sense that the "spontaneous" political act, in suspending the rules of biopolitical sense making that define the positive order of being, makes visible, even available, another dimension of collective existence. Hence, instead of a patriotism that valorizes giving up life's joys for the national democratic Thing (whereby the patriot ascends to the One) or encourages endless small acts of "privatized patriotism," we should embrace a patriotism that commands a shift from renunciation (in its long-standing Christian and, now, neoliberal and neonational sense) to enjoyment (in its psychoanalytic sense), thereby gracing citizens with the freedom and collective power to engage in the concrete (re) creation of life.

Here, again, I recall Foucault's words that gave this book its start: "Since memory is actually a very important factor in struggle (indeed, it is [in a kind of dynamic conscious of history] that struggles develop), if one controls [*tenir*: keep, convene, hold on to, put down] people's [the people's] memory, one controls their dynamism [*dynamisme*]. And one also controls their experience [experiment, expertise, practice, taste], their knowledge [*savoir*: awareness] of/about previous struggles."[68] From the *aneconomics* of the "gift of death" to the jouissance (*dynamisme* actualized collectively) that is the gift of the (partial) death drive(s): if we wanted to get hold of a more concrete sense of this different kind of patriotism, we could do no better than return to the second floor of the United States Holocaust Memorial Museum, midway into the permanent exhibition. To get to this point, we would need to have worked our way through nearly 1,800 square feet of displays bearing graphic visual and verbal witness to Hitler's rise to power—from the suspension of citizens' rights via the declaration of an indefinite state of exception and the imposition of martial law, and the regulation of daily life through the aggressive reconfiguration and surveillance of public and even private space, to the manifest management of the biological

Fig. 6 | Beginning of "Ghetto Bridge": Lodz and Warsaw Ghetto murals, the Ringelblum milk can, and the Warsaw Ghetto wall casting on the third floor of the permanent exhibition. Photo: Edward Owen. Film Roll N02422. © United States Holocaust Memorial Museum.

life of the nation, including the manufacture of various technologies for marking the body, the medicalization of the doctrine of Aryan supremacy, and mass executions. By this point, too, we would be disconcertingly aware of Hitler's dreadful ambitions and the reluctance on the part of many powerful nations, including our own, to protest. At this point, in other words, life appears altogether defined by death—not only in the sense that the spirits of those who have already been destroyed by the lethal machine haunt the present but, even more, in the sense that the millions of Jews, Roma, Poles, political dissidents, Soviet prisoners of war, handicapped, homosexuals, Freemasons, and Jehovah's Witnesses that are targets of Nazi persecution appear less as living beings than as specters of a premature death to come. Hence, as we make the trek across a wooden walkway that simulates the bridge Jews were forced to cross in order to enter the ghettos, their large-as-life photographic resemblance crowding us in on all sides, it becomes all but impossible to miss the metaphor: like their brick-and-mortar parameters, the fate of the ghetto's inhabitants had been sealed (fig. 6). We then turn a corner (again, the material metaphor is likely not lost on us) and enter a space wherein the beginning of the "Final Solution" comes into view: the German invasion of the Soviet Union in 1941, which brought with it the mobile killing squads; the slaughter of 33,771 Jews in Babi Yar; and the mass deportations of adults and children to the death camps.

But suddenly and at the heart of an experience in which even our own bodies have been induced to appreciate the weighty and pervasive presence of this destructive biopolitical regime, something we have been trained not to expect takes place: the Warsaw Ghetto uprising. The explanatory panel set to the left side of this humble and anomalous display within a display reads, in part, as follows:

> Between July 22 and mid-September 1942, at least 250,000 Jews were deported from the Warsaw ghetto to the Treblinka death camp. For the 60,000 Jews remaining in the ghetto, deportation seemed inevitable.
>
> Zionists, Bundist and Communist youth groups in the ghetto formed the Jewish Fighting Organization (Zydoowsksa Organizacja Bojowa, or ZOB). Members of the Revolutionary Party formed another resistance group, the Jewish Military Union (Zydowski Zwiazek Wojskowy, or ZZW).
>
> In January 1943, when the Germans launched a second deportation, the ZOB's commander, Mordicai Anielewicz, called for armed resistance: "Not a single Jew should go to the railroad cars. . . . Our slogan must be: 'Let all be ready to die like human beings.'" After a few days the deportation came to a halt.
>
> The Germans intended to begin deporting the remaining Jews on April 19, 1943, the eve of Passover. When they entered the ghetto that morning, its streets were deserted: the inhabitants were hiding in bunkers. On that day, the Jewish fighters rose in revolt.
>
> More than 2,000 heavily armed German soldiers and police were backed by tanks and artillery. The 700 to 750 ghetto fighters had a few dozen pistols and hand grenades.

We then read that although the organized military resistance was broken in three days, individuals and small groups continued to fight the Germans until May 16, 1943, when Jürgen Stroop, a German commander, ordered the ghetto completely destroyed by fire.

So, suddenly—and here where, to give Agamben his due, we have by now been trained to expect nothing but, in his words, impotence, solitude, and silence—we encounter something completely Other. We encounter vitality, solidarity, and speech, those partial objects or indivisible remainders of a love that, if only momentarily but for all time, miraculously lifts the collective out of the conditions of naked existence from which there appears to be no escape.

4

The Culture and History Wars of the Twenty-First Century, or, Can You Be WHITE and Look at This?

On January 6, 2021, a mob of thousands stormed the US Capitol and hundreds breached the Capitol Complex, forcing Congress to suspend the work of certifying the results of the 2020 presidential election. Since that unprecedented day's events, scores of journalists and editorialists, public officials, Democratic senators and representatives to the House, and members of the Select Committee on the January 6 Attack have laid the blame squarely at the feet of former president Donald J. Trump and his team of operatives; the rioters themselves are often dismissed, in the words of United States District Judge Amit Mehta, as "mere pawn[s] in a game directed and played by people who should know better."[1] In hours of evidence presented to the American public by the Select Committee during the summer and fall of 2022, it was shown that the attack was not the unanticipated upshot of a spontaneous political emotion. Quite the contrary, it was the most visible and brazenly violent episode in a choreographed flank assault on the election process and the peaceful transfer of power. Yet few Republicans who currently occupy or intend to seek office have been willing publicly to hold Trump accountable.[2]

By academic standards January 6 barely appears in the rearview mirror we call history. However, the obvious significance of the insurrection prompted scholars to risk analysis in its immediate aftermath, doing so most effectively by contextualizing the day's unfolding within the broader weave of history—political, economic, sociological, and cultural. For all their important methodological and thematic differences, a striking consensus already has emerged with regard to root cause: "political polarization." In the main, scholars agree with journalists, editorialists, and the like that the assembled mob—who marched on Trump's direction from the Ellipse to the Capitol, violently made their way up its steps, broke into its sacred halls, and illegally entered the chamber to

"Stop the Steal"—is best understood as the most extreme, callous, and astonishing expression to date of long-seething hostilities between the Republicans and Democrats, conservatives and liberals, Right and Left. Indeed, with stunning regularity critical assessments of the years, months, days, and hours leading to the insurrection note that, by the time Trump announced his candidacy for the presidency in 2015, nearly every issue was being cast in brutally oppositional terms; moreover, according to the overwhelming majority of accounts, the situation has only deteriorated since.[3] To put it simply, following a decade or more of relative domestic calm, disequilibrium returned to the United States with a vengeance.

Prior to the Capitol insurrection, the most spectacular manifestations of the ever-widening political rift were those leaving a body count in their wake: the Charleston church shooting of 2015, the 2017 Unite the Right rally in Charlottesville, and the nationwide protests in the summer of 2020 sparked by the police murder of George Floyd in Minneapolis.[4] But signs of the intensification of political polarization—albeit less than lethal—appeared at breakneck speed as students on college and university campuses far and wide clashed over the removal of Confederate monuments and the renaming of buildings honoring heroes of the "Lost Cause"; as truckers formed disruptive convoys to protest state-imposed health rules; as tens of thousands of protestors pounded the pavement to demand stricter gun laws; as citizen-consumers fervidly condoned or zealously condemned the criminalization of drag performances and the commendation of LGBTQ+-affirming marketing campaigns; and as parents and school board members brawled with teachers and administrators over COVID-mitigation plans, bathroom policies, anti-racism pedagogy, and book banning. Of course, during near countless incidents, the televisual and print media played a major role in amplifying our differences, their power of magnification increased exponentially by their dangerous supplement—the new social media. With predictable disregard for complexity, detail, and nuance, network news, cable news, and talk radio delivered verbal soundbites and visual images ready for immediate upload and rapid dissemination: "CRT" or "censorship," "woke" bashing or "race hating," "fake news" or "alt-truth," "pro-life" or "pro-choice," "border walls" or "open borders," "all lives matter" or "black lives matter," "stolen election" or "insurrection."[5] As sites for both the production and (re)circulation of highly charged material, social media platforms such as Facebook, Twitter, and Instagram functioned as technologies of near-instantaneous and highly polarized virtual collectivization.[6] Imagined communities, indeed!

On this, then, nearly everyone—from the politicians to the people, from journalists and editorialists to academics and activists—agrees: our country has never been more divided since the Civil War. Having made their way to its concluding chapter, readers of *Reinventing World War II* may be inclined to skepticism given their familiarity with similarly dire declarations issued some thirty or more years ago. It is my hope, however, that the foregoing analysis of the culture and history wars of the eighties and nineties and, even more, the popular means of their redress, can help us appreciate rather than underestimate the seriousness of what is unfolding before our eyes. Over the course of this concluding chapter, then, I want to draw attention to the very real danger today's cultural and social hostilities pose to the future of our union, however virtual, imagined, and discursive both those hostilities and any sense of national belonging may be. I also want to leverage WWII redux as a singularly useful vantage point from which it becomes possible to identify and assess significant differences between that politico-ideological sequence and the one we find ourselves in today. More specifically, analysis of the rhetorical differences between the history and culture wars of the late twentieth century and those of the twenty-first will expose talk of "political polarization" on all sides as less a thumbnail *explanation* of our political present than a rhetorical stopgap that obfuscates by overgeneralization what is alarmingly new about the divided state of our situation.

Because I wish to cut quickly to the crux of the matter, my relatively direct but hardly painless approach to taking measure of the current crisis will be to revisit *The 1619 Project* and *The 1776 Report*, both products of and responses to the culture and history wars of the twenty-first century. As I have already hinted, one of the recommendations to be taken from my analysis of *The 1619 Project* and *The 1776 Report*—of the differences between them as well as the differences between them and WWII redux—is to comprehend the degree to which these emblematic statements of our polarized present are *wildly* different imaginary syntheses, each aiming to become the new national common sense. What is crucial to understand in advance of one or the other securing its hegemonic grip is that both imaginings presage competing but equally consequential mutations in US public and political culture. Furthermore, either imagining will require a dramatic shift in the psychosocial structure of those who have yet to identify with the ascendent account in order to make sense of America and their connection to it. To put it plainly, the rhetorical reading of *The 1619 Project* and *The 1776 Report* that follows will show these are not merely two different visions of and for America; more important, they are antinomic, Other-cancelling worldings. No synthesis. No mediation. (Race) War.

The Difference a Date Makes

On August 18, 2019, the *New York Times Magazine* released its special issue inaugurating *The 1619 Project*. The front cover portends an imposing storm: a full-page photographic image of an overcast sky that grows darker as the eye surveys the chop of an unsettled and unsettling Atlantic Ocean. As the reader looks to the horizon, where air and water meet, the vanishing point is given body and story in a short paragraph of brackish-colored text: "In August of 1619, a ship appeared on this horizon, near Point Comfort, a coastal port in the British colony of Virginia. It carried more than 20 enslaved Africans, who were sold to the colonists. America was not yet America, but this was the moment it began. No aspect of the country that would be formed here has been untouched by the 250 years of slavery that followed. On the four hundredth anniversary of this fateful moment, it is finally time to tell our story truthfully. The 1619 Project."[7] Brain child of staff writer Nikole Hannah-Jones, the expressed aim of *The 1619 Project* and its hundred-page inaugural issue was to "persuade" the American people to take 1619 rather than 1776 as "the year of our nation's birth" since, as Jake Silverstein put it in his editor's introduction, it was "out of slavery—and the anti-black racism it required—[that] nearly everything that has truly made America exceptional [grew]."[8] Silverstein's piece previews the issue's nonfiction essays (each investigates a contemporary US phenomenon, such as the widening wealth gap, by tracing its ties to chattel slavery) and creative works that draw inspiration from historical events—some well-known, others, like the publication of enslaved person Phillis Wheatley's poetry in 1773, not. Silverstein then itemizes some of chattel slavery's and antiblack racism's living legacy as follows: "[America's] economic might, its industrial power, its electoral system, diet and popular music, the inequities of its public health and education, its astonishing penchant for violence, its income inequality, the example it sets for the world as a land of freedom and equality, its slang, its legal system and the endemic racial fears and hatreds that continue to plague it to this day. The seeds of all that were planted long before our official birth date, in 1776, when the men known as our founders formally declared independence from Britain."[9]

Establishing origins, like fixing ends, neither has been nor ever will be innocent or disinterested, despite every effort to appear as such. But the editor of and contributors to *The 1619 Project*, especially Hannah-Jones, have been atypically forthright about their interest in resetting the nation's timeline, explicitly calling their readers' attention to the entailments for the country of doing so. Indeed, Silverstein's introduction accentuates the "wake work" that the new origin story will demand from *all* Americans on the way toward building a democratic society whose principles and order exceed "the liberal imagination" and the always already "restricted vision of freedom" it imperfectly extends.[10] Here I quote Silverstein at some length given the significance of his words for the analysis to come:

> The goal of The 1619 Project . . . is to reframe American history by considering what it would mean to regard 1619 as our nation's birth year. Doing so requires us to place the consequences of slavery and the contributions of black Americans at the very center of the story we tell ourselves about who we are as a country. . . .
>
> A word of warning: There is gruesome material in these pages, material that readers will find disturbing. That is, unfortunately, as it must be. American history cannot be told truthfully without a clear vision of how inhuman and immoral the treatment of black Americans has been. By acknowledging this shameful history, by trying hard to understand its powerful influence on the present, perhaps we can prepare ourselves for a more just future.
>
> That is the hope of this project.[11]

By nearly every measure, *The Project*'s launch was an unmitigated success. As Hannah-Jones remarks in her preface to the expanded edition of *The 1619 Project: A New Origin Story*, published in 2021, demand for the Sunday *New York Times* special magazine issue far outstripped supply. Soon after its release, informal and formal reading groups met to discuss *The Project* in homes, libraries, museums, and cultural centers across the country, and liberal-minded politicians positively remarked on it during the 2020 campaign season. Even more, numerous "educators in all fifty states" began to integrate it into their lesson plans, their efforts facilitated by online access to reading guides and plans for students of all levels, prepared by a "community of educators" and supported by a partnership between the New York Times and the Pulitzer Center.[12]

But not all reaction to *The 1619 Project* was positive; in point of fact, much of the attention was flagrantly antagonistic toward and ferociously dismissive of the work. Following an early wave of criticism printed in right-wing magazines that typically targeted Hannah-Jones's lead magazine essay, the World Socialist Website began disseminating a series of lectures, essays, and interviews in 2019 and 2020. These pieces challenged *The Project*'s overriding argument that understanding chattel slavery and its attendant antiblack racism is the key to understanding persistent and, in many areas, increasing inequities of the present. Soon thereafter anthologized in a volume tellingly titled *The New York Times' "1619 Project" and the Racialist Falsification of History*, the published pieces collectively made the case for regarding *The Project*, as David North put it in his foreword, as "promoting a false narrative that portrays American history as a perpetual war between the races."[13] Its singularly disorienting blind spot, North argued, was "the working class" or "class struggle, which has been the dominant factor in American social history for the past 150 years, and in which African American workers have fought heroically alongside their white brothers and sisters."[14] Furthermore, North advanced an account of the motivation behind *The Project* that was as incendiary as it was predictable given his theoretical and political commitments: "The interaction of racialist ideology as it has developed over several decades in the academy and the political agenda of the Democratic Party is the motivating force behind the 1619 Project. Particularly under conditions of extreme social polarization, in which there is growing interest in and support for socialism, the Democratic Party—as a political instrument of the capitalist class—is anxious to shift the focus of political discussion away from issues that raise the specter of social inequality and class conflict. This is the function of history that places race at the center of its narrative."[15] In short, according to North and his collaborators, prizing race over class was *The 1619 Project*'s fatal flaw, its contributors and adherents foolishly playing into the hands of "the most powerful and ruthless capitalist class on the planet."[16]

It has often been said that adversity makes strange bedfellows; the odd alliance that emerged out of opposition to *The 1619 Project* was no exception. What do Trump and the MAGA Republicans, the international Trotskyists, the National Association of Scholars, several academic historians ("even many on the left," as Arkansas Republican senator Tom Cotton emphatically pointed out),[17] conservative members of state legislatures and local school boards, political scientist Adolph Reed Jr., former civil rights leader Bob Woodson and the Woodson Center's 1776 Unites initiative, evangelical websites such as The Flag and the Cross, and Emory University scholar of black diaspora Michael M. Wright, for example, have in common? A quarrel of one kind or another with *The 1619 Project*. Although the World Socialist Website had already begun to present its case to readers, the objections of five established American historians—Victoria Bynum, James M. McPherson, James Oakes, Sean Wilentz, and Gordon Wood—who collectively sent a letter to the editor, provided the talking points for what quickly became a nationwide and federally funded campaign to discredit *The Project*.[18] In the letter, published in the paper on December 29, 2019, the signatories "expressed [their] strong reservations about important aspects of The 1619 Project," the first three of which were directed specifically at Hannah-Jones's opening piece. First, they stated that her assertion that "the founders declared the colonies' independence of Britain 'in order to ensure slavery would continue'" is "false." Second, they claimed that her contention that "'for the most part,' black Americans have fought their freedom struggles 'alone'" is "distorted." And third, they insisted that her representation of Abraham Lincoln's commitment to black equality as evolving and less than steadfast from the start is "misleading." Additionally, they pointed out that *The Project*, presented as an authoritative account with "the imprimatur and credibility of *The New York Times*," had not been transparent about the identity of the historians involved, or about "the extent of their involvement as 'consultants' and fact checkers."[19] Without mention of the historians' expressed "applau[se]" of "all efforts to address the enduring centrality of slavery and racism to our history," the historians' letter served as singularly effective fodder for what Hannah Grossman, writing for *Fox News*, coyly dubbed "the bipartisan backlash" against the darkening of American history.[20]

Arguably, late spring of 2020 is the moment when the gloves on both sides of the culture and history wars of the twenty-first century came off. The Right and the Left had been primed for battle. As already noted, in August 2019 *The 1619 Project* hit newsstands. In September the widely covered formal impeachment inquiry of President Trump began. In December the House voted to impeach. The new year began with the Senate's trial of Trump, and the World Health Organization put governments on notice that cases of a mysterious pneumonia had been reported in Wuhan, China, as much as a month ago. By the end of February, the Senate had acquitted Trump, Ahmaud Arbery—a twenty-five-year-old black man jogging in Georgia—had been chased and gunned down by white neighborhood vigilantes, and we were given a name, COVID-19, for a fast-spreading and mysterious disease. Within a month the United States was the world leader in cases. People were dying by the thousands, even more were desperately ill, the country virtually shut down to slow the contagion, we entered a global recession, and Hollywood film producer and serial rapist Harvey Weinstein was sentenced to twenty-five years in prison, thanks in no small part to a robust #MeToo movement.

Then, on May 25, Minneapolis police officer Derrek Chauvin, with three other officers in tow, held George Floyd on the ground in a choke hold, knees to his neck and back, for nearly ten minutes. Floyd died, face and torso pressed to the pavement under Chauvin's weight. On May 26 at 1:46 a.m., seventeen-year-old Darnella Frazier, a witness to Floyd's slaying, posted cell phone video of the murder to Facebook and Instagram with the tag line "They killed him right in front of cup foods over south on 38th and Chicago!! [*sic*] No type of sympathy </3 </3. #POLICEBRUTALITY." The video went viral, and protests erupted in more than two thousand cities. By early June, approximately sixty-two thousand National Guard troops were deployed in cities across the country, many of whom were mobilized in units coded in shamelessly euphemistic terms (e.g., Operation Legend, Operation Diligent Valor, and the Protecting American Communities Task Force) and authorized to use riot-control tactics to manage the growing Black Lives Matter protests. Retroactively, the Department of Homeland Security cited Trump's Executive Order 13933 as licensing their mobilization without the permission of individual states.[21]

"Protecting American Monuments, Memorials, and Statues and Combating Recent Criminal Violence" was the first of four Executive Orders that signaled the Trump administration's full-throttled entry into the culture and history wars and the unambiguous alliance of MAGA conservatives with the radical and alt-Right. The stated purpose of two of the orders, the aforementioned EO 13933 and EO 13934 ("Building and Rebuilding Monuments to American Heroes"), was to "stand strong" against the "assault on our collective national memory" and the "desecrat[ion of] our common inheritance" by "rioters, arsonists, and left-wing extremists."[22] In the main, EO 13933 reaffirmed "the rule of law" and the attorney general's readiness "to prosecute [offenders] to the full extent permitted under Federal law," including "withholding federal support tied to public spaces from State and local governments that have failed to protect public monuments, memorials, and statues from destruction or vandalism" as well as "from State and local law enforcement agencies" that, "whether because of sympathy for the extremists behind this violence or some other improper reason, casts doubt on the management of these law enforcement agencies."[23]

Executive Order 13934 called for the establishment of a Task Force for Building and Rebuilding Monuments to American Heroes and a National Garden of American Heroes. "Rebuilding" was the operative political term. The primary purpose of the National Garden, to be "opened expeditiously," was to serve as a safe haven for any and all monuments "vandalized, destroyed, or removed" by local governments in response to "protests" "in recent weeks . . . across America."[24] In addition to ensuring the talismans to the Lost Cause would be put out of harm's way, the National Garden would serve as a site for displaying new "lifelike or realistic representations" of individuals "who have contributed positively to America throughout our history."[25] To the usual roster of national heroes (from the founding fathers to the Wright Brothers, from Susan B. Anthony to Harriet Tubman and Martin Luther King Jr.), Trump's order recommended the likenesses of Daniel Boone, Henry Clay, Davy Crockett, Billy Graham, Douglas MacArthur, George S. Patton Jr., Ronald Reagan, and Antonin Scalia be added.

Executive Orders 13950 and 13958 were twined, conceptually and politically. The former, "Combating Race and Sex Stereotyping," prohibited all executive departments and agencies (including, not incidentally, the NEH, NEA, and the Smithsonian Institution), the uniformed Services, federal contractors, and federal grant recipients from "promot[ing] race or sex stereotyping or scapegoating," and the dissemination of "divisive concepts."[26] To combat an "ideology . . . rooted in the pernicious and false belief that America is an irredeemably racist and sexist country, that some people, simply on account of their race or sex, are oppressors," EO 13950 issued a federal gag order on the following:

> concepts that (1) one race or sex is inherently superior to another race or sex; (2) the United States is fundamentally racist or sexist; (3) an individual, by virtue of his or her race or sex, is inherently racist, sexist, or oppressive, whether consciously or unconsciously; (4) an individual should be discriminated against or receive adverse treatment solely or partly because of his or her race or sex; (5) members of one race or sex cannot and should not attempt to treat others without respect to race or sex; (6) an individual's moral character is necessarily determined by his or her race or sex; (7) an individual, by virtue of his or her race or sex, bears responsibility for actions committed in the past by other members of the same race or sex; (8) any individual should feel discomfort, guilt, anguish, or any other form of psychological distress on account of his or her race

> or sex; or (9) meritocracy or traits such as a hard work ethic are racist or sexist, or were created by a particular race to oppress another race. The term "divisive concepts" also includes any other form of race or sex stereotyping or any other form of race or sex scapegoating.[27]

Almost immediately, the order began to serve as template language for legislators and policymakers in red states seeking to eliminate anti-sexism and anti-racism programs; decimate diversity, equity, and inclusion initiatives; and purge CRT (the conservative, alt-, and extreme Right's shorthand for any and all of the "divisive concepts" enumerated in the order) from the nation's primary and secondary schools as well as its public colleges and universities. More on this anon.

Although in September he had already announced his intention to form a task force to counter *The 1619 Project*, Trump signed Executive Order 13958, "Establishing the President's Advisory 1776 Commission," on November 2. The Commission's general charge was stated in no uncertain terms: "to challenge, and correct . . . the recent attacks on our founding [that] have highlighted America's history related to race."[28] In coordination with a wide array of federal agencies, all the Commission's efforts were to "prioritize the American founding and foundational principles" in order that "rising generations" not succumb to "a crippling self-doubt that could cause them to abandon faith in the common story that binds us to one another across our differences."[29] In that spirit, the Commission's immediate task was to "produce a report for the President . . . which shall be publicly disseminated, regarding the core principles of the American founding and how these principles may be understood to further enjoyment of 'the blessings of liberty' and to promote our striving 'to form a more perfect Union.'"[30] Although Trump gave the Commission one year to produce its report, Biden's electoral win made it necessary that the work proceed at warp speed. *The Report* was delivered to the American people on Martin Luther King Jr. Day 2021—only two months after the order had been signed, twelve days after the Capitol had been stormed, and two days prior to Biden's inauguration.

Strictly speaking, *The 1776 Report* is twenty pages long, the main text punctuated by ten photos and nine large-font block quotations. Also included in the volume are four appendices ranging from three to eight pages, making for a slim volume of only forty-one pages. *The Report* itself is divided into six sections—an introduction, "The Meaning of the Declaration," "A Constitution of Principles," "The Task of National Renewal," and a conclusion—and the appendices include a reprint of the Declaration of Independence as well as three supplemental essays titled "Faith and American Principles," "Created Equal or Identity Politics," and "Teaching Americans About their Country." Authorship is nowhere assigned other than on the front cover, which lists "The President's Advisory 1776 Commission"; and on the final page, which lists the names of the chair, vice chair, executive director, sixteen Commission members, and its ex officio members.[31] Nowhere in *The Report* is a scholarly citation to be found.

Within one day of *The Report's* release, *Politico* published "A Big Chunk of Trump's 1776 Report Appears Lifted from an Author's Prior Work." Written by Tina Nguyen, the article questioned the originality and scholarly integrity of the Commission's work, citing multiple paragraphs from a 2008 opinion piece penned by Thomas Lindsay (also an appointed member of the Commission) that appear nearly word for word in *The Report*. In addition to itemizing multiple historians' damning indictments of the Commission's work—*The Report*'s assertion, for example, that "George Washington 'freed all the slaves in his family estate' by the end of his life," when, in fact, "Washington had only freed one slave upon his death, and requested that the rest of his slaves be freed after the death of his wife," several of whom "remained in bondage, [having been] transferred to her grandchildren"—the *Politico* piece drew public attention to the close relationship been Trump's appointees and multiple conservative think tanks, institutes, and private institutions, not the least of which is the notoriously conservative and Christian Hillsdale College.[32] Its president, Larry P. Arnn, chaired the Commission, and dean of the Van Andel Graduate School of Government at Hillsdale College's Washington, DC, campus, Matthew Spalding, served as executive director. Together, they hosted on college grounds the only two meetings of the Commission, and the institution's website hosts its ongoing efforts, albeit now as a PAC "dedicated to electing school board members nationwide who want to reform our public education system by promoting patriotism and pride in American history" and "committed to abolishing critical race theory and 'The 1619 Project' from the public school curriculum."[33]

On January 20, the American Historical Association roundly "condemned" *The Report*, summarily denouncing its treatment of its "two main themes"—a "homage to the Founding Fathers" and "a screed against a half-century of historical scholarship"—as "a form of government indoctrination of American students" that "elevate[s] ignorance about the past to a civic virtue."[34] Signed by forty-seven other professional and academic organizations, the rebuke commanded the attention of network, cable, print, and internet news outlets; even the politically tepid *NBC News* characterized *The Report* as "published by a group of conservative political operatives and academics" and "rife with false assertions intended to distort well-documented accounts about how discrimination was enshrined by the nation's founders and continues to persist in various forms, hundreds of years later."[35] Among its other embarrassments, *The Report* was criticized widely for its strategic omissions from the historical record (for example, it makes no mention whatsoever of the Tulsa race massacre or, for that matter, the realities of slavery);[36] its misleading appropriation of the words of historical figures (such as those lifted out of Martin Luther King Jr.'s "I Have a Dream" speech); and distortions of historical events and motivations (among others, "paint[ing] slave-owning leaders such as George Washington and James Madison as pioneers who 'set the stage for abolition'"[37] and asserting strong ideological affinities between twentieth-century Progressive reformers and Mussolini[38]). All told, in the words of Valerie Strauss writing for the *Washington Post*, "The report is the latest salvo in what many historians have called a long-running assault by right-wing conservatives on how schools teach U.S. history."[39]

Only "the latest salvo," to be sure, as a torrent of support for and efforts to enact policies on the state and local levels based on *The Report* flowed from multiple platforms and sources. The editorial board of the *Wall Street Journal*, the newspaper of record for business and financial news, delivered what was perhaps the most muscular defense—and, notably, on January 15, five days before *The Report* was released on the White House website. The paper, obviously having been provided advanced copy of some or all the text, preemptively doubled down on *The Report*'s pivotal thesis, boldly rephrasing it as follows: "The Declaration of Independence's claim that 'all men are created equal' was a revolution in itself, a turning point in world history. To reduce America to its violations of that principle, as do many contemporary writers, is to miss the distinguishing part of the story that roused freedom lovers and terrified tyrants everywhere—and still does."[40] The editorial goes on to single out appendix 3, applauding its explanation of "how identity politics divides Americans into victims and oppressors," and, like *The Report*, directly attributes the sowing of today's partisan hostilities to the academy: "Can anyone be surprised to hear that undergraduate history enrollments lately have hit new lows, facing worse drop-offs than any other department? It's hardly an edifying experience when professors always emphasize the bad, always expose and deconstruct, or always trace the 'dynamics' of power and identity, rather than striving to understand America's historical actors as they understood themselves."[41] Following a quick condemnation of the Commission's claim that identity politics are to blame for current social and economic inequalities, that they are "as unjust as the old hierarchies of the antebellum South," and that "slavery was a unique evil," the editorial concludes on a reassuring note for their readership: "The report is correct in understanding our freedom and prosperity as 'direct results of America's unity, stability, and justice, all of which in turn rest on the bedrock of our founding principles.' Today that is taken as a conservative interpretation, though liberals once believed it too. It also happens to be true."[42]

Most support for *The 1776 Report* was similar in kind, which is to say, a declaration of unqualified support for the mission "to promote 'patriotic education'" loosely tethered to temperate critiques of its execution. Writing for the *Washington Examiner*, for example, Kaylee McGhee White acknowledges that "*The 1776 Report* is not perfect" but "its central thesis is exactly right: A good education will teach students to understand one's country and aspire to its ideals in spite of its flaws."[43] Christine Rosen, senior fellow at the American Enterprise Institute, went one step further, supplementing her enthusiasm for the mission ("the argument for less ideologically driven historical education could not come at a more critical moment"), albeit couched in critique (from "it reads like a rather hastily thrown together pamphlet" to "it lacks supporting notes or a bibliography" and "it makes sweeping statements grounded too much in present political polemic than in complicated historical fact") with a refutation of the widely circulated claim that Trump had not appointed even a single professional historian to the Commission: "This is not true. The Commission's head, Hillsdale College President Larry Arnn, has a Ph.D. in government, as does Charles Kessler, editor of the *Claremont Review*. Victor Davis Hanson, also on the Commission, is, in fact, a professional historian and has long been a prominent contributor to the fields of military history and classics (he currently holds a position at the Hoover Institution at Stanford University). Disagree with Hanson's outspoken political views all you like, but his credentials as a professional historian are sound."[44] Arguably, others not defending the Commission members' fitness to the mission was a win for both the Commission and the cause. It avoided shinning a bright light on their flimsy credentials and political and ideological homogeneity. It is simply a fact that Arnn, Kessler, and Hanson do not have doctoral degrees in American history (or any other area of historical study, for that matter; Hanson earned his PhD in classics from Stanford). It is also a fact that they have published monographs whose titles disclose an unmistakable embrace of traditional Western values, and whose place of publication would cause any self-respecting scholar to doubt the works' integrity and rigor.[45] Arnn published both his biography of Churchill and his *Liberty and Learning: The Evolution of American Education* with Hillsdale College Press, an arm of the college for which, as already noted, he serves as president. Excepting Arnn's two monographs and the twenty-three volume *Churchill Documents* (for which Arnn served as coeditor on six volumes), the press lists no other scholarly works under its name. Arnn also published *The Founders' Key: The Divine and Natural Connection Between the Declaration and the Constitution and What We Risk by Losing It* with Thomas Nelson Publishers, "a world leading publisher and provider of Christian content."[46] Kessler published *I Am the Change: Barak Obama and the Crisis of Liberalism* with Broadside Books, a subsidiary of HarperCollins that "specializes in conservative nonfiction"; and *Crisis of the Two Constitutions: The Rise, Decline, and Recovery of American Greatness* with Encounter Books, which, under the editorship of Roger Kimball, "continues to advance [the] love of liberty and the cultural achievements of the West against a rising tide of collectivist sentiment and the soft totalitarianism of intellectual conformity."[47] Hanson, likely the most widely known of the three, published *Why the West Has Won* (Doubleday) and coauthored with John Heath *Who Killed Homer? The Demise of Classical Education and the Recovery of Greek Wisdom* (Free Press). He is better known for his regular contributions to the *National Review*.

If few persons were willing to deliver an unqualified endorsement of *The Report*,[48] many more were prepared to profess the overall rightness of its "principled" story and to do the political work requisite to having its spirit mandated by law. According to "Tracking the Attack on Critical Race Theory," a study conducted by a team of researchers at the UCLA School of Law, no fewer than 563 anti-CRT measures were introduced "between January 1, 2021 and December 31, 2022 [by] federal, state, and local government officials," and "nearly half—241—were enacted or adopted."[49] Notably, "in every state except Delaware, at least one anti-CRT measure was introduced"[50] that, in the words of Arkansas's "Saving American History Act of 2021," protects the state's interest in promoting "an accurate account of the history of the United States of America in public schools and forming young people into knowledgeable and patriotic citizens" by prohibiting "the use of public school funds to teach the 1619 Project curriculum" and "to reduce funds distributed to public schools that teach the 1619 Project Curriculum."[51] By the end of March 2023, the researchers had tracked "at least 50 new anti-CRT bills" whose aspirations had evolved.[52] Indeed, following the initial wave of proposed legislation in Iowa, Georgia, and Arkansas that explicitly targeted *The 1619 Project*, bills began to be crafted that extended that relatively narrow reach by banning all instruction which suggests any "person bears personal responsibility for and must feel guilt, anguish, or other form of psychological distress for systemic racism and sexism," an injunction lifted directly from EO 13940.[53] Of course, right-wing governors in a number of states such as Idaho, Florida, and Virginia had already flexed their executive muscle by prohibiting the dissemination of "inherently divisive concepts." Virginia governor Glenn Youngkin, for example, banned the notion that "an individual, by virtue of his or her race, skin color, ethnicity, sex, or faith, bears responsibility for actions committed in the past by other members of the same race, ethnicity, sex or faith."[54]

The New Desiderata of Race

In the afterword of *Lacan and Race*, Kalpana R. Seshadri writes about race as an atypically stubborn regime of vision supported by a fundamental fantasy of wholeness that may best be summarily stated in the following words: "There is only one race . . . and it is white."[55] I want to work toward the closing critical and theoretical gesture of this book by reading *The 1619 Project* and *The 1776 Report* as rhetorics that can teach us something about today's racism and our political future. Two warrants for such a reading emerge over the course of the debate itself. First, both sides in the debate indict the other for having written irresponsible history. In the debate's own terms, historical responsibility is measured by the account's fidelity or lack thereof to the facts: charges leveled by each side against the other for having gotten the facts wrong, having twisted the facts, having called up some facts but not others, and having pressed facts into the service of a thinly veiled ideological and political agenda. But what the protracted to and fro of the debate in the political, public, and professional spheres itself signifies, among other things, is the futility in the near or long run of earning anything like consensus by appeal to the facts.[56] In fact, David Waldstreicher, historian of early nineteenth-century America at City University of New York and contributor to *The 1619 Project*, suggests that the debate over the historical merit of *The 1619 Project* and *The 1776 Report* has been ongoing and will likely continue indefinitely, whether in the mainstream media or the halls of academe. Writing for the *Boston Review* about objections to *The 1619 Project* and, by extension, their representation in/as *The 1776 Report*, Waldstreicher remarks, "This dispute reflects deep fault lines in the field of U.S. history."[57] Indeed, on his account, the contest between "the establishment view" and "a growing number of scholars . . . who question [it]" has its own history; "though it rarely spills out into public view in quite the way it has recently, there is a longstanding debate within the academy" over the facts, not the least of which is "just how revolutionary the American Revolution really was."[58] One could say, then, that the jury is (still) out on the facts, or, that we have come upon an impasse. And it is precisely at the point of deadlock that it becomes critically useful and not just theoretically justified to view history "as negotiable determinant" rather than as fact.[59]

Second, although parties on both sides of the debate invoke facts—on the one hand, in August 1619 a ship carrying more than twenty enslaved Africans landed on a coastal port in the British colony of Virginia, who were sold to the colonists; on the other, on July 4, 1776, "the unanimous declaration of the thirteen united States of America" was issued, thereby instituting the United States of America—neither lays claim to writing a history that is disciplined in the modern, strict sense of the word. In fact and as I have shown above, both *The 1619 Project* and *The 1776 Report* invite—if not implore—their readers to read and reuse them as rhetorics by explicitly presenting reasons for doing so, and not only on the front end. As was pointed out above, neither the texts nor their contributors claim value-neutrality. And why would they? In light of the prior analysis of the *Enola Gay* controversy and the history wars of the nineties, the lasting significance of which was a dramatic reconfiguration of the rules for writing history as such, we should not be particularly surprised by these two exemplars at this conjuncture: history's unabashed return as rhetoric, as a techne whose aim is heuristic rather than hermeneutic and whose end is by definition outside itself[60]—histories as what Aristotle long ago classed as "productive knowledges" bequeathed to their readers.[61] Expressly self-identifying as such, let us read them at their word: as rhetorics in the general sense and, more narrowly, as partisan pedagogies of American citizenship for the twenty-first century. Of course, to read these two texts as rhetorics is also to suspend provisionally the injunction to appraise their truth value by appeal to one or another conception of historical objectivity. It also reopens the question, by what alternative measure will their relative value or merit be determined? Here, again, I activate the ethico-political: what are the ethico-political entailments of these two pedagogies for collective life in the United States, today, tomorrow, and into the future?

The 1619 Project and *The 1776 Report* have more in common than their similarly pedagogical but divergent ambitions. First, readers of *Reinventing World War II* should be struck immediately by WWII's near complete absence from or negligible presence in both documents, especially the latter. Nowhere in a report that heaps conventional praise on the nation and delivers explicit instruction in how to "rais[e] new generations of citizens who not only know the self-evident truths of our founding, but act worthy of them" will the reader encounter the words "World War II" or the "Second World War," and no reference whatsoever is made to "the greatest generation."[62] The war makes its appearance on page 13 of *The Report* but in a decidedly nondramatic fashion in a subsection titled "Fascism." The passage aims to singularize America's commitment to its founding principles by recoding the defeat of authoritarianism in Italy and Germany as a David versus Goliath morality tale in which, against all odds, American principles battle not only (Progressive) forces at home but also (Fascist and then Communist) regimes abroad: "Before the Nazis could threaten America in our own hemisphere, the United States built an arsenal of democracy, creating more ships, planes, tanks, and munitions than any other power on earth. Eventually, America rose up, sending millions of troops across the oceans to preserve freedom."[63] With two more sentences, *The Report* dispenses with WWII altogether: "Everywhere American troops went, they embodied in their own ranks and brought with them the principles of the Declaration, liberating peoples and restoring freedom. Yet, while Fascism died in 1945 with the collapse of the Axis powers, it was quickly replaced by a new threat, and the rest of the 20th century was defined by the United States' mortal and moral battle against the forces of Communism."[64]

Over its one hundred pages, *The 1619 Project* invokes WWII only six times: to note the second occurrence in history of forced migration (the first, of course, being the Atlantic slave trade); to mark the inauguration of the postwar Interstate Highway System expansion that fractured black communities; to date the exodus of black Americans from the South in search of jobs; to explicitly demystify the myth of the Good War by exposing its lived contradictions for black American servicemembers (both a nonfictional recounting and a fictional rendition of the brutal beating by police of Bernard Woodard, a stateside black WWII hero on his way home); and to account partially for the emergence of the civil rights movement (that black Americans defended democracy abroad but returned to segregation and second-class citizenship at home incited the "second sustained effort" to "make democracy real").[65] A great deal could be said about how shifting the historical frame has lessened the impact of the Good War. However, my present purpose calls me only to underscore a patently obvious, but for that no less significant, rhetorical trait: the displacement of WWII as totalizing nodal point by both texts. The Commission installs the Revolutionary War and the signing of the Declaration of Independence in that privileged place; *The 1619 Project* proceeds without a cathected totalizing suture that proactively or retroactively lends to every element its meaning or sense. Likewise, not even lip service is paid by *The Report* or *The Project* to multiculturalism, the dominant political rationality of WWII redux whose cunningly dedifferentiating mode of practical reasoning facilitated belonging to the "We" of "the People" during the eighties and nineties. *The Report* emphatically champions a monoculturalism expressly predicated on "a large measure of commonality in manners, customs, language, and dedication to the common good."[66] No one is even whistling that old "unity in diversity" tune today. *The 1619 Project* audaciously celebrates a black American ethos, the widespread recognition of which will be founded on the thorough dismantling of the bicameral rationality which is both cause and effect of the "racial caste system" that persists in the United States.[67]

Save what I have suggested to this point, these two texts could not be more different, but not only substantively or ideologically, as critics and champions alike routinely point out. With regard to form and style they are simply incommensurate. I have already drawn attention to *The 1619 Project*'s atypical format, but some elaboration is in order. Both the inaugural magazine issue and the extended volume bear no resemblance to conventional historiography. Traversing genres and forms, *The 1619 Project* is a series of nonfiction essays punctuated usually between but sometimes within by fictional essays, poetry, and artistic works, a rhetorical mosaic or assemblage of sorts. The series is ordered chronologically, the forced arrival of Africans to the eastern shore marking the beginning of the "new origin story." Furthermore, the nonfiction essays, although sequenced chronologically with respect to a significant historical event, do not proceed in chronological fashion. That is, they do not unfold in a linear manner, as histories typically do, from past to present to future. All of them take a contemporary problematic—Americans' addiction to sugar, for example—as their point of departure and then track its traces into the past. In a word, they are genealogies, not histories. *The 1776 Report*, by contrast, embeds the Commission's chronologically ordered but unconventionally periodized iteration of American history in an expressly interested exegesis of "the principles of the American founding" or what the writers call "the universal truths of equality, liberty, justice, and government by consent."[68] Furthermore, *The Project* literally is polyvocal, and in nearly every case resolutely embodied, the nonfiction pieces, poems, artwork and photographs eloquently lending flesh and bone and breath to concepts and events; *The Report* is univocal and doggedly disembodied. The active voice is predominant in *The Project*. The passive voice saturates *The Report*'s historical account, the active voice kicking in only when discussion is focused on forces opposed to the status quo.[69] The indicative and subjunctive moods are predominant in *The Project*; *The Report* toggles between the indicative and imperative moods. *The Project* unabashedly tarries, in words and images, with the historical sublime, and in a style that is always accessible and oftentimes vernacular.[70] *The Report*'s writing strains to maintain the balance and temperance of the middle style, but its images collectively provide the much-needed aesthetic counterpressure to keep it in place by virtue of their overfamiliarity or, dare one say, their banality.[71]

These rhetorical differences matter. For *The 1619 Project*, I submit, they collectively communicate not good or bad history but African American popular counter-memory. These are their stories, popular counter-memories in Foucault's sense of the term: written and created by African American individuals laboring collectively in the interest of the formation of the African American people. *The 1619 Project*, then, as increasing the American people's knowledge of African Americanness, of its (hi)stories of survival, struggle, suffering, and death as well as of perseverance and progress and prosperity, improbable (hi)stories in light of an enduring climate of anti-blackness.[72] Hence, I extend here an argument I advanced in the introduction to *Reinventing World War II* while at the same time advancing one answer to the question of rhetorical merit: the value, indeed power, of *The 1619 Project* resides in its ability to incite the dynamism of black Americanness, to rouse black Americans, individually and together, to continue the transformation of democracy in the United States from a potentiality into an actuality, a necessary and interminable task. To provide the spark that incites the dynamism of black people, inspiring them to finish suffering their own impotentiality, their nonbeing, is, I reiterate, the origin of human power and the root of human freedom to lend new form (*bíos*) to collective life (*zoë*).

But that is not all. So far it has been my argument that *The 1619 Project* successfully stages, substantively and stylistically, popular counter-memory that does not anchor identity, racial and national, but whose effectivity will take us some distance toward securing it: the be/coming of blackness to/in America, the coming into black Americanness. But this popular counter-memory is not by the authors' and creators' own design only black. Whiteness had been there from the start and all along the way. Thus, my second answer to the question of rhetorical merit: what must certainly be terrifying for white Americans who read *The 1619 Project* is our inexorable confrontation with the historicity of whiteness. As Kalpana Seshadri-Crooks deftly explains at length in *Desiring Whiteness: A Lacanian Analysis of Race*, only a small selection of which I quote here:

> Any encounter with the historicity, the purely symbolic origin of the signifier, inevitably produces anxiety. It is necessary for race to seem more than its historical and cultural origin in order to aim at being. Race must therefore disavow or deny knowledge of its own historicity, or risk surrendering to the discourse of exceptionality, the possibility of wholeness and supremacy. Thus race secures itself through visibility. Psychoanalytically, we can perceive the object cause of racial anxiety as racial visibility, the so-called pre-discursive marks on the body (hair, skin, bone), which serve as the desiderata of race. In other words, the bodily mark, which (like sex) *seems to be more than symbolic*, serves as a powerful prophylactic against the anxiety of race as a discursive production.[73]

To come face to face with the historicity of whiteness by bumping up against its material effects as a visual-discursive regime whose rhetorics have been tirelessly set to work to (re)secure its status as given by God or nature—the ostensibly pre-political facticity of hair, skin, bone—rather than made and held in place by (wo)men. Importantly, over the pages of *The 1619 Project* the visible desiderata of race include not just hair, skin, and bone but, also, those "fundamental principles" of equality, liberty, justice, and government by consent. Even those principles, which according to *The 1776 Report* were "named [by the founding fathers] at the outset to be both universal—applying to everyone—and eternal: existing for all time," are emptied of their imagined pure substance or content and returned to its readers as patently catachrestical concept metaphors.[74] In the absence of a proper referent, their recitation summons into that gaping void a centuries-long history of abuse in word and deed whose end is yet to come.

Whither, then, the so-called great American experiment? I repeat the dire warning I issued on the front end of this closing chapter: should proponents of *The 1776 Report* insist on the rightness of their "American story" for "the task of national renewal," and should they continue to draw on all available institutional resources (including but hardly limited at this time to federal Executive Orders and state-level legislation as well as unprecedented decisions of the US Supreme Court's unmistakably right-wing majority) to secure its hegemonic power, the outbreak of violent race war is all but inevitable. It is, perhaps, worth remarking that *The 1776 Report* itself suggests as much, albeit by rhetorical indirection. That is to say, over the course of its forty pages, this looming inevitability makes itself felt as the negation of the not yet, expressed in/as the desire to quell any and all opposition to the white (male) twenty-first century neoliberal status quo *in advance*. Sometimes the negation is stated in a stunningly explicit way, the report openly issuing, for example, on its very first page a warning to readers who dare to even dream of change: *The 1776 Report* "provide[s] necessary—and wise—cautions against unrealistic hopes and checks against pressing partisan claims or utopian agendas too hard or too far."[75] But the report's most guileful rhetorical feature is its *preemptive* safeguarding of white privilege by foreclosure of any encounter with the historicity of whiteness and, thus, its desublimation and the crisis of desubjectivation that is always desublimation's effect (see chapter 3).[76] Indeed, *The Report* aims to support a system of race founded on the belief that being is "something more than symbolic" and that the "principles of the American founding" transcend their imperfect translation into the norms, customs, rights, and laws at any given time.[77] As stated in the report's conclusion, "America's founding principles are true not because any generation—including our own—has lived them perfectly, but because they are based upon the eternal truths of the human condition."[78] There are the founding principles; everything else is just history. What passes between them is the enduring contradictions of the universal (white) and the particular (black) whose mundane sublation might just as well be called the actually existing racism of everyday American life. This late neoliberal (and Judeo-Christian) dialectic for democratic capitalism "naturally" functions as alibi for the trivialization of antiblackness as well as the near complete erasure of the difficult labor of its overcoming. *The Report*'s authors give all credit for "the remarkable American story [that] unfolds" to the "founding principles" themselves: "Comprising actions by imperfect human beings, the American story has its share of missteps, errors, contradictions, and wrongs. These wrongs have always met resistance from the clear principles of the nation, and therefore our history is far more one of self-sacrifice, courage, and nobility."[79]

I repeat myself: *The 1619 Project* and *The 1776 Report* are not exemplars of merely two different visions of and for America; they are antinomic, Other-cancelling worldings. No synthesis. No mediation. (Race) War.[80] Have we already reached the point of deadlock? A bit of very good news is that we still don't know for certain.

Notes

Introduction

1. There is a vast scholarly and transdisciplinary literature on the US culture industry's enthusiastic uptake of WWII after President Franklin Delano Roosevelt addressed the nation following Japan's attack on Pearl Harbor that I will not try to cite here. For a general overview of this phenomenon and its collapse at the end of the Cold War, see Tom Engelhardt's *End of Victory Culture*.

2. As readers will soon discover, I am interested in advancing an argument about *popular* memory as a distinct rhetorical form and one to be distinguished from collective memory considered more broadly. Hence, over the course of the book I use the terms of the time (such as "Americans" and even "real Americans") that, importantly, make no effort to mark important historical and geopolitical differences between, say, North Americans and South Americans.

3. For my analysis of the G. W. Bush administration's response to 9/11, see Biesecker, "No Time for Mourning."

4. An impressive number of scholars have attended to the culture wars of the eighties and nineties, some of whom I engage below. For additional scholarly overviews and accounts, see Bradley, *Courts and the Culture Wars*; Bolton, *Culture Wars*; Gates, *Loose Canons*; Hartman, *War for the Soul of America*; Hunter and Wolfe, *Is There a Culture War?*; Jay, *American Literature and the Culture Wars*; Nash, Crabtree, and Dunn, *History on Trial*; Nolan, *American Culture Wars*; Scatamburlo, *Soldiers of Misfortune*; Zimmerman, *Whose America?*

5. Schlesinger, *Disuniting of America*, 22.

6. Hirsch, *Cultural Literacy*, xi, xii.

7. Bloom, *Closing of the American Mind*, 7.

8. Gitlin, *Twilight of Common Dreams*, 88.

9. Phillips, "English-Only Debate," 42.

10. Here I borrow the title of John A. Hall and Charles Lindholm's book *Is America Breaking Apart?* The authors' optimistic reading of the state of the situation in the United States at the time and, more specifically, their central claim that the threat was a ruse, runs counter to the argument I am advancing here and over the course of the book.

11. Fukuyama, "End of History?," 1, 4.

12. For a helpful and nuanced discussion of the differences between Freudian and Lacanian conceptualizations of fantasy, see Evans, *Introductory Dictionary of Lacanian Psychoanalysis*.

13. Žižek, *Sublime Object of Ideology*, 118.

14. Žižek, *Sublime Object of Ideology*, 123.

15. Žižek, *Sublime Object of Ideology*, 33.

16. Rose, *States of Fantasy*, 9.

17. Rose, *States of Fantasy*, 8.

18. "Iteration" is a term that appears in multiple essays and books written by Derrida. For a singularly clear discussion of it in the context of Speech Act Theory, see "Signature Event Context."

19. In *Read My Desire* Copjec—by way of Freud's *Totem and Taboo*—delivers an exemplary explanation of the fundamental notion that the principle of any regime's institution may not appear positively in it.

20. Pease, *New American Exceptionalism*, 31.

21. Pease, *New American Exceptionalism*, 27.

22. Pease, *New American Exceptionalism*, 34.

23. On the fabulous textuality of the Cold War, see Derrida's "No Apocalypse, Not Now."

24. Pease, *New American Exceptionalism*, 180.

25. Pease, *New American Exceptionalism*, 174.

26. Pease boldly takes up the task of identifying and analyzing a variety of fantasies that, prior to 9/11, were gunning to fill the ideological gap. Ultimately, I suggest his insights into Bush's War on Terror are predicated on a blindness to the return of WWII that washed over the country in the years leading up to 9/11.

27. Scholars from a wide array of disciplines have used a handful of names to indicate the shifting economic landscape I am writing about here. I have chosen to stick with the rather old-fashioned term "Post-Fordism" rather than, say, "Late Capitalism" because I am seeking to mark a dominant mutation in the mode of production of value in the United States whose complex relation to the dominance of finance capitalism and global exchange (made possible by electronification) had yet to come home to roost at the level of the common sense at the time. For an atypically nuanced examination of that complex relation, see Spivak, "What's Left of Theory."

28. Duggan, *Twilight of Equality?*, xii.

29. This account of neoliberal economic thinking is greatly influenced by Daniel T. Roger's *Age of Fracture*. Another valuable source is O'Gourman's *The Iconoclastic Imagination*, which views neoliberalism as a social philosophy. It suggests that neoliberal economics transforms its key principle—the importance of an unseen economic order—into an ideology that challenges and changes social and political institutions. O'Gourman argues that three major American events—the Kennedy assassination, Reagan's response to the *Challenger* explosion, and CNN's coverage of 9/11—led people to question visible representations and trust in unseen forces. However, my own analysis of American political and public culture from 1985 to 2005 leads to different conclusions. I believe that neoliberalism is a deeply biopolitical cultural and political system, that the relationship between the visible and invisible is not binary, and that understanding what's happening to the people requires attention to popular culture as well as economics and politics.

30. Rogers, *Age of Fracture*, 63.

31. Foucault, *Birth of Biopolitics*, 240.

32. Hall, *Hard Road to Renewal*, 133.

33. At this point in my argument, it is important to underscore the difference between knowledges or truths and Truth. Given the trajectory of the book, the following example is worth noting at the start: it is true, we do in fact know, that the Holocaust took place. The Truth of the Holocaust is another matter altogether.

34. In the past, I overlooked the crucial role of power when considering the archive and rhetoric. See Biesecker, "Of Historicity, Rhetoric."

35. Foucault, *Archaeology of Knowledge*, 54.

36. Foucault, "Truth and Power," 131.

37. I understand that popular memory and commemoration are closely related to public and vernacular memory. However, I want to focus on its unique rhetorical aspect. Ekaterina V. Haskins, in her book *Popular Memories*, explores how participatory forms of commemoration have changed the concept of democratic citizenship. For Haskins, "popular" is synonymous

with "participatory." This view differs significantly from the argument I am making. For rhetorical analyses of public, collective and/or vernacular memory, see Blair and Michael, "AIDS Memorial Quilt"; Dickinson, "Memories for Sale"; Dickinson, Blair, and Ott, *Places of Public Memory*; Dunn, *Queerly Remembered*; Gallagher, "Memory and Reconciliation"; Hariman and Lucaites, *No Caption Needed*; Haskins, "'Put Your Stamp on History'"; Parry-Giles and Parry-Giles, "Collective Memory"; Pezzullo, "Touring 'Cancer Alley,' Louisiana"; Phillips, *Framing Public Memory*; Stormer, "In Living Memory"; Trollinger, *Selling the Amish*; Vivian, *Public Forgetting*; Zelizer, "Reading the Past."

38. It is hardly a coincidence that the fellowship between Enders and Yahzee is founded on their both having been schooled in Christianity.

39. Foucault, "Film and Popular Memory," 91–92, translation modified.

40. Foucault, "Powers and Strategies," 52.

41. Agamben, *Potentialities*, 182.

42. Derrida has taught us, of course, that any strategy is outstripped in the long and short run by a larger play of forces that are determining but indeterminate in the strict sense. In other words, we are played as we play any game. Spivak explains it thus: "As we play tennis, we are also played by the rules of thermodynamics. Those rules are our handle on the thing thinging, the play of the world in which our play in the world is held. Very broadly put (that's all I can manage), this is a rewriting of what Kant describes as the transcendental: 'We will call the principles whose application stays wholly and completely within the limits of possible experience immanent, but those that would fly beyond these boundaries transcendent principles.' . . . To remember we are played, not only playing" ("Afterword," 358). It is crucial to keep this double bind in mind—a persistent reminder to beware of one's own unacknowledged aspirations. In this case, my desire that my "strategy of reading" be taken up and put to good use by others.

43. Derrida, "Structure, Sign, and Play," 255.

44. Derrida, "Structure, Sign, and Play," 254–55.

45. For a singularly aggressive and impactful exception to the neo-Aristotelian orthodoxy in the field at the time, see Black, *Rhetorical Criticism*.

46. Biesecker, "Rethinking the Rhetorical Situation."

47. The graphematics of iterability in a nutshell: "Every sign, linguistic or nonlinguistic, spoken or written (in the current sense of this opposition), in a small or large unit, can be *cited*, put between quotation marks, in so doing it can break with every given context, engendering an infinity of new contexts in a manner which is absolutely illimitable. This does not imply that the mark is valid outside of a context, but on the contrary that there are only contexts without any center or absolutely anchoring" (Derrida, *Limited Inc*, 12).

48. Derrida, *Limited Inc*, 136.

49. Derrida, "*Différance*," 11.

50. Biesecker, "Rethinking the Rhetorical Situation," 121.

51. In addition to Kornbluh's book and Rooney's essay, both of which I invoke below, see the following for a sampling of the work in new formalism: Eyers, *Speculative Formalism*; Levine, *Forms*; and Wolfson and Brown, *Reading for Form*. Of course, to identify the rage for formlessness as the reigning orthodoxy is not to suggest that scholarship on form had disappeared. To the contrary, it is arguable that serious work—philosophical, theoretical, and critical—by the likes of Alain Badiou, a whole host of Lacanians (including Slavoj Žižek, Joan Copjec, and A. Kiarina Kordela), Marxist-feminist-deconstructionist Gayatri Chakravorty Spivak, and Marxist cultural and literary theorist Fredric Jameson not only never stopped attending to form but, in many cases, insisted that form has been and is still the secret.

52. Kornbluh, *Order of Forms*, 2.

53. Kornbluh, *Order of Forms*, 19.
54. Derrida, "Structure, Sign, and Play," 249.
55. Rooney, "Form and Contentment," 34.
56. Alexander, "Can You Be BLACK?"

Chapter 1

1. Harwit, *Exhibit Denied*, 435. Heyman's comments were reported in newspapers the following day.
2. Wallace, "Culture War," 174.
3. Young, "Dangerous History," 208.
4. Koundoura, "Multiculturalism or Multinationalism," 69.
5. Harwit, *Exhibit Denied*, 392.
6. Wallace, "Culture War," 186.
7. Wallace, "Culture War," 187.
8. Harwit, *Exhibit Denied*, 169.
9. Harwit, *Exhibit Denied*, 214.
10. Harwit, *Exhibit Denied*, 215.
11. Harwit, *Exhibit Denied*, 52.
12. Dower, "Three Narratives of Our Humanity," 89.
13. Harwit, *Exhibit Denied*, 323.
14. See, for example, Hallion's letter to Harwit in which he writes, "Unit (400) of the exhibit, [dealing with the aftermath of the bombings at Hiroshima and Nagasaki], strikes me as possibly tasteless. I am not opposed to selective photographs that show graphic injury or damage—but the power of a broken person is overwhelming, and may leave visitors with the mistaken impression that nearly all victims of the Pacific were Japanese" (qtd. in Harwit, *Exhibit Denied*, 203).
15. Harwit, *Exhibit Denied*, 257.
16. It is important to note that the newly installed introductory photo exhibit would have doubled the size of the planned installation. See Harwit, *Exhibit Denied*, 305. Also, according to numerous accounts, including Harwit's own, the proverbial final straw was the team's intention to include newly "discovered" figures estimating the number of American casualties in the event of a Pacific invasion.
17. On the theoretical and critical elaboration of the counter-monument, see Young, *Texture of Memory*, 48.
18. Hogan, "Hiroshima in History and Memory," 5.
19. Moll, *Price for Peace*.
20. Moll, *Price for Peace*.
21. Moll, *Price for Peace*.
22. D-Day Museum website, https://www.ddaymuseum.org/museum_general.html (accessed July 22, 2004).
23. Moll, *Price for Peace*.
24. Rhetorical scholar, historian, and war veteran Robert P. Newman presents an account and analysis of the controversy that vehemently opposes the one I tender here. Out of respect for his scholarship, and appreciation and gratitude for his teaching, mentoring, and friendship, I single it out. See "*Enola Gay* at Air and Space."
25. Wallace, "Culture War," 335.
26. I take the notion of "logics of failed revolt" from Peter Starr's book of the same name.

27. Derrida, "White Mythologies," 207.
28. Brown, *States of Injury*, 74.
29. Brown, *States of Injury*, 55.
30. Berlant, "Subject of True Feeling," 45.
31. In *Democracy and Other Neoliberal Fantasies*, a book whose claims accumulate at breathtaking speed, political theorist Jodi Dean takes identity politics or victim politics as the historical point of departure for her scathing critique of the Left, its cowardly complicity with a communicative capitalism that fits hand in glove with the new millennial neoliberal agenda.
32. Foucault, *Fearless Speech*, 170. It is in the two days of hearings that followed the *Enola Gay* controversy that we can see how truth telling is literally or materially brought into coincidence with the exercise of power: the overwhelming majority of members of the Senate hearings committee are themselves WWII veterans who, as I note in the body of the chapter, repeatedly invoke their own experience as evidence of the truth.
33. Approximately midway through *Archaeology of Knowledge*, Foucault presents what we may, with caution, read as a thumbnail description of the general conditions of possibility for discursive change:

> So the subject of the statement should not be regarded as identical with the author of the formulation—either in substance, or in function. He is not in fact the cause, origin, or starting-point of the phenomenon of the written or spoken articulation of a sentence; nor is it that meaningful intention which, silently anticipating words, orders them like the visible body of its intuition; it is not the constant, motionless, unchanging focus of a series of operations that are manifested, in turn, on the surface of discourse through the statements. It is a particular, vacant place that may in fact be filled by different individuals; but, instead of being defined once and for all, . . . this place varies—or rather it is variable enough to be able either to persevere, unchanging, through several sentences, or to alter with each one. (95)

It is in this sense that identity politics can be considered a statement: a space of enunciation, effective speech, or utterance that was taken up by the Right, put to new uses, deployed for different ends.
34. The reader will note that "personal experience" is the narrative device that organizes later popular culture representations of WWII. *Band of Brothers*, like *Price for Peace*, uses the personal testimony of WWII veterans to, in the case of the former, frame the episode and, in the case of the latter, to punctuate the documentary record.
35. Additional instances: Colonel Charles D. Cooper, director of publications, Retired Officers Association: "This testimony of The American Legion has been prepared at the direction of and under the review of our National Commander, William M. Detweiler. . . . His experience on this issue is real, and this testimony has his full support and approval—and thus, represents the position of the more than 3.1 million men and women who comprise Legion membership." *Smithsonian Institution Management Guidelines for the Future, Before the Committee on Rules and Administration*, 104th Cong., 20 (1995).
36. *Air Force Magazine*, July 1995, 23.
37. *Smithsonian Institution Management Guidelines for the Future, Before the Committee on Rules and Administration*, 104th Cong., 37 (1995).
38. *Smithsonian Institution Management Guidelines for the Future, Before the Committee on Rules and Administration*, 104th Cong., 38 (1995).
39. Scott, "Experience," 25.

40. *Smithsonian Institution Management Guidelines for the Future, Before the Committee on Rules and Administration*, 104th Cong., 7 (1995).

41. Linenthal, "Anatomy of a Controversy," 59.

42. For a detailed account of the suppression of the catalog, see Harwit, *Exhibit Denied*, 414–17.

43. As before, the repudiation of the so-called life of the mind in the nineties is predicated on—indeed traffics in—a set of discursively manufactured antagonisms that have long exerted mass appeal:

> Intellect is pitted against feeling, on the ground that it is somehow inconsistent with warm emotion. It is pitted against character, because it is widely believed that intellect stands for mere cleverness, which transmutes easily into the sly or the diabolical. It is pitted against practicality, since theory is held to be opposed to practice, and the "purely" theoretical mind is so much disesteemed. It is pitted against democracy, since intellect is felt to be a form of distinction that defies egalitarianism. . . . Who cares to risk sacrificing warmth of emotion, solidity of character, practical capacity, or democratic sentiment in order to pay deference to a type of man who at best is deemed to be merely clever and at worst may even be dangerous? (Hofstadter, *Anti-Intellectualism in American Life*, 45–46)

However, the anti-intellectualism that resurfaces in the nineties is marked by an important difference that will be the focus of the discussion that follows.

44. *Guidelines for the Consideration of Memorials under the Commemorative Works Act, Before the Subcommittee on Libraries and Memorials of the Committee on House Administration*, 103rd Congress, 64 (1994) (hereafter cited in chapter 1 as *Subcommittee on Libraries and Memorials*).

45. That understanding and all the practical entailments thereof (not the least of which is public policy) are to be given over completely to "experience" is one of the implications of Susan Sontag's meditations in *Regarding the Pain of Others*, which closes on the following enigmatic note: "'We'—this 'we' is everyone who has never experienced anything like what they went through—don't understand. We don't get it. We truly can't imagine what it was like. We can't image how dreadful, how terrifying war is; and how normal it becomes. Can't understand, can't imagine. That's what every soldier, and every journalist and aid worker and independent observer who has put in time under fire, and had the luck to elude the death that struck down others nearby, stubbornly feels. And they are right" (125–26).

46. It is no surprise that people within academia also downplay leftist "intellectual" work by making it seem far removed from everyday life. For an example, see Richard Rorty's *Achieving Our Country*:

> We now have, among many American students and teachers, a spectatorial, disgusted, mocking Left rather than a Left which dreams of achieving our country. This is not the only Left we have, but it is the most prominent and vocal one. Members of this Left find America unforgivable, as Baldwin did, and also unachievable, as he did not. This leads them to step back from their country and, as they say, "theorize" it. It leads them to do what Henry Adams did to give cultural politics preference over real politics, and to mock the very idea that democratic institutions might once again be made to serve social justice. It leads them to prefer knowledge to hope." (36)

Furthermore, given that one of my project's audiences is rhetorical theorists, critics, and historians, it is important to note that substituting personal experience for rigorous analysis is happening even among fellow scholars. Indeed, in response to a portion of this book-length project that I had submitted for publication in one of the field's flagship journals, I received this response from an anonymous reviewer: "There literally is no positive moment in the essay. Would *any* commemoration of the WWII dead satisfy this critic? This was a war in which, for example, Raymond Williams proudly served as a tank commander and, so far as I can tell, only Patrick Buchanan currently wishes we hadn't fought. Silly me—I still carry my father's WWII dogtags as a sign of pride and remembrance. I guess I am hopelessly unhip . . . well, whatever. I cannot imagine the author of this essay being attached enough to any value to wish to die for it. Too bad." I respond to this "review" in chapter 4.

47. *Subcommittee on Libraries and Memorials*, 25.
48. Amos, *ABC News Nightline* transcript, 2.
49. Mason, "Proudly Display the *Enola Gay*," 22.
50. *Subcommittee on Libraries and Memorials*, 13.
51. Yardley, "Dropping a Bomb of an Idea," B2.
52. *Subcommittee on Libraries and Memorials*,10.
53. Ringle, "At Ground Zero," A1.
54. *Subcommittee on Libraries and Memorials*, 68.
55. Foucault, "Discourse on Language," 224.
56. Foucault, "Questions of Method," 75.
57. Scarry, *Body in Pain*, 14.
58. Qtd. in Gitlin, *Twilight of Common Dreams*, 217.
59. Renshon, "America at a Crossroads," 3.
60. Gitlin, *Twilight of Common Dreams*, 217.
61. Mason, "Proudly Display the *Enola Gay*," 23.
62. Mason, "Proudly Display the *Enola Gay*," 22.
63. Spielberg, *Saving Private Ryan*.
64. Brokaw, *Greatest Generation*, 11.
65. Brokaw, *Greatest Generation*, 390.
66. McDaniel, "Brothers in Battle," 2.
67. Brown, *States of Injury*, 73.
68. Derrida, *Given Time*, 7.

Chapter 2

1. Takaki, *Different Mirror*, 92.
2. As Kaja Silverman explains in *Threshold of the Visible World*, the given-to-be-seen may be defined as "the operation within the field of vision of the system of intelligibility which is synonymous with the dominant fiction." It "depends for its hegemonic effects on the slotting of the eye into a particular spectatorial position—into a metaphoric geometral point. The latter can then be best defined as *the position from which we apprehend and affirm those elements of the screen which are synonymous with the dominant fiction*" (179). Although I invoke this phraseology from the Lacanian lexicon to underscore the spectral or visual character of national identification, the ensuing analysis aims to apprehend the role of rhetoric in transactions that seek to libidinally secure fidelity to the nation.
3. Will, "Statue Sweepstakes," 64.
4. Spivak, "Subaltern Studies," 271.
5. From "About the Memorial: World War II Memorial Homepage," https://www.wwii memorial.com (accessed September 3, 1999):

> The concept for the memorial is an ensemble of a lowered plaza surrounding the Rainbow Pool, parapet walls surmounted by transparent architectural arms of stone and metal and two monumental memorial arches. The memorial will include iconography, inscriptions and sculpture as part of the final design. . . . Bronze laurel wreaths are suspended from the oculus of each arch . . . [which] overlook the memorial plaza and Rainbow Pool. . . . The floor of the memorial plaza is an orchestrated blend of green spaces and paved surfaces surrounding the Rainbow Pool. A central ceremonial area is placed at the western apex of the memorial plaza. A curvilinear granite wall is embedded into the waterfalls that navigate the vertical transition between the Reflecting Pool and the Rainbow Pool. Inscriptions honoring the fallen and all who served and a flame of freedom will be incorporated into the ceremonial area. . . . In the center of the plaza, the fountains of the reconstructed Rainbow Pool will be restored to their former splendor as part of the memorial.

6. Both substantively and stylistically, public debate (or lack thereof) over the World War II Memorial differs markedly from the lengthy and often heated rhetorical struggles that emerged over other proposals to recognize the nation's fallen heroes by raising a structure on their behalf on the mall (e.g., the Vietnam Veterans Memorial, the Vietnam Women's Memorial, and the Women in Military Service for America Memorial). See *Guidelines for the Consideration of Memorials under the Commemorative Works Act, Before the Subcommittee on Libraries and Memorials of the Committee on House Administration*, 103rd Congress, 2 (1994).

7. An interesting exception was delivered by Judy Scott Feldman, chair of the National Coalition to Save Our Mall, during her testimony before the Commission of Fine Arts. She objected vigorously to the proposed memorial's "imperial and triumphal design" that was "unacceptably reminiscent of Fascist and Nazi regimes." Molotsky, "Panel Backs World War II Memorial on Mall in Washington," A1.

8. Molotsky, "Panel Backs World War II Memorial on Mall in Washington," A1. Across the country, forty-three newspapers (including the *New York Times*, the *Washington Post*, and *USA Today*) printed at least one article or editorial opposing the site (though many of those were reprints of the same original piece).

9. Kidder, "War Memorial," 3C.

10. Clinton, "Remarks by President Clinton."

11. The memorial's statement of purpose is as follows:

> The World War II Memorial will be the first national memorial dedicated to all who served in the armed forces and Merchant Marines of the United States during World War II and acknowledging the commitment and achievement of the entire nation. All military veterans of the war, the citizens on the home front, the nation at large, and the high moral purpose and idealism that motivated the nation's call to arms will be honored. Symbolic of the defining event of the twentieth century in American history, the memorial will be a monument to the spirit, sacrifice, and commitment of the American people, to the common defense of the nation and to the broader causes of peace and freedom from tyranny throughout the world. It will inspire future generations of Americans, deepening their appreciation of what the World War II generation accomplished in securing freedom and democracy. Above all, the memorial will stand for all time as an important symbol of American national unity, a timeless reminder of the moral strength and awesome power that can flow when a free people are at once united and bonded together in a common and just cause. ("About the Memorial")

12. Clinton, "Clinton Salutes Veterans," 4A.

13. These statements contest Arthur Danto's theoretical claim that a clear distinction is to be made between monuments and memorials: "We erect monuments so that we shall always remember, and build memorials so that we shall never forget. Thus we have the Washington Monument but the Lincoln Memorial. Monuments commemorate the memorable and embody the myths of beginnings. Memorials ritualize remembrance and mark the reality of ends. . . . The memorial is a special precinct, extruded from life, a segregated enclave where we honor the dead. With monuments we honor ourselves" ("Vietnam Veterans Memorial," 153).

14. Schribman, "Put the Memorial," 3C.

15. Kidder, "War Memorial," 3C.

16. Clinton, "Remarks on Responsible Citizenship," 5.

17. Popular and academic examinations of the National Mall enact a stubbornly hermeneutic focus on individual memorials and monuments, foreclosing any apprehension of how the piecemeal construction of additional monuments or memorials alters the rhetorical force of the Mall's totality, however provisional that totality may be.

18. Another way to describe the aim of my analysis would be to say that it seeks to extend Michael McGee's 1975 call for the rhetorical accounting of the discursive production of a <people> by attending not only to the "material forces, events, and themes in history *only as they have already been mediated or filtered by the Leader whose words [we have typically studied]*" but also to those other enunciative sites through which national affiliation is (re)produced ("In Search of 'the People,'" 249).

19. "Memorial Moratorium," 2A.

20. Foucault, "Truth and Power," 46.

21. There is a vast theoretical and critical literature on the relationships among the nation, the media, and the discursive production of the citizen-subject in the late twentieth century. This analysis takes several of its cues from Berlant's analysis of infantile citizenship in *Queen of America*, Grossberg's account of the politically disaffected citizen in *We Gotta Get Out of This Place*, and Miller's treatment of the cultural citizen in *Technologies of Truth*. It is notable that all three of these analyses were published during the period under examination here and, on my view, are aging well.

22. Clinton, "Responsible Citizenship."

23. Meacham, "Caught in the Line of Fire," 50.

24. Qtd. in Caldwell, "Spielberg at War," 48.

25. Arnold, "'Private Ryan' Revives a Genre," E3.

26. Arnold, "'Private Ryan' Revives a Genre," E3.

27. Wolcott, "Tanks for the Memories," 73.

28. For an alternative analysis of the film written by a cultural historian, see Bodnar, "*Saving Private Ryan*." Other rhetoric scholars have examined the film as well, coming to very different conclusions largely because, as I will suggest, they do not read the film in the context of the discursive formation of which it is a significant part. See Owen, "Memory, War and American Identity"; Ehrenhaus, "Why We Fought"; and Hasian, "Nostalgic Longings."

29. Elshtain, "Spielberg's America," C73.

30. Wolcott, "Tanks for the Memories," 75.

31. Meacham, "Caught in the Line of Fire," 50.

32. Qtd. in Charles, "Guts and Glory," 162.

33. Berlant, *Queen of America*, 57.

34. While the film explores the sacrifices and heroism of American soldiers, its portrayal of women is problematic, often sexist and misogynistic. This is especially evident in scenes

outside of combat, where soldiers engage in "intimate" conversations." Consider, for example, the Brooklyn bad boy's recounting of Mrs. Rachel Cherbowitz's advice from the dressing room of his mother's shop that "if [he's] ever scared" he "close [his] eyes and remember these" "44EEs" or "massive things"; and Ryan's jovial recollection of "the last night the four [Ryan brothers] were together," memorable for the brothers' thwarted rape of Alice Jardine, "a girl who just took a nose dive from the ugly tree and hit every branch coming down." Furthermore, although there are no fantasy rape scenarios in Brokaw's *Greatest Generation*, I argue that certain women fare no better there. The book subtly moves from emphasizing traditional "family values" to promoting a broader, neoliberal "national family" by strategically re-membering and repositioning female bodies and desire. Out of this emerges a newly determined abject feminine: the "feminist" who refuses to submit her agency to the will of the national family.

35. It is not without consequence that *Saving Private Ryan* structurally elides the sixties and seventies—those socially and politically tumultuous decades in US history during which citizens literally took to the streets.

36. Rothstein, "Rescuing the War Hero," E2.

37. Brokaw has since edited and published several other best-selling books for which WWII serves as the central reference, organizing theme, or point of departure. See, for example, *Album of Memories* and *Greatest Generation Speaks*, both which were reissued in audio format.

38. Goldstein, "World War II Chic," 47.

39. Brokaw, *Greatest Generation*, 15, xx.

40. Brokaw, *Greatest Generation*, 388–89.

41. Brokaw, *Greatest Generation*, 388.

42. Brokaw, *Greatest Generation*, xx.

43. Miller, *Well-Tempered Self*.

44. My discussion of disincorporation is indebted to Warner's theorization in "Mass Public."

45. Brokaw, *Greatest Generation*, 200–201.

46. *The Greatest Generation* encourages dismantling welfare and privatizing social services, sometimes boldly, sometimes subtly. See, for example, the story of James and Dorothy Dowling, during which Brokaw writes, "James Dowling was orphaned soon after he was born. His mother died when he was only six months old and his father was unable to care for this baby and his four brothers and sisters. *In those simpler times, when much of social welfare was a matter of good-hearted people*, the plight of James and his siblings was made known in the church. The minister announced that someone had to take in these children. James and two of his brothers were taken home by the Conklins, Clarence and Anna" (46, emphasis added). Or Brokaw's closing words to "The Dumbos," a vignette recounting the postwar trials and tribulations of four couples "in the small South Dakota city of Yankton": "Outside of our own families, to those of us growing up in Yankton at the time, these World War II couples were emblematic of the values that shaped our lives. In many respects, *their marriages and the way they conducted them were a form of community service*" (249, emphasis added).

47. Brokaw, *Greatest Generation*, 200.

48. Brokaw, *Greatest Generation*, 17.

49. Brokaw, *Greatest Generation*, xxx.

50. Brokaw, *Greatest Generation*, xxx.

51. Kuhn, *Family Secrets*, 17.

52. The literature on the relation of the visual image or the photograph and the verbal text is extensive. Some classic works are Barthes, *Mythologies*; Barthes, "Rhetoric of the Image";

Berger, *Ways of Seeing*; Mitchell, *Picture Theory*; Sontag, *On Photography*; and Tagg, *Burden of Representation*.

53. See Cartwright, *Screening the Body*.

54. Brown, *States of Injury*, 57.

55. Brokaw, *Greatest Generation*, 356.

56. Foucault, "Preface," xix.

57. Witt, *Day the Nation Said "Thanks!,"* 96.

58. On the minimalist aesthetic (and, I would add, rhetoric) of monumental material culture, see, for example, Blair, Jeppeson, and Pucci, "Public Memorializing in Postmodernity"; Bodnar, *Remaking America*; Gillis, *Commemorations*; Savage, *Standing Soldiers, Kneeling Slaves*; and Sturken, *Tangled Memories*.

59. Witt, *Day the Nation Said "Thanks!,"* 94.

60. Phelan, *Unmarked*, 7.

61. Lacan, *Four Fundamental Concepts of Psychoanalysis*, 93.

62. The argument I am advancing here is not that WIMS never could perform a radical, interruptive politics. I am claiming that at this particular time-place, in the context of the discourse formation of which it is a part, it is not doing so. It may be worthwhile to note that one of the implications of this analysis for thinking about rhetoric more generally is that the popular "polysemy thesis" often begs rather than answers the question, "What rhetorical work is being done by or through this text?" Although grasping the polysemic nature of all discourse and practice is an important first step, a rigorous rhetorical analysis proceeds to discern those forces that operate provisionally to secure—through processes of articulation, disarticulation, and rearticulation—the effectivity of the text, utterance, or practice. For a cogent review of the literature in the field and a call to sharpen our theoretical assumptions and critical practice, see Ceccarelli, "Polysemy."

63. Indeed, the exhibit's handheld script is replete with various gestures of pointing: "See the uniform of Navy nurse Doris Yetter"; "Notice the hand-made clothespin used by Madeline Ullom"; "Also in the exhibit is a pair of custom-made mosquito boots, worn by Army nurses in Africa"; "Notice the photograph of a woman packing a parachute." For an extensive analysis of the deployment of the constative utterance in museums of natural history and fine art, see Bal, *Double Exposures*.

64. I borrow the term "exhibition rhetoric" from Ferguson, "Exhibition Rhetorics." There he tethers together Enzensberger's expanded concept of the "cultural industries" ("to include advertising, education, and any institutional use of media techniques intended for vast audiences or what is now often referred to cynically as 'infotainment,'" 176) and a classical conception of rhetoric ("a strategic system of representation," 176) to argue that "the will to influence is at the core of any exhibition" (179). Rhetorical scholars have been studying museums and exhibits for some time, delivering impressive insights. See, for example, Atwater and Herndon, "Cultural Space and Race"; Armanda, "Memorial Agon"; Brady, "Mediating Indigenous Voice in the Museum"; Dickinson, Ott, and Aoki, "Spaces of Remembering and Forgetting"; Fried, "Personalization of Collective Memory"; Johnson, "'Psychiatric Power"; Kelly and Hoerl, "Genesis in Hyperreality"; McAlister, "Uncanny Architrope"; Olson, *Constitutive Visions*; Ott, Aoki, and Dickinson, "Ways of (Not) Seeing Guns"; Palewicz and Hasian, "Mourning Absences"; Trollinger and Trollinger, *Righting America at the Creation Museum*; Weiser, *Museum Rhetoric*; Zagacki and Gallagher, "Rhetoric and Materiality."

65. It should be noted that the Integration Act exhibit, originally placed next to a wholly separate exhibit documenting the history of the memorial's emergence, was moved to a display case situated between the WWII and new Korean War exhibits. Wilma L. Vaught, personal interview with the author, Washington, DC, June 6, 2000.

66. Miller, *Technologies of Truth*, 265.

Chapter 3

1. Schudson, *Watergate in American Memory*, 13. WWII's relative insignificance for political public culture in the late eighties was "confirmed" by a Gallup follow-up question. "When asked to list two major events, people again mentioned Vietnam most often (34.4 percent), followed by the Reagan presidency (20.2), the assassinations (17.8), and then Watergate (17.4), ahead of the Great Depression (16.8), the civil rights movement (15.9), the Kennedy presidency (15.4), and World War II (13.6)."

2. Rorty, *Achieving Our Country*.

3. Badiou, *Ethics*, 47.

4. Clinton, "Veterans Day National Ceremony."

5. Derrida, *Other Heading*, 41.

6. Huyssen, *Twilight Memories*, 250.

7. Paul Williams's *Memorial Museums* examines the hybrid institution's appearance in multiple countries around the world, seeking to answer a crucial question posed by their very presence or existence:

> A vital issue is whether older categories of analysis remain suitable for describing this new commemorative form—"memorial museum" is a compound made necessary by the complication of conventional museological categories. On initial consideration, the memorial museum spells an inherent contradiction. A *memorial* is seen to be, if not apolitical, at least safe in the refuge of history. . . . A history *museum*, by contrast, is presumed to be concerned with interpretation, contextualization, and critique. The coalescing of the two suggests that there is an increasing desire to add both a moral framework to the narration of terrible historical events and more in-depth contextual explanations to commemorative acts. (8)

8. Cole, *Selling the Holocaust*, 147.

9. Gourevitch, "Genocide Pop."

10. Linenthal, *Preserving Memory*, 112.

11. Landsberg, *Prosthetic Memory*, 138. As she puts it earlier in the book, "One goal of this book is to explore the ability of prosthetic memories to produce empathy and social responsibility as well as political alliances that transcend race, class, and gender. A sensuous engagement with the past, this book contends, is the foundation for more than individual subjectivity; it becomes the basis for mediated collective identification and the production of potentially counterhegemonic public spheres" (21).

12. Miller, *Well-Tempered Self*, 73–74.

13. Landsberg, *Prosthetic Memory*, 112, 135.

14. Landsberg, *Prosthetic Memory*, 135.

15. Landsberg, *Prosthetic Memory*, 129–32.

16. Landsberg, *Prosthetic Memory*, 132–33.

17. Landsberg, *Prosthetic Memory*, 135.

18. Landsberg, *Prosthetic Memory*, 139.

19. Meister, "'Never Again,'" 7.

20. Novick, *Holocaust in American Life*, esp. 207–38.

21. Zelizer, *Remembering to Forget*, 171–201.

22. For a detailed analysis of those many sites, see Young, *Texture of Memory*, esp. 287–322.

23. Young, *Texture of Memory*, 5.

24. Huyssen, "Monument and Memory," 250.

25. Zelizer, *Remembering to Forget*, 212.

26. For Zelizer, journalistic photography "works" when images are clearly attached to referents, real things or real events, in the world. It goes awry when, for all the formal reasons she discusses over the course of the book, images begin to represent other images or function as simulacrums—images of images.

27. The social or psychological logic informing Zelizer's analysis is mimetic and linear: from representation comes identification with pain, followed by the impulse to work toward its mitigation. My analysis draws on Lacanian psychoanalysis, from which a considerably more complicated understanding of human beings and their various relations (including a doubled conceptualization of identification as, on the one hand, imaginary and, on the other, as symbolic) has developed. The literature is vast, but a few book-length treatments that may serve as a point of departure are Borch-Jacobsen, *Lacan*; Fink, *Lacanian Subject*; Grosz, *Jacques Lacan*; MacCannell, *Figuring Lacan*; and Weber, *Return to Freud*.

28. Zelizer, *Remembering to Forget*, 225–26.

29. Zelizer, *Remembering to Forget*, 202.

30. Spivak, "Politics of Interpretations," 118.

31. "I don't believe that there is any perception" (Derrida, "Discussion," 272).

32. Foucault, "Nietzsche, Genealogy, History," 154.

33. Cole, *Selling the Holocaust*, 152.

34. Cole, *Selling the Holocaust*, 158.

35. Cole, *Selling the Holocaust*, 152.

36. Michael Bernard-Donald delivers a unique rhetorical reading of the USHMM by focusing on enduring rhetorical elements like ethos, figure, trope, and kairos. He closely observes patrons' responses to the exhibit and summarily describes "every" visitor's experience:

> The space of the visitor becomes dynamic, in which what happens in spite of us and in front of our eyes before we are cognizant of it, and how we make sense of it, place it into discourse, and do our best to regularize the experience, vie for primacy. In that movement, the visitor's ability to settle on any single understanding, any single memory, is forestalled. The Holocaust, as a specific object of memory, becomes displaced, and the visitor who goes to the museum with an identity for both herself and the event, whose ethos is more or less stable, becomes attuned to the "irruption of the real." (*Figures of Memory*, 151)

Using Michael Hyde's Heideggerian-inspired ethics of "dwelling" and Marc Auge's "non-place" concept, Bernard-Donals then draws the following conclusion about the memorial museum's rhetorical force: "It is at times far more disorienting than they, or the US Holocaust Memorial Council, might wish. The space they inhabit on leaving the museum is a space of exposure, wherein they dwell not in the knowledge that they now know, once and for all, what happened. Rather, that space, insofar as it renders the visitor placeless, called, and called into question, is a virtual, kairotic, and liminal one that casts them into an uncertain ethical and political future" (153). I agree that when patrons step out from the exhibit they are "cast into an uncertain ethical and political future." However, I am arguing that the felt uncertainty is neither as "affective" nor as enduring as Bernard-Donals so suggests. Rather, the exhibit's rhetorical effect is not individual but collective, triggering a crisis of *national* identity for US patrons steeped in the neoliberal national fantasy.

In *American Public Memory and the Holocaust*, Lisa A. Costello patiently attends to the gender politics of Holocaust remembrance by studying Lanzmann's documentary *Shoah*. She argues persuasively that "it is precisely what is *not seen* that allows only the binary norms of gender to dominate what audiences see as the Holocaust ideal." Importantly, however, since the "rhetorical process of gendering" in public memory relies on "discursive, material, and embodied articulations and performances that create and disturb gendered distinctions,'" they "can be challenged" (25).

37. Weinberg and Elieli, *Holocaust Museum in Washington*, 88.

38. Weinberg and Elieli, *Holocaust Museum in Washington*, 96.

39. It is important to point out that "included within but not belonging to" is a thumbnail definition of the Lacanian part-object. The part-object is not a part that belongs to the given whole but, rather, a part that that breaks with it, opening the totalizing scene onto another. For a rich and useful exposition on the part-object and its detotalizing effects, see Copjec, "Narcissism, Approached Obliquely," in *Imagine There's No Woman*.

40. Foucault, "Nietzsche, Genealogy, History," 154.

41. Benjamin, *Arcades Project*, 463.

42. Badiou, *Being and Event*, 99. Badiou defines "excrescent" as that which is represented but not presented (96).

43. Derrida, *Other Heading*, 35.

44. Butler, "Contingent Foundations," 17.

45. This is, of course, one of the crucial hegemonic functions of the heteronormative couple in Brokaw's *Greatest Generation* as well as across the assemblage of texts that collectively constitute the ethnonational state fantasy more broadly.

46. Poovey, *Making a Social Body*, 3.

47. Badiou, "Democratic Materialism," 20.

48. Agamben, *Means Without End*, 138–39.

49. Copjec, *Imagine There's No Woman*, 28–29.

50. Badiou, "Being by Numbers," 87.

51. Copjec, *Imagine There's No Woman*, 29.

52. Copjec, *Imagine There's No Woman*, 29.

53. Copjec, *Imagine There's No Woman*, 34.

54. Copjec, *Imagine There's No Woman*, 34.

55. Copjec, *Imagine There's No Woman*, 30.

56. Copjec, *Imagine There's No Woman*, 32.

57. It is crucial to underscore that this subject is autonomous in the sense of freed from the given state of situation but is not "sovereign" in the neoliberal sense of the term.

58. Copjec, *Imagine There's No Woman*, 79–80.

59. Copjec, *Imagine There's No Woman*, 66.

60. Copjec, "*Gia Savoir Sera*," 132.

61. Copjec, *Imagine There's No Woman*, 37.

62. The rhetoric and politics of the national count—of what is counted, who is counted, what and who is excluded, how the count is orchestrated, et cetera—in US history warrants extended study. A certain *kind* or *manner* of "counting," as I noted from the start of my analysis of *Saving Private Ryan*, is a fundament of the ethnonational neoliberal fantasy that is the focus of this book. However, it is worth pointing also to the role of the count in more recent commemorative controversies, not the least of which was the battle over who would be counted in the 9/11 Memorial Museum. It is my intention to study this in the near future. For a foray into that project and, more specifically, a rhetorical examination of the relation of the count to the attribution of neonational value, see Biesecker, "From General History to Philosophy."

63. These are the last four words on the last page of Brokaw's *The Greatest Generation*.

64. This sacrificial logic was invoked as a warrant for the loss of life of service members during the recent evacuation of US citizens and Afghans who worked alongside the US

government during "the longest war in American history." As President Biden put it in his address to the nation:

> The extraordinary success of this mission was due to the incredible skill, bravery and selfless courage of the United States military and our diplomats and intelligence professionals. For weeks, they risked their lives. . . . Risking their lives, not for professional gains but to serve others. Not in a mission of war but in a mission of mercy. Twenty service members were wounded in the service of this mission. Thirteen heroes gave their lives. I was just at Dover Air Force Base for the dignified transfer. We owe them and their families a debt of gratitude we can never repay, but we should never, ever forget. (Biden, "Transcript of Biden's Speech")

65. Copjec, *Imagine There's No Woman*, 151.
66. Copjec, "*Gia Savoir Sera*," 133.
67. Copjec, *Imagine There's No Woman*, 78.
68. Foucault, "Film and Popular Memory," 91–92, translation modified.

Chapter 4

1. Wade, "Judge Blames Trump."

2. There were often-noted exceptions. For their service on the Select Committee, Republicans Liz Cheney and Adam Kinzinger were formally censured by the Republican Party, thereby withholding "any and all support of them . . . for their behavior which has been destructive to the U.S. House of Representatives, the Republican Party, and [the] republic." See Republican National Committee, "Resolution to Formally Censure." Cheney lost to her opponent in the Republican primary by a landslide, and the jury is still out on her political prospects. In October 2021, Kinzinger announced he would not pursue another term in the House. Then senator from Utah and former Republican presidential hopeful Mitt Romney also drew sharp rebukes from members of his party for voting twice to impeach Trump. The Utah GOP's resolution to censure him failed by a vote of 711–98. See Reston and Pellish, "Utah GOP Vote to Censure."

3. For a detailed historical account of Trump's highly polarizing campaign against Hillary Clinton, see Stuckey, *Deplorable*.

4. Albeit impossible to tally, it is nevertheless crucial to mark the (unofficial) body count that anti-LGBTQ+ hate crimes and legislation as well as antiabortion legislation (continue to) leave in their wake.

5. For a detailed rhetorical analysis of the signifying chain that runs from "black lives matter" to "blue lives matter" to "white lives matter" to "all lives matter," see Biesecker, "From General History to Philosophy."

6. I am more ambivalent than is Jodi Dean on the entailments of the new social media for democracy in the United States, her grim assessment predicated on what she takes to be their near-complete capture by communicative capitalism. The counter-conduct prompted by a video recording of the murder of George Floyd, discussed at greater length below, encourages me to guard the question. See Dean, *Democracy and Other Neoliberal Fantasies*.

7. Silverstein, *1619 Project*.

8. Silverstein, "Editor's Note."

9. Silverstein, "Editor's Note."

10. For "wake work," see Sharpe, *In the Wake*; and Hartman, *Scenes of Subjection*, xxxiii.

11. Silverstein, "Editor's Note."

12. Hannah-Jones, "Preface," xxiv; *The 1619 Project*: Education Portal, https://pulitzercenter.org/education/k-12-programs-and-resources/1619-project-education-portal (accessed December 29, 2023).

13. North, "Foreword," xxvi.

14. North, "Foreword," xxvi.

15. North, "Foreword," xxiv.

16. Mackaman and North, "It Is All Just a Metaphor," 316.

17. Cotton and Buck, "When *New York Times*."

18. With the exception of Wilentz, the historians who served as signatories made substantive contributions in the form of interviews and essays to the World Socialist Website project and the published volume that followed.

19. Bynum et al., "Letter to the Editor."

20. Bynum et al., "Letter to the Editor"; Grossman, "Why Schools Adopted *The 1619 Project*."

21. Department of Homeland Security, "DHS Announces New Task Force."

22. Trump, "Protecting American Monuments"; Trump, "Building and Rebuilding Monuments."

23. Trump, "Protecting American Monuments."

24. Trump, "Building and Rebuilding Monuments."

25. Trump, "Building and Rebuilding Monuments."

26. Trump, "Combating Race and Sex Stereotyping."

27. Trump, "Combating Race and Sex Stereotyping."

28. Trump, "Establishing the President's Advisory 1776 Commission."

29. Trump, "Establishing the President's Advisory 1776 Commission."

30. Trump, "Establishing the President's Advisory 1776 Commission."

31. Trump appointed Larry P. Arnn, Hillsdale College president, as the commission's chair. Carol Swain, a former Vanderbilt University law professor, was named vice chair. Matthew Spalding, a professor at Hillsdale College, was the executive director. The members, drawn from right-wing think tank, fund-raising, and political circles, included Phil Bryant, Jerry Davis, Michael Farris, Gay Hart Gaines, John Gibbs, Mike Gonzalez, Victor Davis Hanson, Charles Kesler, Peter Kirsanow, Thomas Lindsay, Bob McEwen, Ned Ryan, and Julie Strauss Levin.

32. Nguyen, "Big Chunk of Trump's Report."

33. See 1776 Project PAC, https://1776projectpac.com/ (accessed January 1, 2024).

34. American Historical Association, "AHA Condemns Report."

35. Clifton, "How the Trump Administration's '1776 Report.'"

36. Trollinger, "*1776 Report*."

37. Clifton, "How the Trump Administration's '1776 Report.'"

38. This "bizarre" association was pointed out in the statement prepared by the American Historical Association cited above and was recirculated countless times by champions and detractors of *The 1776 Report*.

39. Strauss, "Trump's 'Patriotic Education' Report."

40. Editorial Board, "*1776 Report*."

41. Editorial Board, "*1776 Report*."

42. Editorial Board, "*1776 Report*."

43. White, "Media Are Lying."

44. Rosen, "Slandering *The 1776 Report*."

45. The unmistakable articulation of Christian nationalism and political conservativism, and its profound influence on life in the United States today, is duly noted but only superficially

explored in this concluding chapter. For a sobering introduction to this complex configuration, see Gorski and Perry, *Flag and the Cross*; and Stewart, *Power Worshippers*.

46. Thomas Nelson Publishers, "Company Profile," https://www.thomasnelson.com/about-us/company-profile (accessed January 1, 2024).

47. Encounter Books, "About," https:// www.encounterbooks.com/about (accessed January 1, 2024).

48. Jeff Minick's "A Must-Read for Patriots" is one of the exceptions to the general rule. Following what may generously be described as a sophomoric summary of the document, the author castigates the Biden administration for its near immediate dissolution of the 1776 commission and its order to have *The Report* removed from all federal websites. He sees such action as "draw[ing] a line in the sand. On one side stand all those who love America, liberty, and justice under the law. On the other side are those who reject our founding principles and are working to abolish them." Without even a hint of irony, his closing note "encourages readers to purchase this gem of Americana."

49. Waxman, "Exclusive."

50. Waxman, "Exclusive."

51. State of Arkansas, "House Bill 1231: The Saving American History Act of 2021," February 8, 2021, https://legiscan.com/AR/text/HB1231/id/2278186.

52. Waxman, "Exclusive."

53. Florida's SB 266, for instance, which went into effect on July 1, 2023, requires that "general-education core courses may not distort significant historical events or include a curriculum that teaches identity politics . . . or is based on theories that systemic racism, sexism, oppression, and privilege are inherent in the institutions of the United States and were created to maintain social, political, and economic inequities." See Blest, "Florida Just Passed." As Brian Leiter elaborated on his blog, "As state-mandated ideological indoctrination goes, this is remarkably brazen" ("Viktor Desantis's War").

54. Youngkin, "Executive Order Number One." A lot could be said in this chapter about the introduction of "ethnicity" and "faith" to the fated list. (Presumably, this would remove the Christian Crusades and the Spanish Inquisition from the world history curriculum, for example.) However, it is necessary that I draw readers' attention to the elision of "skin color" from the final clause of the sentence. "Race" serves here, and elsewhere, as cover term that leads us toward a scientifically debunked but stubbornly enduring concept of biological and racialized essentialism. There is more excellent theoretical and critical literature on this issue than can possibly be cited here. For a start, readers may do no better than throw themselves into the theoretical thick of it by way of the infamous debate between Anthony Appiah and David Goldberg. See Appiah, "Illusions of Race"; and Goldberg, *Racist Culture*.

55. Seshadri, "Afterword," 299.

56. This idea differs greatly from the claim that what we call facts don't matter for the writing of history. As the groundbreaking work of historian Saidiya Hartman, among others, has taught us, the facts matter even when they are missing. As she puts it in "A Note on Method" in *Wayward Lives, Beautiful Experiments*, a brilliant example of what I call a popular memory text:

> Every historian of the multitude, the dispossessed, the subaltern, and the enslaved is forced to grapple with the power and authority of the archive and the limits it sets on what can be known, whose perspective matters, and who is endowed with the gravity and authority of historical actor. . . . The aim is to convey the sensory experience of the city and to capture the rich landscape of black social life. To this end, I employ a mode of close narration, a style which places the voice of narrator and character in inseparable relations, so that the vision, language, and rhythms of the wayward shape and arrange the text. (xii–xiv)

Of course, the seminal test case on the question of the limits of the archive, of "historical fact and objectivity," is the Holocaust. Holocaust denial is the absurd epitome of the objectivist stance.

57. Waldstreicher, "Hidden Stakes of the 1619 Controversy."

58. Waldstreicher, "Hidden Stakes of the 1619 Controversy."

59. Spivak, "In a Word," 23.

60. Before its disciplinization in the nineteenth century, history was a rhetorical art. "It is well known," Hayden White writes, "that the transformation of historical studies into a science . . . was to be achieved by the liberation of history from its status as a genre of rhetoric" ("Historicality as a Trope of Political Discourse," 176). He adds that this change was long in progress and was evident in the "Father of History's fixation on the fact" as his main concern. But the deconstructionist faces a double bind here. In the words of Derrida, "Historical truth must itself escape from the historicist reduction for historicism itself to be possible and at a certain level legitimate" (*Heidegger*, 109). At the time White penned his essay, Derrida's early seminar on Heidegger had yet to be published but it wrestled with precisely the same dilemma. It is not simply "historical all the way down," since any notion of the historical is predicated on the ahistorical if it is to make sense.

61. For an expert engagement with rhetoric as a productive knowledge, see Atwill, *Rhetoric Reclaimed*.

62. President's Advisory 1776 Commission, *1776 Report*, 16.

63. President's Advisory 1776 Commission, *1776 Report*, 14.

64. President's Advisory 1776 Commission, *1776 Report*, 14.

65. Silverstein, *1619 Project*, 24.

66. President's Advisory 1776 Commission, *1776 Report*, 4.

67. It is worth remarking that *The 1619 Project* is also to be distinguished from Afropessimism, both substantively and stylistically. Rhetorically, I would argue, they are two distinct modes of speech and thought. See, for example, Wilderson, *Afropessimism*; and Sexton, *Amalgamation Schemes*. Scholars generally align Saidiya Hartman's and Christina Sharpe's work with Afropessimism; I have yet to be persuaded. Close and comparative rhetorical analyses of these scholars' work is desperately needed.

68. President's Advisory 1776 Commission, *1776 Report*, 1.

69. The passive voice is wittingly deployed to make the case for the natural unfolding of those democratic founding principles. For example, the conclusion to the Civil War is stated in the following way: "'This conflict was resolved, but at the cost of more than 600,000 lives.' As historian William Trollinger forcibly puts it, "That's it. And note the passive voice: 'conflict was resolved.' No mention of who was responsible for the deaths. No mention of the fact that the South was determined, by any means necessary, to maintain slavery as an institution, and so instigated this war. No mention of the fact that the Confederates maintained that they were the ones who were truly loyal to the sentiments of the Declaration and Constitution. No mention of the Confederates at all. Only, the 'conflict was resolved'" ("*1776 Report*"). Trollinger delivers a bulleted list of other substantive objections to *The 1776 Report* that aim at the very heart of the Commission's beating ideological and political agenda.

70. Drawing on Schiller's theory of imagination, Hayden White argued in the 1980s for bringing back the historical sublime to the discipline of history. Exorcised from the craft on the way toward its modernization, White explains, the displacement of the historical sublime by "'objectivity,' 'modesty,' 'realism,' and 'social responsibility'" ("Politics of Historical Interpretation," 81) set the field on its conservative and bourgeois course:

> To the extent that [radical and reactionary historians alike] succeed in [rendering history's manifest confusion comprehensible to either reason, understanding, or aesthetic

> sensibility], these ideologies deprive history of the kind of meaninglessness that alone can goad living human beings to make their lives different for themselves and their children, which is to say, to endow their lives with a meaning for which they alone are fully responsible. Once can never move with any politically effective confidence from an apprehension of "the way things actually are or have been" to the kind of moral insistence that they "should be otherwise" without passing through a feeling of repugnance for and negative judgment of the condition that is to be superseded." (72–73)

Paul Gilroy's "'Not a Story to Pass On'" may be read as the productive and dangerous supplement to White's argument for a course correction in the field of history. In this chapter of *The Black Atlantic* Gilroy explores a long and uninterrupted history of black writers putting the historical sublime to work to deconstruct the tradition-modernity binary on which White's (racialized) argument rests.

71. As previously noted, *1776 Report* includes ten visual images: Emmanuel Leutze's rendition in oil of *Washington Crossing the Delaware*, a photo of Martin Luther King Jr. waving to the crowd on the Mall, John Turnbull's rendition in oil of the Declaration of Independence, a photographic reproduction of the first page of the US Constitution, a stock photographic image of Frederick Douglass, a stock photographic image of Abraham Lincoln, a photograph of Ronald Reagan speaking at the Brandenburg Gate, a photographic head shot of Martin Luther King Jr. during the 1963 March on Washington for Jobs and Freedom, a photographic image of elementary school children raising their hands in a classroom, and a close-up photograph of the Lincoln Memorial.

72. Hartman's *Wayward Lives* is exemplary for its effort to recover the poetics of life amid precarity.

73. Seshadri-Crooks, *Desiring Whiteness*, 8.

74. President's Advisory 1776 Commission, *1776 Report*, 1.

75. President's Advisory 1776 Commission, *1776 Report*, 1.

76. It is clearly the case that any scholarly work whose aim, like Susan Neiman's *Learning from the Germans*, is to encourage a sincere reckoning with slavery and its living legacy—one consequence of which is the desublimation of the United States as exemplary nation—runs afoul of all "divisive concepts" legislation and, thus, can no longer be assigned reading in classrooms across the country without considerable risk to the teacher.

77. Seshadri-Crooks, *Desiring Whiteness*, 9.

78. President's Advisory 1776 Commission, *1776 Report*, 20.

79. President's Advisory 1776 Commission, *1776 Report*, 1.

80. By training, academics are not given to forecasting. However, informed speculation on this question has seen its way into print. Additional support for my rather grim view may be found in Gerstle, *Rise and Fall*; Marche, *Next Civil War*; Martin and Burns, *This Will Not Pass*; Niewert, *Alt-America*; and Richardson, *How the South Won*.

Bibliography

Agamben, Giorgio. *Means Without End: Notes on Politics*. Translated by Vincenzo Binetti and Cesare Casarino. Minneapolis: University of Minnesota Press, 2000.

———. *Potentialities: Collected Essays in Philosophy*. Edited and translated by Daniel Heller-Roazen. Stanford, CA: Stanford University Press, 1999.

Alexander, Elizabeth. "Can You Be BLACK and Look at This? Reading the Rodney King Video(s)." *Public Culture* 7, no. 1 (1994): 77–94.

American Historical Association. "AHA Condemns Report of Advisory 1776 Commission." January 20, 2021. https://www.historians.org/news-and-advocacy/aha-advocacy/aha-statement-condeming-report-of-advisory-1776-commission-(january-2021).

Amos, Deborah. *ABC News Nightline* transcript, October 25, 1994. LexisNexis.

Appiah, Anthony. "Illusions of Race." In *In My Father's House: Africa in the Philosophy of Culture*, 28–46. New York: Oxford University Press, 1992.

Armanda, Bernard, J. "Memorial Agon: An Interpretive Tour of the National Civil Rights, Museum." *Southern Communication Journal* 63, no. 3 (1998): 235–43.

Arnold, Martin. "'Private Ryan' Revives a Genre." *New York Times*, July 30, 1998, E3.

Atwater, Deborah F., and Sandra L. Herndon. "Cultural Space and Race: The National Civil Rights Museum and Museum Africa." *Howard Journal of Communications* 14, no. 1 (2003): 15–28.

Atwill, Janet. *Rhetoric Reclaimed: Aristotle and the Liberal Arts Tradition*. Ithaca, NY: Cornell University Press, 1998.

Badiou, Alain. *Being and Event*. Translated by Oliver Feltham. London: Continuum, 2005.

———. "Being by Numbers, an Interview with Lauren Sedowsky." *Artforum*, October 1994, 84–87.

———. "Democratic Materialism and the Materialist Dialectic." In *Logic of Worlds: Being and Event 2*, translated by Alberto Toscano, 1–9. London: Continuum, 2009.

———. *Ethics: An Essay on the Understanding of Evil*. Translated by Peter Hallward. London: Verso, 2001.

Bal, Mieke. *Double Exposures: The Practice of Cultural Analysis*. New York: Routledge, 1996.

Barthes, Roland. *Mythologies*. Translated by Annette Lavers. New York: Hill and Wang, 1972.

———. "The Rhetoric of the Image." In *Image Music Text*, translated by Stephen Heath, 32–51. London: Fontana Press, 1977.

Benjamin, Walter. *The Arcades Project*. Edited by Rolf Tiedeman. Translated by Howard Eiland and Kevin McLaughlin. Cambridge, MA: Harvard University Press, 1999.

Berger, John. *Ways of Seeing*. New York: Viking Penguin, 1997.

Berlant, Lauren. *The Queen of America Goes to Washington City: Essays on Sex and Citizenship*. Durham, NC: Duke University Press, 1997.

———. "The Subject of True Feeling: Pain, Privacy, and Politics." In *Cultural Studies and Political Theory*, edited by Jodi Dean, 42–62. Ithaca, NY: Cornell University Press, 2000.

Bernard-Donals, Michael. *Figure of Memory: The Rhetoric of Displacement at the United States Holocaust Memorial Museum*. Albany: State University of New York Press, 2016.

Biden, Joe. "Transcript of Biden's Speech on the U.S. Withdrawal from Afghanistan." *New York Times*, August 31, 2021. https://www.nytimes.com/2021/08/31/us/politics/transcript-biden-speech-afghanistan.html.

Biesecker, Barbara A. "From General History to Philosophy: Black Lives Matter, Late Neoliberal Molecular Biopolitics, and Rhetoric." *Philosophy and Rhetoric* 50, no. 4 (2017): 409–30.

———. "No Time for Mourning: The Rhetorical Production of the Melancholic Citizen-Subject in the War on Terror." *Philosophy and Rhetoric* 40, no. 1 (2007): 147–67.

———. "Of Historicity, Rhetoric: The Archive as Scene of Invention." *Rhetoric and Public Affairs* 9, no. 1 (2006): 124–31.

———. "Rethinking the Rhetorical Situation Through the Thematic of *Différance*." *Philosophy and Rhetoric* 22, no. 2 (1989): 110–30.

Black, Edwin. *Rhetorical Criticism: A Study in Method*. New York: Macmillan, 1965.

Blair, Carole, Marsha S. Jeppeson, and Enrico Pucci Jr. "Public Memorializing in Postmodernity: The Vietnam Veterans Memorial as Prototype." *Quarterly Journal of Speech* 77, no. 3 (1991): 263–88.

Blair, Carole, and Neil Michael. "The AIDS Memorial Quilt and the Contemporary Culture of Public Commemoration." *Rhetoric and Public Affairs* 10, no. 4 (2007): 595–626.

Blest, Paul. "Florida Just Passed Its 'Stop WOKE' Anti-CRT Bill." *Vice News*, March 11, 2022. https://www.vice.com/en/article/wxdbwb/stope-woke-act-florida-crt-bill.

Bloom, Alan. *The Closing of the American Mind: How Higher Education Has Failed Democracy and Impoverished the Souls of Today's Students*. New York: Simon & Schuster, 1987.

Bodnar, John. *Remaking America: Public Memory, Commemoration, and Patriotism in the Twentieth Century*. Princeton, NJ: Princeton University Press, 1992.

———. "*Saving Private Ryan* and Postwar Memory in America." *American Historical Review* 106, no. 3 (2001): 805–17.

Bolton, Richard. *Culture Wars: Documents from the Recent Controversies in the Arts*. New York: The New Press, 1992.

Borch-Jacobsen, Mikkel. *Lacan: The Absolute Master*. Translated by Douglas Brick. Stanford, CA: Stanford University Press, 1991.

Brady, Miranda. "Mediating Indigenous Voice in the Museum: Narratives of Place, Land, and Environment in New Exhibition Practice." *Environmental Communication* 5, no. 2 (2011): 202–20.

Brand, Amanda N. "White Masculine Abjection, Victimhood, and Disavowal in Rape Culture: Reconstituting Brock Turner." *Quarterly Journal of Speech* 108, no. 2 (2022): 148–71.

Brokaw, Tom. *An Album of Memories: Personal Histories from the Greatest Generation*. New York: Random House, 2001.

———. *The Greatest Generation*. New York: Random House, 1998.

———. *The Greatest Generation Speaks: Letters and Reflections*. New York: Random House, 1999.

Brown, Wendy. *States of Injury: Power and Freedom in Late Modernity*. Princeton, NJ: Princeton University Press, 1995.

———. *Undoing the Demos: Neoliberalism's Stealth Revolution*. New York: Zone Books, 2015.

Butler, Judith. "Contingent Foundations." In *Feminists Theorize the Political*, edited by Judith Butler and Joan W. Scott, 3–21. New York: Routledge, 1992.

Bynum, Victoria, James M. McPherson, James Oakes, Sean Wilentz, and Gordon S. Wood. "Letter to the Editor." *New York Times Magazine*, December 20, 2019. https://www.nytimes.com/2019/12/20/magazine/we-respond-to-the-historians-who-critiqued-the-1619-project.html?.

Caldwell, Christopher. "Spielberg at War." *Commentary* 106, no. 4 (October 1998): 48.
Cartwright, Lisa. *Screening the Body: Tracing Medicine's Visual Culture*. Minneapolis: University of Minnesota Press, 1995.
Ceccarelli, Leah. "Polysemy: Multiple Meanings in Rhetorical Criticism." *Quarterly Journal of Speech* 84, no. 4 (1998): 395–415.
Charles, Nick. "Guts and Glory." *People Weekly*, October 12, 1998, 162.
Clifton, Derrick. "How the Trump Administration's '1776 Report' Warps the History of Racism and Slavery." *NBC News*, January 20, 2021. https://www.nbcnews.com/news/nbcblk/how-trump-administration-s-1776-report-warps-history-racism-slavery-n1254926.
Clinton, William Jefferson. "Clinton Salutes Veterans, Dedicates Memorial Site." *Los Angeles Times*, November 12, 1995, 4A.
———. "Remarks by President Clinton at the Tomb of the Unknown Soldier, Arlington National Cemetery." *Federal News Service*, November 11, 1995. LexisNexis.
———. "Remarks on Responsible Citizenship and Common Ground." *American Review*, July 6, 1995, 5.
———. "Veterans Day National Ceremony." United States Department of Veterans Affairs, November 11, 1995. https:// department.va.gov/veterans-day-speech/remarks-by-president-william-jefferson-clinton-veterans-day-national-ceremony-6/.
Cole, Tim. *Selling the Holocaust: From Auschwitz to Schindler; How History Is Bought, Packaged, and Sold*. New York: Routledge, 1999.
Copjec, Joan. "*Gia Savoir Sera*: The Science of Love and the Insolence of Chance." In *Alain Badiou: Philosophy and Its Conditions*, edited by Gabriel Riera, 119–36. Albany: State University of New York Press, 2005.
———. *Imagine There's No Woman: Ethics and Sublimation*. Cambridge, MA: MIT Press, 2004.
———. *Read My Desire: Lacan Against the Historicists*. Cambridge, MA: MIT Press, 1995.
Costello, Lisa A. *American Public Memory and the Holocaust: Performing Gender, Shifting Orientations*. New York: Lexington Books, 2019.
Cotton, Tom, and Ken Buck. "When *New York Times* Fake News Replaces American History." *National Review*, June 30, 2021. https://www.nationalreview.com/2021/06/when-new-york-times-fake-news-replaces-american-history.
Danto, Arthur. "The Vietnam Veterans Memorial." *The Nation*, August 31, 1985, 152–55.
Dean, Jodi. *Democracy and Other Neoliberal Fantasies: Communicative Capitalism and Left Politics*. Durham, NC: Duke University Press, 2009.
Department of Homeland Security. "DHS Announces New Task Force to Protect American Monuments, Memorials, and Statues." July 1, 2020. https://www.dhs.gov/news/2020/07/01/dhs-announces-new-task-force-protect-american-monuments-memorials-and-statues.
Derrida, Jacques. "*Différance*." In *Margins of Philosophy*, translated by Alan Bass, 1–28. Chicago: University of Chicago Press, 1982.
———. "Discussion." In *The Structuralist Controversy: The Languages of Criticism and the Sciences, of Man*, edited by Richard Macksey and Eugenio Donato, 265–72. Baltimore: Johns Hopkins University Press, 1970.
———. *Given Time: 1. Counterfeit Money*. Translated by Peggy Kamuf. Chicago: University of Chicago Press, 1992.
———. *Heidegger: The Question of Being and History*. Translated by Geoffrey Bennington. Chicago: University of Chicago Press, 2016.
———. *Limited Inc*. Translated by Alan Bass and Samuel Weber. Evanston, IL: Northwestern University Press, 1988.

———. "No Apocalypse, Not Now (Full Speed Ahead, Seven Missiles, Seven Missives)." Translated by Catherine Porter and Philip Lewis. *Diacritics* 14, no. 2 (1984): 20–31.
———. *The Other Heading: Reflections on Today's Europe.* Translated by Pascale-Anne Brault and Michael B. Naas. Bloomington: Indiana University Press, 1992.
———. "Signature Event Context." In *Limited Inc*, translated by Alan Bass and Samuel Weber, 1–24. Evanston, IL: Northwestern University Press, 1988.
———. "Structure, Sign, and Play in the Discourses of the Human Sciences." In *The Structuralist Controversy: The Languages of Criticism and the Sciences of Man*, edited by Richard Macksey and Eugenio Donato, 247–65. Baltimore: Johns Hopkins University Press, 1972.
———. "White Mythologies: Metaphor in the Text of Philosophy." In *Margins of Philosophy*, translated by Alan Bass, 207–71. Chicago: University of Chicago Press, 1982.
Dickinson, Greg. "Memories for Sale: Nostalgia and the Construction of Identity in Old Pasadena." *Quarterly Journal of Speech* 83, no. 1 (1997): 1–27.
Dickinson, Greg, Carole Blair, and Brian L. Ott, eds. *Places of Public Memory: The Rhetoric of Museums and Memorials.* Tuscaloosa: University of Alabama Press, 2010.
Dickinson, Greg, Brian L. Ott, and Eric Aoki. "Spaces of Remembering and Forgetting: The Reverent Eye/I at the Plains Indian Museum." *Communication and Critical/Cultural Studies* 3, no. 1 (2006): 27–47.
Dower, John W. "Three Narratives of Our Humanity." In *History Wars: The* Enola Gay *and Other Battles for the American Past*, edited by Edward T. Linenthal and Tom Engelhardt, 63–96. New York: Henry Holt, 1996.
Duggan, Lisa. *The Twilight of Equality? Neoliberalism, Cultural Politics, and the Attack on Democracy.* Boston: Beacon Press, 2003.
Dunn, Thomas R. *Queerly Remembered: Rhetorics for Representing the GLBTQ Past.* Columbia: University of South Carolina Press, 2016.
Edgar, Amanda Nell, and Holly Willson Holladay. "'Everybody's Hard Times Are Different': Country as a Political Investment in White Masculine Precarity." *Communication and Critical/Cultural Studies* 16, no. 2 (2019): 122–39.
Editorial Board. "*The 1776 Report*: A Trump Commission Tries to Correct the Historical Record." *Wall Street Journal*, January 15, 2021. https://www.wsj.com/articles/the-1776-report-11610754084.
Ehrenhaus, Peter. "Why We Fought: Holocaust Memory in Spielberg's *Saving Private Ryan*." *Critical Studies in Media Communication* 18, no. 3 (September 2001): 321–37.
Elshtain, Jean Bethke. "Spielberg's America." *Tikkun* 13 (November/December 1998): C73.
Engelhardt, Tom. *The End of Victory Culture: Cold War America and the Disillusioning of a Generation.* New York: Basic Books, 1995.
Evans, Dylan. *An Introductory Dictionary of Lacanian Psychoanalysis.* London: Routledge, 1996.
Eyers, Tom. *Speculative Formalism: Literature, Theory, and the Critical Present.* Evanston, IL: Northwestern University Press, 2017.
Ferguson, Bruce. "Exhibition Rhetorics: Material Speech and Utter Sense." In *Thinking About Exhibitions*, edited by Reesa Greenberg, Bruce W. Ferguson, and Sandy Nairne, 175–90. New York: Routledge, 1996.
Fink, Bruce. *The Lacanian Subject: Between Language and Jouissance.* Princeton, NJ: Princeton University Press, 1995.
Foucault, Michel. *The Archaeology of Knowledge and the Discourse on Language.* Translated by A. M. Sheridan Smith. New York: Pantheon Books, 1972.
———. *The Birth of Biopolitics: Lectures at the College de France, 1978–79.* Edited by Michel Senellart. Translated by Graham Burchell. New York: Palgrave Macmillan, 2008.

———. "The Discourse on Language." In *"The Archaeology of Knowledge" and "The Discourse on Language,"* 215–37. Translated by A. M. Sheridan Smith. New York: Pantheon Books, 1972.

———. *Fearless Speech*. Edited by Joseph Pearson. Los Angeles: Semiotext(e), 2001.

———. "Film and Popular Memory." In *Foucault Live: Interviews, 1966–84*, edited by Sylvere Lotringer, translated by John Johnston, 89–106. New York: Semiotext(e), 1989.

———. "Nietzsche, Genealogy, History." In *Language, Counter-Memory, Practice: Selected Essays and Interviews*, edited by Donald F. Bouchard and translated by Donald F. Bouchard and Sherry Simon, 139–64. Ithaca, NY: Cornell University Press, 1977.

———. "Powers and Strategies." In *Michel Foucault: Power, Truth, Strategy*, edited by Meaghan Morris and Paul Patton, 49–58. Sydney: Feral, 1967.

———. "Preface." In *The Order of Things: An Archaeology of the Human Sciences*, xvi–xxiv. New York: Routledge, 2005. First published in English in 1970 by Tavistock (London).

———. "Questions of Method." In *The Foucault Effect: Studies in Governmentality*, edited by Graham Burchell, Colin Gordon, and Peter Miller, 73–86. Chicago: University of Chicago Press, 1991.

———. "Truth and Power." In *Power: The Essential Works of Foucault, 1954–1984*, edited by James D. Faubion, 3:111–33. New York: The New Press, 2001.

———. "Truth and Power: Interview with Alessandro Fontano and Pasquale Paswuino." Translated by Paul Patton and Meaghan Morris. In *Michel Foucault: Power, Truth, Strategy*, edited by Meaghan Morris and Paul Patton, 29–48. Sydney: Feral, 1967.

Fried, Amy. "The Personalization of Collective Memory: The Smithsonian's September 11 Exhibit." *Political Communication* 23, no. 4 (2006): 387–405.

Fukuyama, Francis. "The End of History?" *National Interest* 16 (Summer 1989): 3–18.

Gallagher, Victoria J. "Memory and Reconciliation in the Birmingham Civil Rights Institute." *Rhetoric and Public Affairs* 2 (1999): 303–20.

Gates, Henry Louis, Jr. *Loose Canons: Notes on the Culture Wars*. Oxford: Oxford University Press, 1992.

Gerstle, Gary. *The Rise and Fall of the Neoliberal Order: America and the World in the Free Market Era*. New York: Oxford University Press, 2022.

Gillis, John R. *Commemorations: The Politics of National Identity*. Princeton, NJ: Princeton University Press, 1994.

Gilroy, Paul. "'Not a Story to Pass On': Living Memory and the Slave Sublime." In *The Black Atlantic: Modernity and Double Consciousness*, 187–223. London: Verso, 1993.

Gitlin, Todd. *The Twilight of Common Dreams: Why America Is Wracked by Culture Wars*. New York: Metropolitan Books, 1995.

Goldberg, Todd. *Racist Culture: Philosophy and the Politics of Meaning*. Cambridge: Blackwell, 1993.

Goldstein, Richard. "World War II Chic." *Village Voice*, January 19, 1999, 47.

Gorski, Philip S., and Samuel L. Perry. *The Flag and the Cross: White Christian Nationalism and the Threat to American Democracy*. New York: Oxford University Press, 2022.

Gourevitch, Philip. "Genocide Pop." *Washington Post*, January 16, 1994. http://www.washingtonpost.com/archive/lifestyle/style/1994/01/16/genocide-pop/66b2e1f0-d207-4b21-bf66-aee28329e9c4/.

Griswold, Charles L. "The Vietnam Veterans Memorial and the Washington Mall: Philosophical Thoughts on Political Iconography." *Critical Inquiry* 12, no. 4 (Summer 1986): 688–719.

Grossberg, Lawrence. *We Gotta Get Out of This Place: Popular Conservatism and Postmodern Culture*. New York: Routledge, 1992.

Grossman, Hannah. "Why Schools Adopted *The 1619 Project* as a Curriculum When It Was Full of Historical Errors." *Fox News*, April 11, 2022. https://www.foxnews.com/media/schools-1619-project-curriculum-historical-errors.

Grosz, Elizabeth. *Jacques Lacan: A Feminist Introduction*. London: Routledge, 1990.

Gunn, Joshua. *Political Perversion: Rhetorical Aberration in the Time of Trumpeteering*. Chicago: University of Chicago Press, 2020.

Gutkin, Len. "The Review: Indoctrination Nation." *Chronicle of Higher Education*, June 5, 2023. https://www.chronicle.com/newsletter/the-review/2023-06-05.

Hall, John A., and Charles Lindholm. *Is America Breaking Apart?* Princeton, NJ: Princeton University Press, 1999.

Hall, Stuart. *The Hard Road to Renewal: Thatcherism and the Crisis of the Left*. New York: Verso, 1988.

Hannah-Jones, Nikole. "Preface: Origins." In *"The 1619 Project": A New Origin Story*, edited by Nikole Hannah-Jones, Caitlin Roper, Ilena Silverman, and Jake Silverstein, xvii–xxxiii. New York: One World, 2021.

Hariman, Robert, and John Louis Lucaites. *No Caption Needed: Iconic Photographs, Public Culture, and Liberal Democracy*. Chicago: University of Chicago Press, 2007.

Hartman, Andrew. *A War for the Soul of America: A History of the Culture Wars*. Chicago: University of Chicago Press, 2016.

Hartman, Saidiya. "A Note on Method." In *Wayward Lives, Beautiful Experiments: Intimate Histories of Riotous Black Girls, Troublesome Women, and Queer Radicals*, xiii–xv. New York: Norton, 2019.

———. *Scenes of Subjection: Terror, Slavery, and Self-Making in Nineteenth-Century America*. New York: Norton, 2022.

Harwit, Martin. *An Exhibit Denied: Lobbying the History of the* Enola Gay. New York: Copernicus, 1996.

Hasian, Marouf, Jr. "Nostalgic Longings, Memories of the 'Good War,' and Cinematic Representations in *Saving Private Ryan*." *Critical Studies in Media Communication* 18, no. 3 (September 2001): 338–58.

Haskins, Ekaterina V. *Popular Memories: Commemoration, Participatory Culture, and Democratic Citizenship*. Columbia: University of South Carolina Press, 2015.

———. "'Put Your Stamp on History': The USPS Commemorative Program *Celebrate the Century*." *Quarterly Journal of Speech* 89, no. 1 (2003): 1–18.

Hirsch, E. D. *Cultural Literacy: What Every American Needs to Know*. Boston: Houghton Mifflin, 1987.

Hofstadter, Richard. *Anti-Intellectualism in American Life*. New York: Random House, 1966.

Hogan, Michael, J. "Hiroshima in History and Memory: An Introduction." In *Hiroshima in History and Memory*, edited by Michael J. Hogan, 1–10. Cambridge: Cambridge University Press, 1996.

Hunter, James Davison, and Alan Wolfe. *Is There a Culture War? A Dialogue on Values and American Public Life*. Washington, DC: Brookings Institution Press, 2006.

Huyssen, Andreas. "Monument and Memory in a Postmodern Age." *Yale Journal of Criticism* 6, no. 2 (1993): 249–62.

———. *Twilight Memories: Marking Time in a Culture of Amnesia*. New York: Routledge, 1995.

Jay, Gregory. *American Literature and the Culture Wars*. Ithaca, NY: Cornell University Press, 1997.

Johnson, Davi. "'Psychiatric Power: The Post-Museum as a Site of Rhetorical Alignment," *Communication and Critical/Cultural Studies* 5, no. 4 (2008): 344–62.

Johnson, Paul Elliott. *I the People: The Rhetoric of Conservative Populism in the United States*. Tuscaloosa: University of Alabama Press, 2022.

Kelly, Casey Ryan. *Apocalypse Man: The Death Drive and the Rhetoric of White Masculine Victimhood*. Columbus: Ohio State University Press, 2020.

Kelly, Casey Ryan, and Kristen E. Hoerl. "Genesis in Hyperreality: Legitimizing Disingenuous Controversy at the Creation Museum." *Argumentation and Advocacy* 48, no. 3 (2012): 123–41.

Kidder, Rolland. "War Memorial Will Be in Its Proper Setting." *Buffalo News*, June 6, 1998, 3C.

King, Claire Cisco. "It Cuts Both Ways: *Fight Club*, Masculinity, and Abject Hegemony." *Communication and Critical/Cultural Studies* 6, no. 4 (2009): 366–85.

———. *Washed in Blood: Male Sacrifice, Trauma, and the Cinema*. New Brunswick, NJ: Rutgers University Press, 2012.

Kornbluh, Anna. *The Order of Forms: Realism, Formalism, and Social Space*. Chicago: University of Chicago Press, 2019.

Koundoura, Maria. "Multiculturalism or Multinationalism." In *Multicultural States: Rethinking Identity and Difference*, edited by David Bennett, 69–88. New York: Routledge, 1998.

Kuhn, Annett. *Family Secrets: Acts of Memory and Imagination*. New York: Verso, 1995.

Lacan, Jacques. *Four Fundamental Concepts of Psychoanalysis*. Edited by Jacques-Alain Miller. Translated by Alan Sheridan. New York: Norton, 1979.

Landsberg, Allison. *Prosthetic Memory: The Transformation of American Remembrance in the Age of Mass Culture*. New York: Columbia University Press.

Leiter, Brian. "Viktor Desantis's War on Higher Education in Florida . . . This Is What It Looks Like on the Ground." *Leiter Reports: A Philosophy Blog*, May 30, 2023. https://leiterreports.typepad.com/blog/2023/05/viktor-desantiss-war-on-higher-educationon-the-ground.html.

Levine, Caroline. *Forms: Whole, Rhythm, Hierarchy, Network*. Princeton, NJ: Princeton University Press, 2015.

Linenthal, Edward T. "Anatomy of a Controversy." In *History Wars: The* Enola Gay *and Other Battles*, edited by Edward T. Linenthal and Tom Engelhardt, 9–62. New York: Henry Holt, 1996.

———. *Preserving Memory: The Struggle to Create America's Holocaust Museum*. New York: Columbia University Press, 1995.

MacCannell, Juliet Flower. *Figuring Lacan: Criticism and the Cultural Unconscious*. Lincoln: University of Nebraska Press, 1986.

Mackaman, Thomas, and David North. "It Is All Just a Metaphor: The *Times* Attempts Yet Another Desperate Defense." In *The New York Times' "1619 Project" and the Racialist Falsification of History*, edited by David North and Thomas Mackaman, 311–18. Oak Park, MI: Mehring Books, 2021.

Marche, Stephen. *The Next Civil War: Dispatches from the American Future*. New York: Avid Reader Press, 2022.

Martin, Jonathan, and Alexander Burns. *This Will Not Pass: Trump, Biden, and the Battle for America's Future*. New York: Simon & Schuster, 2022.

Mason, Herbert Molloy, Jr. "Proudly Display the *Enola Gay*." *VFW*, March 1995, 20–23.

McAlister, Faber. "An Uncanny Architrope: Impossible Ghosts of Empire at the Brontë Museum." *Quarterly Journal of Speech* 109, no. 3 (2023). https://doi.org/10.1080/00335630.2023.2193236.

McDaniel, Mike. "Brothers in Battle." *Houston Chronicle*, September 9, 2001, 2.

McGee, Michael. "In Search of 'the People': A Rhetorical Alternative." *Quarterly Journal of Speech* 61, no. 3 (1975): 235–49.

Meacham, Jon. "Caught in the Line of Fire." *Newsweek*, July 13, 1998, 48–54.

Meister, Robert. "'Never Again': The Ethics of the Neighbor and the Logic of Genocide." *Postmodern Culture* 15, no. 2 (2005). https://www.doi.org/10.1353/pmc.2005.0010.

"Memorial Moratorium." *Baltimore Sun*, September 9, 1999, 2A. LexisNexis.

Miller, Toby. *Technologies of Truth: Cultural Citizenship and Popular Media*. Minneapolis: University of Minnesota Press, 1998.

———. *The Well-Tempered Self: Citizenship, Culture, and the Postmodern Subject*. Baltimore: Johns Hopkins University Press, 1993.

Minick, Jeff. "A Must-Read for Patriots: *The 1776 Report*." *Epoch Times*, February 17, 2021. https://www.theepochtimes.com/bright/a-must-read-for-patriots-the-1776-report-3696259.

Mitchell, W. J. T. *Picture Theory: Essays on Verbal and Visual Representation*. Chicago: University of Chicago Press, 1994.

Moll, James, dir. *Price for Peace: From Pearl Harbor to Nagasaki*. National D-Day Museum, 2002.

Molotsky, Irvin. "Panel Backs World War II Memorial on Mall in Washington." *New York Times*, July 21, 2000, A1.

Nash, Gary, Charlotte Crabtree, and Ross Dunn. *History on Trial: Culture Wars and the Teaching of the Past*. New York: Vintage Books, 2000.

Neiman, Susan. *Learning from the Germans: Race and the Memory of Evil*. New York: Picador, 2019.

Newman, Robert P. "*Enola Gay* at Air and Space." In Enola Gay *and the Court of History*, 97–133. New York: Peter Lang, 2004.

Nguyen, Tina. "A Big Chunk of Trump's 1776 Report Appears Lifted from an Author's Prior Work." *Politico*, January 19, 2021. https://www.politico.com/news/2021/01/19/trump-1776-report-plagiarism-460464.

Niewert, David. *Alt-America: The Rise of the Radical Right in the Age of Trump*. London: Verso, 2017.

Nolan, James L., Jr. *The American Culture Wars: Current Contests and Future Prospects*. Charlottesville: University Press of Virginia, 1996.

North, David. "Foreword." In *The New York Times' "1619 Project" and the Racialist Falsification of History*, edited by David North and Thomas Mackaman, xi–xxvi. Oak Park, MI: Mehring Books, 2021.

Novick, Peter. *The Holocaust in American Life*. New York: Houghton Mifflin, 1999.

O'Gourman, Ned. *The Iconoclastic Imagination: Image, Catastrophe, and Economy in America from the Kennedy Assassination to September 11*. Chicago: University of Chicago Press, 2016.

Olson, Christa. *Constitutive Visions: Indigeneity and Commonplaces of National Identity in Republican Ecuador*. University Park: Penn State University Press, 2014.

Ott, Brian L., Eric Aoki, and Greg Dickinson. "Ways of (Not) Seeing Guns: Presence and Absence at the Cody Firearms Museum." *Communication and Critical/Cultural Studies* 8, no. 3 (2011): 215–39.

Owen, A. Susan. "Memory, War and American Identity: *Saving Private Ryan* as Cinematic Jeremiad." *Critical Studies in Media Communication* 19, no. 3 (2002): 249–82.

Palewicz, Nicholas S., and Marouf A. Hasian Jr. "Mourning Absences, Melancholic Commemoration, and the Contested Public Memories of the National September 11 Memorial Museum." *Western Journal of Communication* 80, no. 2 (2016): 140–62.

Parry-Giles, Shawn J., and Trevor Parry-Giles. "Collective Memory, Political Nostalgia, and the Rhetorical Presidency: Bill Clinton's Commemoration of the March on Washington, August 28, 1998." *Quarterly Journal of Speech* 86, no. 4 (2000): 417–37.

Pease, Donald E. *The New American Exceptionalism*. Minneapolis: University of Minnesota Press, 2009.

Pezzullo, Phaedra C. "Touring 'Cancer Alley,' Louisiana: Performances of Community and Memory for Environmental Justice." *Text and Performance Quarterly* 23 (2003): 226–52.

Phelan, Peggy. *Unmarked: The Politics of Performance*. New York: Routledge, 1993.

Phillips, Andrew. "The English-Only Debate." *Maclean's*, May 5, 1997, 42.

Phillips, Kendall. *Framing Public Memory*. Tuscaloosa: University of Alabama Press, 2004.

Poovey, Mary. *Making a Social Body*. Chicago: University of Chicago Press, 1995.

President's Advisory 1776 Commission. *The 1776 Report*, January 2021. https://trump whitehouse.archives.gov/wp-content/uploads/2021/01/The-Presidents-Advisory -1776-Commission-Final-Report.pdf.

Renshon, Stanley A. "America at a Crossroads: Political Leadership, National Identity, and the Decline of Common Culture." In *One America? Political Leadership, National Identity, and the Dilemmas of Diversity*, edited by Stanley A. Renshon, 3–27. Washington, DC: George Washington University Press, 2001.

Republican National Committee. "Resolution to Formally Censure Liz Cheney and Adam Kinzinger and to No Longer Support Them as Members of the Republican Party." *New York Times*, February 4, 2022. https://www.nytimes.com/interactive/2022/02 /04/us/rnc-resolution-censure-cheney-kinziger.html.

Reston, Maeve, and Aaron Pellish. "Utah GOP Vote to Censure Mitt Romney Fails While Senator Is Booed at Convention." *CNN*, May 1, 2021. https://www.cnn.com/2021/05 /01/politics/mitt-romney-utah-gop-trump/index.html.

Richardson, Heather Cox. *How the South Won the Civil War: Oligarchy, Democracy, and the Continuing Fight for the Soul of America*. New York: Oxford University Press, 2020.

Ringle, Ken. "At Ground Zero: Two Views of History Collide over Smithsonian A-Bomb Exhibit." *Washington Post*, September 26, 1994, A1.

Rogers, Daniel T. *Age of Fracture*. Cambridge, MA: Harvard University Press, 2011.

Rooney, Ellen. "Form and Contentment." In *Reading for Form*, edited by Susan J. Wolfson and Marshall Brown, 25–48. Seattle: University of Washington Press, 2006.

Rorty, Richard. *Achieving Our Country: Leftist Thought in Twentieth-Century America*. Cambridge, MA: Harvard University Press, 1999.

Rose, Jacqueline. *States of Fantasy*. New York: Oxford University Press, 1996.

Rosen, Christine. "Slandering *The 1776 Report*." *Commentary*, January 21, 2021. https://www .commentary.org/christine-rosen/slandering-the-1776-report.

Rothstein, Edward. "Rescuing the War Hero from 1990s Skepticism." *New York Times*, August 3, 1998, E2.

Rowland, Allison L. "Small Dick Problems: Masculine Entitlement as Rhetorical Strategy." *Quarterly Journal of Speech* 109, no. 1 (2023): 26–47.

Savage, Kirk. *Standing Soldiers, Kneeling Slaves: Race, War, and Monument in Nineteenth-Century America*. Princeton, NJ: Princeton University Press, 1997.

Scarry, Elaine. *The Body in Pain: The Making and Unmaking of the World*. New York: Oxford University Press, 1985.

Scatamburlo, Valerie L. *Soldiers of Misfortune: The New Right's Culture War and the Politics of Political Correctness*. New York: Peter Lang, 1998.

Schlesinger, Arthur J., Jr. *The Disuniting of America: Reflections on a Multicultural Society*. New York: Norton, 1992.

Schribman, David. "Put the Memorial, Like the War, at the Center." *Buffalo News*, April 26, 1997, 3C.

Schudson, Michael. *Watergate in American Memory: How We Remember, Forget, and Reconstruct the Past*. New York: Basic Books, 1992.

Scott, Joan. "Experience." In *Feminists Theorize the Political*, edited by Judith Butler and Joan Scott, 22–40. New York: Routledge, 1992.

Seshadri, Kalpana R. "Afterword: There Is Only One Race . . ." In *Lacan and Race: Racism, Identity, and Psychoanalytic Theory*, edited by Sheldon George and Derek Hook, 299–304. New York: Routledge, 2021.

Seshadri-Crooks, Kalpana. *Desiring Whiteness: A Lacanian Analysis of Race*. London: Routledge, 2000.

Sexton, Jared. *Amalgamation Schemes: Antiblackness and the Critique of Multiracialism*. Minneapolis: University of Minnesota Press, 2008.

Sharpe, Christina. *In the Wake: On Blackness and Being*. Durham, NC: Duke University Press, 2016.

Silverman, Kaja. *The Threshold of the Visible World*. New York: Routledge, 1996.

Silverstein, Jake. "Editor's Note." In *The 1619 Project*. Special issue, *New York Times Magazine*, August 19, 2019. https://www.nytimes.com/interactive/2019/08/14/magazine/1619-america-slavery.html.

———, ed. *The 1619 Project*. Special issue, *New York Times Magazine*, August 19, 2019. https://www.nytimes.com/interactive/2019/08/14/magazine/1619-america-slavery.html.

Sontag, Susan. *On Photography*. New York: Doubleday, 1977.

———. *Regarding the Pain of Others*. New York: Farrar, Straus and Giroux, 2003.

Spielberg, Steven, dir. *Saving Private Ryan*. DreamWorks Pictures, Paramount Pictures, Amblin Entertainment, 1998.

Spivak, Gayatri Chakravorty. "Afterword." In *Jacques Derrida: Of Grammatology, 40th Anniversary Edition and Newly Revised Translation*, 345–68. Translated by Gayatri Chakravorty Spivak. Baltimore: Johns Hopkins University Press, 2016.

———. "In a Word: Interview." In *Outside in the Teaching Machine*, 1–24. London: Routledge, 1993.

———. "The Politics of Interpretations." In *In Other Worlds: Essays in Cultural Politics*, 118–33. New York: Routledge, 1998.

———. "Subaltern Studies: Deconstructing Historiography." In *In Other Worlds: Essays in Cultural Politics*, 270–304. New York: Routledge, 2006. First published in 1998 by Routledge (New York).

———. "What's Left of Theory." In *An Aesthetic Education in the Era of Globalization*, 191–217. Cambridge, MA: Harvard University Press, 2012.

Starr, Peter. *Logics of Failed Revolt: French Theory After May '68*. Stanford, CA: Stanford University Press, 1995.

Stewart, Katherine. *The Power Worshippers: Inside the Dangerous Rise of Religious Nationalism*. New York: Bloomsbury, 2019.

Stormer, Nathan. "In Living Memory: Abortion as Cultural Amnesia." *Quarterly Journal of Speech* 88, no. 3 (2002): 265–83.

Strauss, Valerie. "Trump's 'Patriotic Education' Report Excuses Founding Fathers for Owning Slaves and Likens Progressives to Mussolini." *Washington Post*, January 19, 2021. https://www.washingtonpost.com/education/2021/01/19/trump-patriotic-education-report-slavery-fascists.

Stuckey, Mary E. *Deplorable: The Worst Presidential Campaigns from Jefferson to Trump*. University Park: Penn State University Press, 2021.

Sturken, Marita. *Tangled Memories: The Vietnam War, the AIDS Epidemic, and the Politics of Remembering*. Berkeley: University of California Press, 1997.

Tagg, John. *The Burden of Representation: Essays on Photographies and Histories*. Minneapolis: University of Minnesota Press, 1993.

Takaki, Ronald. *A Different Mirror: A History of Multicultural America*. Boston: Little, Brown, 1993.

Trollinger, Susan L. *Selling the Amish: The Tourism of Nostalgia*. Baltimore: Johns Hopkins University Press, 2012.

Trollinger, Susan L., and William Vance Trollinger Jr. *Righting America at the Creation Museum*. Baltimore: Johns Hopkins University Press, 2016.

Trollinger, William Vance, Jr. "*The 1776 Report*: A Crime Against History." *Righting America: A Forum for Scholarly Conversation About Christianity, Culture and Politics in the US*, January 28, 2021. https://rightingamerica.net/the-1776-report-a-crime-against-history.

Trump, Donald J. "Building and Rebuilding Monuments to American Heroes: Executive Order 1394." *Federal Register*, July 3, 2020. https://www.federalregister.gov/documents/2020/07/08/2020-14872/building-and-rebuilding-monuments-to-american-heroes.

———. "Combating Race and Sex Stereotyping: Executive Order 13950." *Federal Register*, September 22, 2020. https://www.federalregister.gov/documents/2020/09/28/2020-21534/combating-race-and-sex-stereotyping.

———. "Establishing the President's Advisory 1776 Commission: Executive Order 13958." *Federal Register*, November 2, 2020. https://www.federalregister.gov/documents/2020/11/05/2020-24793/establishing-the-presidents-advisory-1776-commission.

———. "Protecting American Monuments, Memorials, and Statues and Combating Recent Criminal Violence: Executive Order 13933." *Federal Register*, July 2, 2020. https://www.federalregister.gov/documents/2020/07/02/2020-14509/protecting-american-monumnets-memorials-and-statues-and-combating-recent-criminal-violence.

Vivian, Bradford. *Public Forgetting: The Rhetoric and Politics of Beginning Again*. University Park: Penn State University Press, 2010.

Wade, Peter. "Judge Blames Trump for Jan. 6, Tells Rioter 'You Were a Pawn in a Game.'" *Rolling Stone*, November 19, 2020. https://www.rollingstone.com/politics/politics-news/judge-blames-trump-jan-6-riot-1260527/.

Waldstreicher, David. "The Hidden Stakes of the 1619 Controversy." *Boston Review*, January 24, 2020. https://www.bostonreview.net/articles/david-waldstreicher-hidden-stakes-1619-controversy.

Wallace, Mike. "Culture War, History Front." In *History Wars: The* Enola Gay *and Other Battles for the American Past*, edited by Edward T. Linenthal and Tom Engelhardt, 171–98. New York: Henry Holt, 1996.

Warner, Michael. "The Mass Public and the Mass Subject." In *The Phantom Public Sphere*, edited by Bruce Robbins, 234–56. Minneapolis: University of Minnesota Press, 1993.

Watson, Bradley C. S. *Courts and the Culture Wars*. Boston: Lexington Books, 2003.

Waxman, Olivia B. "Exclusive: New Data Shows the Anti–Critical Race Theory Movement Is 'Far from Over.'" *Time*, April 6, 2023. https://time.com/6266865/critical-race-theory-data-exclusive.

Weber, Samuel. *Return to Freud: Jacques Lacan's Dislocation of Psychoanalysis*. Cambridge: Cambridge University Press, 1991.

Weinberg, Jeshajahu, and Rina Elieli. *The Holocaust Museum in Washington*. New York: Rizzoli International Publications, 1995.

Weiser, M. Elizabeth. *Museum Rhetoric: Building Civic Identity in National Spaces*. University Park: Penn State University Press, 2017.

White, Hayden. "Historicality as a Trope of Political Discourse." In *The Ethics of Narrative: Essays on History, Literature, and Theory, 1998–2007*, edited by Robert Doran, 165–85. Ithaca, NY: Cornell University Press, 2022.

———. "The Politics of Historical Interpretation: Discipline and De-Sublimation." In *The Content of the Form: Narrative Discourse and Historical Representation*, 58–82. Baltimore: Johns Hopkins University Press, 1987.

White, Kaylee McGhee. "The Media Are Lying About *The 1776 Report*." *Washington Post*, January19, 2021. https://www.washingtonexaminer.com/opinion/the-media-are-lying-about-the-1776-report?.

Wilderson, Frank B., III. *Afropessimism*. New York: Norton, 2020.

Will, George F. "The Statue Sweepstakes." *Newsweek*, August 26, 1991, 64.

Williams, Paul. *Memorial Museums: The Global Rush to Commemorate Atrocities*. New York: Berg, 2007.

Witt, Linda. *The Day the Nation Said "Thanks!": A History and Dedication of the Women in Military Service for America Memorial*. Washington, DC: Military Women's Press, 1999.

Wolcott, James. "Tanks for the Memories." *Vanity Fair* 456 (August 1998): 73.

Wolfson, Susan J., and Marshall Brown, eds. *Reading for Form*. Seattle: University of Washington Press, 2006.

Woo, John, dir. *Windtalkers*. Metro-Goldwyn-Mayer and Lion Rock Productions, 2002.

Yardley, Jonathan. "Dropping a Bomb of an Idea." *Washington Post*, October 10, 1994, B2.

Young, James E. *The Texture of Memory: Holocaust Memorials and Meaning*. New Haven, CT: Yale University Press, 1993.

Young, Marilyn B. "Dangerous History: Vietnam and the 'Good War.'" In *History Wars: The* Enola Gay *and Other Battles for the American Past*, edited by Edward T. Linenthal and Tom Engelhardt, 199–209. New York: Henry Holt, 1996.

Youngkin, Glen. "Executive Order Number One (2022): Ending the Use of Inherently Divisive Concepts, Including Critical Race Theory, and Restoring Excellence in K–12 Public Education in the Commonwealth." Commonwealth of Virginia Office of the Governor, January 15, 2022. https://www.governor.virginia.gov/media/governor virginiagov/governor-of-virginia/pdf/eo/EO-1-Ending-the-Use-of-Inherently-Divisive-Concepts.pdf.

Zagacki, Kenneth, and Victoria Gallagher. "Rhetoric and Materiality in the Museum Park at the North Carolina Museum of Art." *Quarterly Journal of Speech* 95, no. 2 (2009): 171–91.

Zelizer, Barbie. "Reading the Past Against the Grain: The Shape of Memory Studies." *Critical Studies in Mass Communication* 12 (1999): 214–39.

———. *Remembering to Forget: Holocaust Memory Through the Camera's Eye*. Chicago: University of Chicago Press, 1998.

Zimmerman, Jonathan. *Whose America? Culture Wars in the Public Schools*. Cambridge, MA: Harvard University Press, 2002.

Žižek, Slavoj. *The Sublime Object of Ideology*. London: Verso, 1989.

Index

RSA·STR

THE RSA SERIES IN TRANSDISCIPLINARY RHETORIC

Other titles in this series:

Nathan Stormer, *Sign of Pathology: U.S. Medical Rhetoric on Abortion, 1800s–1960s*

Mark Longaker, *Rhetorical Style and Bourgeois Virtue: Capitalism and Civil Society in the British Enlightenment*

Robin E. Jensen, *Infertility: A Rhetorical History*

Steven Mailloux, *Rhetoric's Pragmatism: Essays in Rhetorical Hermeneutics*

M. Elizabeth Weiser, *Museum Rhetoric: Building Civic Identity in National Spaces*

Chris Mays, Nathaniel A. Rivers, and Kellie Sharp-Hoskins, eds., *Kenneth Burke + The Posthuman*

Amy Koerber, *From Hysteria to Hormones: A Rhetorical History*

Elizabeth C. Britt, *Reimagining Advocacy: Rhetorical Education in the Legal Clinic*

Ian E. J. Hill, *Advocating Weapons, War, and Terrorism: Technological and Rhetorical Paradox*

Kelly Pender, *Being at Genetic Risk: Toward a Rhetoric of Care*

James L. Cherney, *Ableist Rhetoric: How We Know, Value, and See Disability*

Susan Wells, *Robert Burton's Rhetoric: An Anatomy of Early Modern Knowledge*

Ralph Cintron, *Democracy as Fetish*

Maggie M. Werner, *Stripped: Reading the Erotic Body*

Timothy Johnson, *Rhetoric, Inc.: Ford's Filmmaking and the Rise of Corporatism*

James Wynn and G. Mitchell Reyes, eds., *Arguing with Numbers: The Intersections of Rhetoric and Mathematics*

Ashley Rose Mehlenbacher, *On Expertise: Cultivating Character, Goodwill, and Practical Wisdom*

Stuart J. Murray, *The Living from the Dead: Disaffirming Biopolitics*

G. Mitchell Reyes, *The Evolution of Mathematics: A Rhetorical Approach*

Jenell Johnson, *Every Living Thing: The Politics of Life in Common*

Kellie Sharp-Hoskins, *Rhetoric in Debt*

Jennifer Clary-Lemon, *Nestwork: New Material Rhetorics for Precarious Species*

Nicholas S. Paliewicz, *Extraction Politics: Rio Tinto and the Corporate Persona*

Paul Lynch, *Persuasions of God: Inventing the Rhetoric of René Girard*

Loretta Victoria Ramirez, *The Wound and the Stitch: A Genealogy of the Female Body from Medieval Iberia to SoCal Chicanx Art*

Milton Keynes UK
Ingram Content Group UK Ltd.
UKHW021844271124
451524UK00002B/28

9 780271 097824